SHEILA HANCOCK one of Britain's most highly regarded and popular actors, received a Damehood for services to drama and charity in 2021. Since the 1950s she has enjoyed a career across film, television, theatre and radio. Her first big television role was in the BBC sitcom *The Rag Trade* in the early 1960s. She has directed and acted for the Royal Shakespeare Company and the National Theatre. Following the death of her husband, John Thaw, she wrote a memoir of their marriage, *The Two of Us*, which was a number one bestseller and won the British Book Award for Author of the Year. Her memoir of her widowhood, *Just Me*, also a bestseller, was published in 2007, followed by her bestselling novel *Miss Carter's War*. She lives in London and France.

OLD RAGE

SHEILA HANCOCK

BLOOMSBURY PUBLISHING
LONDON · OXFORD · NEW YORK · NEW DELHI · SYDNEY

BLOOMSBURY PUBLISHING
Bloomsbury Publishing Plc
50 Bedford Square, London, WC1B 3DP, UK
29 Earlsfort Terrace, Dublin 2, Ireland

BLOOMSBURY, BLOOMSBURY PUBLISHING and the Diana logo are trademarks of
Bloomsbury Publishing Plc

First published in Great Britain 2022
This edition published 2023

Extract from *The Collected Poems of Dylan Thomas: The Centenary Edition* published by
Weidenfeld & Nicolson, used with kind permission of the author's
estate © The Dylan Thomas Trust, 2014
Extract from *The English Journey* by J.B. Priestley published by Great Northern
Books © J. B. Priestley, 1934
Extract from Walter de la Mare's *Fare Well* printed with kind permission of
the Literary Trustees of Walter de la Mare and the Society of Authors as their
representative © Walter de la Mare, 1918
Extract from *The Collected Poems of Philip Larkin* published by Faber and Faber
© Philip Larkin, 2003
Extract from *Martha: The Life and Work of Martha Graham* by Agnes De Mille
published by Random House © Agnes De Mille, 1991
Extract from *Collected Poems* by Louis MacNeice published by Faber & Faber,
used with permission from the author's estate © Louis MacNeice, 2007
Extract from *Harold Pinter Plays 3* by Harold Pinter published
by Faber & Faber © Harold Pinter, 2013
'SAD' from *One Hundred Lockdown Sonnets* by Jacqueline Saphra published by Nine Arches
Press, used with kind permission of the author and publisher © Jacqueline Saphra, 2021
And the People Stayed Home by Kitty O'Meara published by Tra Publishing, used with kind
permission of the author and publisher © Kitty O'Meara, 2020

A catalogue record for this book is available from the British Library

ISBN: HB: 978-1-5266-4744-3; TPB: 978-1-5266-4745-0; PB: 978-1-5266-4746-7;
eBook: 978-1-5266-4748-1; ePDF: 978-1-5266-4742-9

2 4 6 8 10 9 7 5 3 1

Typeset by Newgen KnowledgeWorks Pvt. Ltd., Chennai, India
Printed and bound in Great Britain by CPI Group (UK) Ltd, Croydon CR0 4YY

To find out more about our authors and books visit www.bloomsbury.com
and sign up for our newsletters

November 2020

'I am writing in the strictest confidence to inform you that you have been recommended to Her Majesty the Queen for the honour of DBE in the New Year 2021 Honours List. Before the Prime Minister submits your name to Her Majesty the Queen for approval, we would be glad to know that this would be agreeable to you.'

No, no it wouldn't.

I don't feel at all agreeable. I feel sick with inadequacy. A lifetime of getting away with it does not merit reward. What if the Queen disapproves and rejects me?

Prince Philip: It is all going a bit downmarket isn't it?

The Queen: Well, she is very good in Just a Minute.

Prince Philip: But what about Wildcats of St Trinian's?

Should I turn it down? It's hardly in keeping with my Quaker belief of equality. No, that would be dreadfully rude and ungracious.

I can't even discuss it with anyone because it is 'in confidence'. And we are all locked down anyway.

For heaven's sake, why am I not jumping up and down with delight? A while ago, I probably would've been. But recent years have depleted my delight quotient, and jumping up and down is physically beyond me.

Oh Lord, maybe that is why they are giving me this, because I am old, and can cross a stage without falling over, and can handle a canal boat. Can? Could. Should I phone and tell them that may no longer be true?

I have passed supposedly disturbing milestones – my fiftieth, seventieth, even my eightieth birthday – without a qualm, only to be, as I approach ninety, shaken to my core by the shocking realisation that I am now very, very old. Physically, mentally, in my attitude, my health, my outlook, I am suddenly falling apart. 'Old age ain't no place for cissies.' It was the Queen's own mother who quoted this comment made by Bette Davis. The word 'cissies' has somewhat dubious connotations now, but she meant being weak and fearful. Neither of which, when I worked with her in the latter years of her career, Bette, or, it would seem, the Queen Mother, appeared to be. Nor did I, I suppose. Till now. As I hold the letter, this cissy's hand is shaking.

Why have they bestowed this on me? Who are the 'independent Main Honours Committee' that will instruct the prime minister to embarrass the Queen?

Again.

The Queen: First he asks me to prorogue Parliament.
                     Now this.

There is a bit in the letter that says: There is a clear expectation that those invited to receive an honour are, and will continue to be, role models.

What!?

I wish this mystery committee would show me a copy of their 'independent assessment', so I can see what

I have to continue with. Why have they trusted me with this mission? It is very nice of them all to have thought of me, but who do they think I am? Was? Will be? What is my 'role'? Have they miscast me? I am not really the public persona, the show-off, the strong woman, the national treasure, the – the – Dame. Should I confess that to them?

What kind of role model is someone who, like Macbeth, feels 'I have lived long enough. My way of life is fallen into the sere, the yellow leaf'? (Someone who is beyond caring that, in our profession, mentioning Shakespeare's Scottish king by name can be disastrous.) Everything I believed in, and in my small way fought for, has seemingly been abandoned. With Yeats, I feel 'Things fall apart; the centre cannot hold. Mere anarchy is loosed upon the world.' I am hopeless in all senses of the word. Where is the wisdom that is meant to come with age? Where the contentment? My daughters are scarred. My achievements are risible. What an utter, utter waste of time, a lifetime, it has all been. Should they be told that's what I'm really like before they bother the Queen?

I am grateful. They have offered me something wonderful, beyond the wildest ambitions of my mum and dad for their daughter. Three years ago, I might have rejoiced, but now, facing the New Year's Eve when my family would learn about the secret honour, sheltering alone at home, battered by various events, with death uncomfortably near, I am afraid I really don't feel very agreeable.

Not today. Tomorrow may be different. Let's hope. The whole world is living in hope at the moment.

In 2016 I began writing a book that I hoped would be a gentle record of a fulfilled old age. An inspirational journey. It hasn't turned out like that. As I wrote it, my own and the wider world descended into chaos.

Yet it started so well.

2016

January 2016

The year has begun with my friend and neighbour Delena's annual New Year party. A gathering-together of old friends. It is markedly less crowded nowadays, and those that manage it up the stairs are grateful for the resulting availability of seats. I feel positively sprightly compared to one guest with a broken femur, another a failed back operation, two stroke survivors and an assortment of less than successful hip and knee replacements. The general trend of the conversation was the increasing inability to learn lines, the depressing type of roles that we were being called on to play, the lack of projection in younger actors and shock-horror that some are actually being miked. (Good thing too, I think. Makes life much easier.) The moans were conveyed with loud hilarity at past adventures and present ills. One erstwhile roué was still relentlessly flirting from the sofa, undaunted by the fact he couldn't get up off it. Old age was mocked and defied by this joyous gathering.

February 2016

No one demonstrates the resilience of the old better than my sister Billie. After a lifetime of working in variety and cabaret all over the world with her husband, Roy, they retired to live in Norfolk when he could no longer work on the stilts used in their act. Billie had no roots that could be called home, as we moved about so much as children, whereas her husband's family, led by his father, well-known Northern comic and theatre owner Roy Barbour, were well established in Lowestoft and Blackpool, which is why Billie and Roy opted to set up home in the North.

She did her best to settle into this new way of life. When her husband died of a stroke, she stuck out a year living alone in the Broads, working in the local charity shop and trying to adapt to a nice little house instead of her touring caravan or her tiny flat in Paris. She played with the neighbours' children, and, as my father had done when he first lived in a house as opposed to digs, she created a colourful little garden.

Suddenly, on reaching eighty, she freaked out, put her cat in a basket, and went to join a bunch of friends from her past working life living in Antibes. Her best friends Stella, a member of a distinguished circus family, and Nicky, a showgirl, model, half of a fabulous cowboy lasso act, and latterly dress-shop owner, welcomed her with open arms, along with Juliana and Bob, whose enormous rare-breed cats Billie cared for sometimes, staying in their luxury flat overlooking the sea. Her social life was a whirl and, as I discovered when I visited them, the most enormous fun.

I organised a dinner party at her favourite local restaurant to celebrate her ninetieth birthday. Family and friends awaited her entrance, knowing that she had spent weeks getting her nails and hair done and choosing her outfit and jewellery. I was beginning to worry at the lateness of her arrival when a distraught Stella rushed in to say Billie had fallen and could not get up. My son-in-law was left to entertain the motley party guests with his fragmented French, while my daughter Ellie Jane and I dashed round to her flat. We found Billie on the floor. She struggled desperately to pretend she was okay and could go to her party, but was obviously seriously injured.

In France you call the fire brigade if you need an ambulance, and the drama of the incident was somewhat lightened by the arrival of two devastatingly handsome paramedics. Even Billie, who it turned out had broken her hip and was in agony, perked up no end.

After days of medical investigation the doctor told us, with a solemn face, that at her age the likelihood of being able to walk again was minimal, but they would provide her with care and a wheelchair, or she could go into a home. Mercifully I don't think he understood Billie's English swear words, but he did flinch slightly at the flashing of her eyes and her shaking fist.

So my sister went into a splendid rehabilitation centre where she insisted on going to the gym twice a day. A month later she was walking round the grounds on the trainer's arm, and, shortly after that, with merely a stick for support. She just refused to listen to the 'Well, at your age what can you expect?' brigade. The trainer told me it was a complete miracle. Knowing my sister, I would categorise it more as complete bloody-mindedness.

March 2016

My professional life seems to have come full circle. The first theatre to which I was contracted was the Theatre Royal,

Oldham. It is no more. It was on its way to being no more when I worked there fresh from drama school in 1951. The roof leaked so that the audience had to constantly move seats to avoid dripping rainwater, and the dressing rooms had no heating, and cracked black-pitted mirrors surrounded by broken lightbulbs. Before entering you had to bang on the door to tell the mice that their shift was over and they should stop eating the greasepaint. Cut to 2016. We no longer use sticks of make-up made by Leichner, with numbers five and nine mixed in your hand being the favourite for a natural skin tone, but the Southwark Playhouse dressing room I was in recently for a production of a musical called Grey Gardens was no improvement on the Theatre Royal. The mice there were very happy with crumbs of the Jaffa Cakes that the cast were all addicted to. In fact, I have gone down slightly in dressing-room status, as at least in Oldham the men and women were separate; in Southwark we had one room for everyone, with clothes-hanging rails draped with sheets down the middle to separate the sexes. Very soon any semblance of propriety was abandoned, and men and women alike pranced about in their underwear. On the face of it, it doesn't look like progress. I have luxuriated in the Number One dressing room in the Theatre Royal Drury Lane and several other West End theatres, so surely it is a sad plight after six decades of work to be dumped in a rough-and-ready fringe theatre.

Actually, not only was the musical a huge success, with people queuing for returns during its sell-out run, but I loved every minute of being in the venue. To get backstage you have to go through the bar where the audience are carousing before and after the show, which if you're in a flop must be an ordeal, but we had a ball. The show worked better than it would have done – and apparently did in New York, where it was behind a proscenium arch – because we had the audience seated around us within touching distance, giving us actors a thrilling awareness of their deep involvement in the true story of these relatives of the Kennedy family, living in squalor with hundreds of cats, hating and loving one another intensely. One night I dried in a song and turned to someone in the front row, saying, 'I've no idea what comes next.' And he told me. He'd seen the show several times, he loved it so much. It was theatre as it should be. The venue is irrelevant as long as there is that mystical bond between a group of people and a story being told.

Sadly the Theatre Royal was demolished, but there is still a thriving theatre, the Coliseum, in Oldham. Southwark Playhouse and its mice are planning to move to two splendid new spaces in the area.

I, too, am struggling on.

May–June 2016

One of the big advantages of my chosen career for me now is that there is no retirement age. I am not suddenly deemed redundant and unable to work so long as I can remember the words and stumble across the stage or set without bumping into the scenery. I might even be called 'a national treasure' or even 'a legend' for managing to do so. On the other hand, on the day I reached eighty I was considered twice as likely to drive badly as the day before, thus justifying a doubling of my insurance overnight – a totally unproven assumption, as I revealed in a television programme I made about the subject. Luckily my profession continues to consider me employable, although the roles increasingly require me to die or go senile. One that didn't is the film I have made over the last two months that is one of the most fulfilling jobs I have ever had.

When I was sent the script of Edie, about an old woman who, having been for years the carer of her unlovable husband, decides, on his death, to go to Scotland and climb a mountain, I thought there must be some mistake. In my profession I have always been a sort of also-ran. I am happily aware that a bevy of actors has usually been approached for a part before they come to me – although nowadays the bevy is rather reduced as some have dropped off the twig. Despite my success in Grey Gardens, I know that a performance in a fringe theatre does not carry much weight in the film world. This script had a wonderful part in a charming story and I couldn't understand why the many actors ahead of me in the pecking order had not gobbled it up.

I duly met the producer and director in a club, and they had indeed seen me in Grey Gardens and wanted me to play the role. I was about to hug them both, laughingly saying that, 'Of course the climbing will be done with green screen, won't it?'

Silence.

The long and the short of it was that, no, they wanted me to actually climb the bloody mountain.

All was suddenly clear. Many of my contemporaries have the afflictions of old age that would render such extreme demands impossible, and anyway they have already done wonderful leading roles, and would now prefer to put their feet up, or work in a lovely studio with a comfy dressing room. Or at a warm location in a luxurious Winnebago. It is the mark of my still-lethal ambition that I asked the producer to give me a night to think about it.

I talked to the director of the health club where I occasionally did a gentle workout, asking if he thought I could get fit enough to climb a mountain in three months. He blanched only slightly and consulted his top trainer, whose whole life is spent breaking records of one sort or another, and who wasn't going to be defeated by my shrivelled muscles and thinning bones. So, it was all systems go. Every other day in the gym, lifting weights, speeding on the treadmill, developing bulges in arms and legs which hadn't been there for years. In addition, I trained in Richmond Park with an ex-RAF officer at walking in bog and up and down slopes. At the double.

By the time I arrived at Lochinver, where cast and crew were to live together in a hunting lodge, I felt incredibly fit. We had a few days to get to know each other before setting off on the long trip to the foot of the Suilven mountain, filming scenes as we went. It was a challenge. Stumbling over a bog full of horrific Scottish beasties, one minute falling flat on my face over a tussock, the next up to my knees in mud, is not what a nice English girl from Hammersmith is used to. All of the time, looming ahead, was Suilven, getting bigger and bigger the nearer we got to it.

Suilven is a curious mountain, rising vertically from the wilderness with an unusual plum-pudding top. And huge. It took several days to reach its foot, including rowing over a loch, which is not the elegant, gliding sport it appears to be, but rather takes all your strength and gives you blisters.

And I had my first experience since the Brownies of sleeping, or rather not sleeping, in a tent. On the first evening, in an effort to show the right Nature-loving spirit, I pointed out a pretty snake slithering past my tent door, only to have hysterics when one of the crew said it was poisonous. When I eventually staggered to the actual foot of the mountain, my legs were shaking more from fear than exhaustion.

Seeing my stricken face, the first assistant took me aside and said, 'This is your last chance to back out, Sheila. The climb is going to take two or three days, shooting as we go, and we will be sleeping in tents. Once you start there is nowhere for a helicopter to land apart from the top, so you will have to continue.' I looked at the first slope; the crew were already clambering up it, laden with heavy cameras and sound equipment. I had grown fond of these young men and women and the thought of giving up and letting them down was out of the question.

A ghillie, Reuben, a man who knew everything about the geology and history of the landscape, was assigned to work out where I should put my hands and feet when scrambling over the rocks. He was concerned about my age and insisted that I have a break every ten minutes. A plan which soon proved unfeasible for a low-budget film. His technique to keep me going was, if I managed a tricky bit, to reward me with a jelly baby. Kevin Guthrie, who played my young friend, was endlessly solicitous. His main advice was 'Don't look down, for God's sake don't look down.'

The biggest problem for me was the absence of toilets. The mountain is bare of trees or bushes so there is nowhere to hide, plus those Scottish beasties are waiting to bite your bum the minute you squat in their beautiful national park.

To begin with, the crew were told to look the other way, but eventually I went native and behaved like other animals in the wild. Until Calum, a local man, came to my rescue.

I am always fascinated by the effect the presence of a film unit can have on the residents at the location of a shoot. Usually it starts with suspicion and grudging cooperation. Not surprisingly, as film units are a motley crew. They are clothed for the weather and usually unkempt and tired, and at the end of a hard day's shooting they like a drink. In a remote place it can be a frightening invasion of the usual calm and order. Thus it was in Lochinver. The pie shop and the pub were pleased to see us, but the locals were wary of these rogues and vagabonds, as we used to be called. As always, when they became extras, the inhabitants were baffled by the boring repetition and long waits involved in the process of making a film, but once they got to know us most of them were intrigued. There is always much laughter and affection that gels a random group of technicians and actors, all away from home and united in creating a piece of work. Sometimes a local person living a nice, comfortable, steady life finds it exciting.

I remember, several years ago, a film unit descending on the village we then lived in in Wiltshire, taking over the local manor house for the making of an adaptation of Pride and Prejudice. The manor house's owner, a rather cantankerous old woman, at first hid away from the invading army, but was lured into eating on the catering bus. The cheery, disrespectful ribaldry of the crew – 'Hello, my darling, come to join the plebs, have you?' – was something she had never been exposed to and she fell in love with it. The humour, the dedication and the albeit temporary affection enchanted her. When the circus moved on, I imagine she felt very sad, as we all do when a job ends. But for us it is usual.

In Lochinver we were blessed with Calum, who was intrigued by our way of life. He lived and worked locally and started working as an extra with us, or a 'supporting player' as we now call it, but gradually became indispensable. He was knowledgeable about the landscape and could turn his hand and mind to anything. He invented a plastic-and-wooden lavatory for me which he would set up and conceal, and then stand guard while I used it. Calum told me our arrival had changed his life and he was going to rethink everything. He even played a small role in the film, proving himself to be a subtle and charming actor in his first part. He looked out for me, always warning me of the importance of keeping warm, hypothermia being a real threat for someone of my age.

One night I did actually think I might die. We had to camp on a ledge above the clouds. I had thermal underwear, several layers of clothes, hats and gloves, and a supposedly insulated tent. Here comes one of those superlatives I hate but I mean it: I have never been so cold in my life. What I had forgotten, when layering myself up, was the state of my bladder. It was pitch-dark with a sheer drop to oblivion outside my tent. Stripping off and crouching outside, trying not to wake anyone else, I was terrified. And frozen to the bone. I spent the rest of the night with my teeth chattering. Yes, they actually do clack and chatter with cold. When I saw the sun peeping over the distant horizon at dawn, I understood why primitive man worshipped it. How anyone can think that camping is fun is beyond me.

The last lap of the climb was the toughest. Crossing a metre-wide, very long path with a vertical drop either side was the only time I actually wept with fear, my whimpering allayed by an extra helping of jelly babies. After the final rock scramble, egged on by Kevin, flat on my stomach, I wriggled onto the top. In the script, when she reaches the top, Edie is supposed to whoop and dance in triumph. Physically doing the climb, rather than mocking it up with technology, was justified when I realised that, although in terms of the story jumping about and shouting seemed right, in actual fact it was impossible. The sheer wonder of what I experienced as I stood on that unexpectedly grassy summit took my breath away, and I was struck dumb. Miles and miles of wilderness on all sides. No sign of life. Not a road, not a house. Reuben pointed to a dark patch on the ground below and told me geologists had proved it to have been there since the beginning of time.

Throughout my long life I have had a few experiences that have shaken me to the core of my being – transcendental, revelatory. This was one. I did not feel diminished, a tiny human in this vast world; I felt part of it, absorbed, embraced, part of Nature. I felt I belonged to this wild, bleak, magnificent place. My body had lain against the mountain's cliff face, I'd clung to it with my hands, trusted my feet on its stones, and it had befriended me.

The sun was setting and we needed to get it on film. A helicopter took most of the crew off, as they wanted a final shot of Kevin and me, with no one around. The pilot was agitated as we were above the clouds and it was getting dark. The brilliant director of photography, August Jakobsson, wanted a last shot from the helicopter. As it passed, the wind from its blades nearly blew us over the edge and scuppered the whole operation by killing off the leading characters. Eventually, they came back for us. The helicopter ride in the dark, back to base, was the most frightening part of the entire shoot. When we got back, there was drinking and cheering and hugging.

There is nothing better than the feeling that you have done a good job on something; it can be doing the ironing, arranging some flowers, making a child laugh, or climbing a mountain to film a good story. That night a mutual sense of achievement was celebrated with joy.

For me, I was aware that something profound has happened to my – what? My soul?

June 2016

Much as I loved Scotland, I am glad to get back to London and indulge in my usual round of concerts, theatre and long lunches with my mates at my slightly decadent, bohemian club in Soho. My ecstatic reaction to the landscape of the Highlands took me by surprise. I think of myself as a city girl. I love the pace, the people, the easy access to cafés, galleries, theatres and parks. In London I enjoy the jangle of different languages, the kaleidoscope of ethnicity. I relish the unpredictability. I walk its streets and turn down some passageway and find a new mews or building I didn't know was there. It seems an amorphous mass but, if you live here, you know that it is a series of villages each with its own character: elegant Hampstead, raffish Spitalfields, boisterous Brixton. Cities can and do absorb anyone. Areas change according to the influx of new people. Settlers in London have been Roman, Huguenot, Jewish, Irish, Jamaican, Arab, Somali, Indian, Pakistani, Bangladeshi, Chinese – you name it, they've come here. Troublemakers have tried to stop this flow with their hatred and fear, but cities will continue to embrace change, which is probably why most of them would prefer to leave open the doors to Europe. 'The metropolitan elite' is a label currently used as an insult which, if 'elite' is taken to mean aiming high, to be better, to be special, I embrace. These are things all of us should aspire to. For our country, as well as ourselves.

On Suilven I felt that Nature could be my friend. I had never really felt that before. Always slightly on edge, I have gone on family country walks and admired the views, whilst secretly looking forward to visiting the nearest pub. I feel more relaxed in the hubbub of a city than in the quiet of the country. I am less frightened of passing a gang of seemingly threatening youths than of crossing a field of horses or even sheep. A hunt in full cry, shouting, blaring horns, baying hounds, is scarier to me than a noisy demonstration in Trafalgar Square. I am, I suppose, scared of the country, just as the folks who live there are appalled by London.

I blame the war.

As a child whose playground was bombsites, I was more thrilled by collecting shrapnel, machine-gun bullets, shells and bomb fragments than posies of wildflowers. When I was evacuated it was the first time I had lived in the country. I was terrified of the monster cows in the field next door to my billet. I will still walk miles to avoid crossing a field in which they are grazing, however peaceably. I am more at home in rural France because, where I live, there are no animals in the fields.

When I was a child we left King's Cross to live in suburbia. Not only that but my parents gave up working in hotels and pubs and took jobs that meant regular hours, my dad in a factory, my mum in a shop. I don't know how happy they were about that. My dad must have missed the boisterous companionship of being a landlord but the decision could have had something to do with his partiality to a drink – or two – or several. They also probably thought their children needed more stability. In which case, where we moved to was not ideal. During the Blitz, Bexleyheath and the area around it was known as Bomb Alley; it was organised to defend the armament factories Vickers-Armstrongs in Crayford and the Woolwich Arsenal, as well as the docks. With the deafening mobile ack-ack gun behind the house, searchlights, barrage balloons and constant dogfights as the Nazi bombers were confronted by Spitfires overhead, there was no lack of excitement, but when the war ended I found Bexleyheath deadly dull. The bustle and noise of the pub customers in King's Cross, even the odd fight, the winkle and shrimp barrows on Sundays, the Salvation Army bands, the crowds, the buses, the trains that ran under our yard shaking the glasses, were replaced by genteel calm.

On country walks, if there are no actual people around, I will look for traces of them: ruined tin mines in Cornwall, what is left of our mining industry in the Midlands and the North, old barns and farm buildings in the countryside. Halfway up Suilven is a substantial dry-stone wall. It serves no obvious purpose and makes no sense. Its origin is shrouded in mystery but it almost certainly is what is known as a destitution wall. In the Highland Clearances of the eighteenth and nineteenth centuries, many people were driven from their homes and land to accommodate a growth in sheep farming by the landowners. That together with the potato famine, which devastated Scotland as well as Ireland, forced many to emigrate, and those who remained were poverty-stricken. In order to receive meagre subsistence, they were made to work on pointless tasks such as building unnecessary roads, the so-called destitution roads. Most likely some Highlander walked miles from a distant village every day, and then climbed Suilven with massive stones, and constructed this monument to inhumanity.

He used his skill and strength to create something beautiful. I imagine he ended up with more self-respect than the man who tried to humiliate him. The landowner probably laughed with his friends about the ludicrous task he set the Highlander, but I suspect that to have daily communion, in sun and storm, with that magical mountain, crafting something that future generations would admire, means that the labourer had the last laugh.

Alone as he was, he probably felt an affinity to Nature. I remember when John used to ask me to join him looking at the stars at our French home – we no longer see them in big over-lit cities – I would have a quick look and say, 'Yes, lovely', and carry on cooking supper. He would stand there for ages, and I think now that he probably knew that feeling of being part of the universe. And I didn't understand it. How sad that I was too busy to try. On our last visit to our French home, when he was mortally ill, though weak he stood stock-still, for over half an hour, looking at the view of the mountains, forest and blue, blue sky. Then again, on the last evening, he sat outside staring at the stars for a very long time. Is it any wonder that I now, eighteen years after his death, still feel his presence, his energy?

Can I ever, before my own inevitable death, set aside my sensible, rational approach to life and contemplate the inexplicable?

June 2016

The night before the referendum vote as to whether the United Kingdom wishes to leave the European Union, I went on a television debate and tried to explain why I personally want us to remain.

When I arrived at the venue, people were huddled in groups waiting to go into the studio, so I made my way towards the one gathered around Alastair Campbell, Tony Blair's ideas man, hoping for support. They barely acknowledged my arrival, apart from slight irritation that I had interrupted their flow. This was a serious matter and I was just an elderly woman, and a silly actress to boot. When it came to my turn to speak on the debate, I was introduced by Jeremy Paxman with a jolly jibe that I should be voting for Brexit like all the old people. The audience disapproved of his rudeness; I was grateful to him because he got them on my side.

There was a gauge in the studio to demonstrate the effect of the speeches on undecided voters. Unlike most of the other speakers, my reasons for remaining were nothing to do with trade, or how much richer or poorer we would be if we left the European Union. I spoke from the heart, and it must have had some resonance because the gauge shot round to 'Remain' as I spoke, leaving Jeremy open-mouthed, and, bless him, delighted. My grandchildren told me later that my piece had 'gone viral' on the web, which they assured me was paradoxically a good thing.

After the programme, the great and the good congratulated me effusively, including Alastair C. What thrilled me most was a hug from Delia Smith, my saviour at many a social occasion. That was much more impressive to me than the fact that the prime minister, David Cameron, sent out a message on social media telling people to look at what I had said before they voted.

The argument I put forward was one I heard little then and have rarely heard since, whenever Brexit is discussed. The gist of my contribution was that, as a child during the war, I was bombed, and my friends and neighbours killed, by the Germans. I went to bed underground in our damp air-raid shelter and listened to the zooming planes and guns fighting life-and-death battles in the skies above. Our house lost its roof and windows in the bombardment. At seven years old my case was packed, my gas mask put over my shoulder and a label tied to my coat, and I was sent off to the country and billeted on strangers. I was terrified for most of my childhood.

And I hated the Germans.

My first husband, Alec Ross, served in the RAF during the war when he was involved in destroying German cities and killing thousands of their citizens.

And the Germans, in their turn, hated him.

Sometime after VJ Day, the Fricker boy from next door came back skeletal and mute from the horrors he had endured in a Japanese prisoner-of-war camp.

And I hated the Japanese.

Then we did the unthinkable. Not once but twice, we backed the United States in obliterating two huge areas of Japan with atomic bombs. Killing and maiming thousands.

And surely to God they hated us.

But somehow, out of this maelstrom of hatred came the idea of a united Europe. Encouraged by our hero Winston Churchill, the countries that had been involved in two world wars, killing 40 million in the first, and 70 million in the second, would unite to create a better, more peaceful continent. It was a step towards a united world.

After the war my father made me look at pictures of Belsen. One photo in particular is branded on my brain. It is of a terrified naked child standing on a laboratory bench being pointed at with a stick, watched by uniformed Nazi officers and white-coated doctors. My father did not spare my eleven-year-old self the horrors of Dr Mengele's experiments on Jewish and Roma children in the camps. As I cried, he told me, 'For their sake, this must never happen again. It is down to you.'

I am fairly certain my dad, like me, would have rejoiced to see a united Europe based on liberal principles. It was our way of trying to ensure that worldwide strife on this scale would never happen again. A united world. Idealistic? Yes. Difficult? Fearsomely. But essential? Yes. Surely it's only by working together that we can resolve the huge problems of inequality and poverty, the mass movement of populations – which the word 'immigration' does not adequately describe – and the destruction of our planet? The European Union was one faltering, difficult step towards that. Much has gone wrong. But with commitment and will, we could've made something wonderful.

In one day, 23 June 2016, all that has gone. The result was 51.89 per cent to leave and 48.11 per cent to remain. (I will always worry that the 3.78 per cent margin was my fault.)

July 2016

Our country is now riven and fragmented. There are rifts being whipped up between city and country, North and South, young and old. At the height of the pre-referendum war of rhetoric, a young MP, Jo Cox, who once said in the House of Commons that we 'have more in common than that which divides us', was shot and viciously stabbed to death in public by a tragically deluded man shouting, 'Britain first.'

Since the very close result of the referendum, I have somewhat half-heartedly taken part in campaigns to stop some of the damage that I believe will happen if we sever ourselves from our neighbours. Has happened. I suppose I am one of the metropolitan elite, a saboteur, a traitor, a Remoaner, a citizen of nowhere, and all the other put-downs thrown at those of us who voted against leaving. (Not to mention the 30 per cent who did not vote at all. Shame on them.)

Some are furious with people like me, who they think don't understand what it is for a community to lose its identity. I do, my beloved fellow countrymen (and women!), I do.

In Oldham, where I worked for a year in the fifties, I saw the decline of the cotton trade. The influx of workers from Pakistan prepared to work for less money and worse conditions, who became ghettoised in various pockets of the town, plus the destruction of the back-to-back houses, unsanitary, rudimentary, but immaculately kept, and sociable, caused damage to the existing strong, white, working-class culture. When the mills closed, there was a gradual breakdown of a whole way of life, with no intervention early on, when it would have made a difference.

I was staying in Workington when they closed the steelworks, the epicentre of the life of the town. A couple of men rendered unemployed by the closure warned me that older men would no longer be able to advise and keep an eye on the younger, and a soft-toy factory was no replacement for the virile work at the steelworks. They predicted that the whole town would fall apart. When I went back to do a radio show a few years later I could see the signs of decline in this previously buoyant town. I was told by the locals how pleasant life used to be. I was given a sketch by Lowry of the nearby seaside town Maryport, back when it was a beach for families to enjoy, with boats, and sandcastles, and the whippet dogs they used to race. Even that was now polluted, and destroyed by the sea coming from nearby Windscale, as it used to be called, until, after a disastrous accident at the plant, it was renamed Sellafield. Cumbria has not been taken care of.

The mining communities too, where a bitter battle was fought to save not just jobs but a whole way of life, were obliterated and just left to rot. Did no one foresee the social problems that would follow? Or did they just not care?

All of them shamefully ignored by successive British governments. And now they blame the EU.

I am enraged that we have, in my opinion, been manipulated by the unscrupulous campaigning of an unelected political adviser called Dominic Cummings, who plainly despises long-established government procedure and appears willing to tell any lie, or use any simplistic brainwashing slogan, to achieve his fanatical ends, supposedly on behalf of the likes of Nigel Farage, Boris Johnson, Arron Banks and Jacob Rees-Mogg, but actually intent on a revolution far beyond their Brexit dreams.

A like-minded friend suggested that we are like all old people, who don't embrace change, and moan about how wonderful life was when we were young. As I have pointed out, for me it wasn't. War was vile, and poverty was grinding. My generation, and that of my parents, toiled to make things better and succeeded to an amazing degree, but one of those achievements is now on the rubbish dump. Many of the liberal values we fought for are now ridiculed, kindness and respect for minorities has become 'political correctness gone mad', and racism and anti-Semitism are on the rise.

Many Remainers, after fruitlessly trying to make their voices heard, with no leadership, and a pro-Leave press, have become sad but resigned. Not me. I am still in turmoil. I have had two quite serious brushes with depression in my life and I know the signs. I am aware my reaction is bordering on the unhinged.

November 2016

On 5 November, competing with the Guy Fawkes fireworks, a virulent rash exploded on my legs. The irritation took over my whole being in its intensity. I couldn't think of anything else. I have always thought that if I were ever paralysed and unable to communicate, not being able to ask for relief for an unbearable itching would be worse than silent pain. I was unable to sleep or work, and the only temporary balm proved to be, contrary to all advice, having a scalding-hot shower. Remembering my cancer years, when I believed my body was telling me that I needed to get rid of a growing destructive element in my life, I sought to explain my all-consuming, ugly, erupting skin. Could it be that my obsession with the volcanic changes in the world had entered my bloodstream? Was it that picture of Trump and Farage that was all over the press, standing in front of some garish golden doors, like a couple of gleeful louts, Trump, grinning maniacally, doing a thumbs-up sign, and Farage, not sure what to do with his hands in the absence of his customary pint of beer, gesturing awkwardly towards his new best pal, whilst giving one of his usual obscene, gape-mouthed, roaring laughs? Two squalid opportunists, in cahoots in their triumphant boys' adventure of changing the world. And giving me a rash. The bastards.

2016 has been an earthquake of a year. I feel alienated, at least from my country, if not the world. I am reminded of a visit I made to my beloved Auntie Ruby in 1999. After a lifetime of independent spinsterhood, in which she'd bestowed her generous love on me and many others, she eventually had a fall and stairs became a problem, so I found her a nice residential home into which she seemed to settle. After a few months I noticed she had stopped doing her Telegraph crossword. In those days the Telegraph was an excellent newspaper, and she usually spent the morning reading it. When I visited we would discuss world events. One day I went to see her – it was at the height of the revelations of genocide in Kosovo, while the other news was of schoolboys killing their colleagues in Columbine, and a nail bomb exploding in a gay pub in Soho. We would normally have had a good debate about the state of the world, but that day she seemed reluctant to engage. She explained she no longer read her lovely Telegraph. With tears in her eyes, she told me, 'It's not my world now, darling. I don't belong here any more.' I was angry that she would opt out of what she had taught me to challenge with relish, and had become apathetic and detached, preferring to talk about the pleasure of our Victoria sponge and Earl Grey tea. Now I understand.

My dear Auntie Ruby died shortly after that last conversation. Do I, like her, just give up and recognise that I am a dinosaur that has outlived its viability in this new world? My evacuation experience taught me to get up if I was knocked down and fight back, with my fists if necessary. That's easier when you are eight years old, but maybe I could still winch my old bones out of the Slough of Despond. Maybe I should evoke the spirit of Dylan Thomas:

Do not go gentle into that good night,
Old age should burn and rave at close of day;
Rage, rage against the dying of the light.

Right now, I just don't have the energy.

November 2016

Decided to escape to France, hoping the locals won't blame me for Brexit. My friends at Marseilles Airport and the car-hire firm just shake their heads and look at me with pity.

Winter is not the ideal time to visit Provence. It was below freezing when I arrived but I took profound satisfaction in collecting kindling from the field and concocting faggots with painstaking folding of newspaper, then gradually feeding in logs, until the stove roared into life. With no leaves on the trees, I could see the cradle of mountains that encircle the horizon. The landscape palette was brown, black, green, blue, purple, and the quivering silver of the aspen trees. Nature had turned the landscape into a sculpture. As I cuddled down in front of the stove listening to my old-fashioned cassette tapes, I was warmed with pleasure and gratitude that I have this refuge. Whatever the turmoil in the world outside, this place remains constant.

I love being in France. I am, and always will be, British, but from that root grows something larger. I, like my grandchildren, absolutely feel part of a big multicultural European hotchpotch of races, linked together, striving to share our wealth and success and troubles with one another. When I did Who Do You Think You Are?, I discovered I have German ancestry; there are very few of us on this island who do not have blood ties with other Europeans. Way back we were actually joined geographically. That my country is at present cutting through these roots, and forcibly ripping me away, is leaving this gaping, bleeding wound in my life that I have yet to find a way of staunching.

After an evening of wound-licking, the next day I pulled myself together. I was about to put on John's old location jacket to go into Apt, our nearest market town, when I remembered the hem of my fifty-year-old grey corduroy trousers was hanging over my shoes and dragging on the ground, as it had for several months. It was growing fear of old-lady falls and broken hips that made me sit, leg balanced on the table, sewing it back in place with an approximation of the hemstitch I learned at school seventy-odd years ago. People don't stitch and patch and darn like we used to back in the day. All my clothes were made to last, with seams that could be let out and hems that could be lengthened to allow for growth. Dad had leather patches on the elbows of his jacket, sheets were cut in two and remade with less-worn sides to middle, and socks and gloves sported intricate darns woven on a wooden mushroom. All my clothes as a child were remade versions of my mother's or big sister's garments. Never for one moment did it occur to me that I might be hard done by, except when my scholarship provided the fees for my grammar school but I found myself the only girl whose tunic and blouse, and even green serge knickers, were home-made. I was too mortified to appreciate that my mother, who worked in a shop six days a week, must have toiled over the Singer sewing machine until the small hours to provide my uniform.

My trousers now trip-proof, I donned the ancient big black jumper which my mother had knitted for me when another scholarship led to the Royal Academy of Dramatic Art. On this occasion, Kent County Council generously provided me with a modest maintenance fee (which wouldn't happen now), but it didn't stretch to buying one of the sloppy joe jumpers that were all the rage. Mum's trusty knitting needles did the job and I still, to this day, relish its baggy warm embrace. My wardrobe in France is all my cast-offs from London. Unrecognised, I wander around with no make-up, lank unwashed hair and ragged old thrown-together ensembles. In Chiswick I could well be considered a bag lady and social services would step in. Here in France they just accept that Englishwomen are not very chic and don't have a weekly manicure and coiffure done by either a shop or a friend. They assume that I am a bit eccentric, like the very tall Arab who wanders around muttering to himself, and who once startled me by wordlessly forcing a Babybel cheese into my hands, possibly thinking my need was greater than his.

In Apt I am always greeted fondly by our newsagent, Karim, who keeps The Times and a day-old Guardian for me and scans the pages for news of me and two other English actors who live in the area. These cuttings he gives to me discreetly, conscious that I value my anonymity, but unaware that I hate reading anything about myself and so throw away his review or comment without looking at it. I said hello to a couple of old English blokes who take a morning drink at the old-fashioned zinc bar that I frequent for its excellent coffee. They did once tell the Gauloises-smoking, Pernod-quaffing owner I was 'une grande vedette', but his Gallic shrug revealed that he considered Les Anglais' age and alcohol intake to have addled their cheerful brains.

My evolution into a proud European took time. It started when I was fourteen, in 1947. I am not sure how it came about, but two of my teachers – surprisingly jaunty women when stripped of their gowns and teaching demeanour – took me to Paris to spend the summer holiday as an au pair with a friend of theirs, whose husband was the director of the Comédie-Française theatre. I had done a couple of school plays and maybe they thought I merited encouragement.

I don't remember all the details of this, my first venture abroad, but suffice it to say it had a profound effect.

I remember we saw the detritus of battle on the deserted beaches, and Paris must have been a sombre place, but my recollection is of mind-blowing sophistication. War and want had rendered my childhood devoid of much in the way of worldly pleasures. I am sure there was a stratum of society in Britain that knew about olive oil and wine, but for me, who had only ever tasted our annual Christmas bottle of Barsac, drinking wine at every meal was a revelation. I was taken to a Jacques Fath fashion show and saw the difference between dressmaking and couture. I stood transfixed in the Jeu de Paume gallery before Van Gogh's inch-deep Starry Night, displayed amongst the first real paintings I had ever seen. My boss Madame Touchard's sex life was quite unlike my mum's, who I was not even sure had one, and seemed a lot of fun. I cycled all over the then traffic-free Paris, so it became, and still is, my favourite city in the world, next to London.

In a few short weeks I saw what goodies the world had to offer. I had left behind a world of bomb craters and destruction and found a whole new beautiful place. I was too young to detect the complex wounds of war and occupation in France.

Then in 1949, when I was sixteen, I sewed a Union Jack on a knapsack and with two friends set off to hitch-hike around France, Belgium and Holland, getting various jobs to support ourselves on the way. We were overwhelmed by the hospitality and gratitude we received.

The final stage of my European odyssey was twenty-five years ago, when John and I bought the house in rural France. It seemed a very grown-up thing to buy a property abroad but that's what we did. Primitive, no central heating, just a wood-burning stove, no pool, no kitchen, rudimentary bathroom, in a small hameau surrounded by lavender and cherry orchards. To begin with, the French were wary of us, but over the years it became our home, to which we sped whenever we weren't working in England. When John died, in 2002, the agony of his absence made me consider selling the house, but I realised I needed the uncomplicated empathy of my French neighbours. It is unbelievable that John and I, then just I, have lived in Provence for twenty-five years.

This hameau, when I first arrived, consisted of Roger, a French vineyard worker, and his family; Pierre, a retired miner; André and Denis, two brothers who were born and raised in a small cottage; and Monsieur Cros, a schoolteacher, and his family. Into this close community came an English couple and an American woman. What a culture shock that must've been. Over the past twenty years, the vineyard was sold to a Swedish businessman who had always dreamed of working on the land, and spends his retirement painstakingly changing the local wine from boxed plonk to a very acceptable rosé. The American woman has been replaced by two Parisians whose second home it is, although one of them went to school in the area and his father used to be mayor. The miner has left to enjoy his generous pension on the coast and instead we have a delightful young woman whom we have watched fall in love and have two children, who wave to me in my kitchen as they cavort naked in the sun. The Swede has tastefully developed a barn into a modern dwelling and another outbuilding into a pottery for his wife. We have grown at ease with one another without invading anyone's privacy.

A few years ago an Englishwoman with a German husband moved in down the lane, and their warm sociability has woven us into a very close community. They arrange occasional boules matches on our ramshackle rough pitch, and we had a secret party for Denis's eightieth birthday and mourned together André's death. So, life has not stood still over the years in this little hameau. The feeling of deep fondness and complete trust that exists between us has developed gradually. I still can't understand 50 per cent of what Denis says in his Provençal accent but I know he is there for me should I need him.

Getting ready to return to London, I decided to check the postbox at the end of the track. I went via the ancient oak, embracing it as I always do, digging my fingers into its bark, thanking it for being. I stood for a while admiring the blaze of the sunset. Then I banged on the iron postbox and listened for wasps. After cautiously unlocking the door, I was about to tear up the advertising material that had ignored my 'Pas de Publicité' notice when I spotted the name of our village in an article on the cover of the local mairie news. It took me a while to translate but its meaning was devastatingly clear. The commune has to build seventy-five new residences by government edict, and our hameau is one of the hamlets designated for expansion.

Blood really does run cold in response to shock. Our ramshackle, ancient, primitive, intimate group of homes is to be desecrated by new building. Strangers will come and break up our little community. Twenty-five years of only slight gradual change, the security of a shared way of life, will be ruined.

The intricate web we have woven over the years will be destroyed by expansion. These newcomers won't understand our way of life. Why can't things stay the same?

'I want my village back.'

November 2016

I had to get back to do some dubbing on a series called Delicious that I had been working on in Cornwall. I have ambivalent feelings towards Cornwall, which voted overwhelmingly to leave the EU. While I was filming there during the campaign, I had many an argument with local film crew members, but I did understand why they felt the way they did – the South-West, too, has been neglected. In the wake of another industrial collapse, that of the tin mines, the natives of Cornwall are forced into servicing surfers, second-homers and troublesome tourists whose picnics have turned the seagulls into fat savage predators. There is work in the summer but none in the winter, which is why Cornwall is one of the poorest counties in the UK. I discovered that many people had no idea how much support had come to the area from the European Union. What's more, after the very successful Leave campaign, they did not care. They just wanted out. Mind you, some Cornish folk hate people from Devon, and given half a chance would build a wall along the Tamar and keep everyone out, let alone nasty Europeans. They hoist their slightly sinister black-and-white Cornish flag and make plans to cut through the border and set Cornwall adrift as an angry little island, living off fish cooked by Rick Stein.

There is one pub that we used to go to where the locals welcomed us with open arms, and we relished the fish, the cider and the yarns of the old regulars. One day one of them told me that his friend, whom I will call Tom, wanted to talk to me but was too shy. Tom and I found a quiet corner and this old man hesitantly told me his story.

Tom was born during the war. His mother, let's call her Eileen, was not married, which in those days was a shameful situation: 'I was illegitimate.' It was even more frowned upon because she had been 'going with' an American serviceman. I remember well how reviled the GIs were. They were considered sloppy and spoiled compared with our British troops. Especially risible was their loose-limbed marching. They seemed to have a lot of money to spend and – even more riling for the local men – the girls all thought they were lovely. So did the kids. They were endlessly kind to us vaccies, with copious supplies of goodies. 'Got any gum, chum?' was our password to piles of chewing gum, candies and cookies. And they were great dancers. At village socials they whirled the girls around in a way far removed from the stiff stumblings of the local lads. But to 'go with' one of these attractive men was considered a betrayal of the English men who were away fighting.

'She tried to get rid of me' – Tom said this several times. Maybe it was something his poor ostracised mother would say to him when the strain of being treated as a slut, while single-handedly trying to bring up a child by taking in washing, and cleaning up at the Big House, became too much. I dread to think what that desperate young girl did to herself to try to abort the baby she knew would ruin her life. Because of course the GI left, and Eileen told Tom she never heard from him again.

It was ten years before anyone in the village spoke to her – ten years before Tom said she became 'respectable'. He was adamant that that was the timescale. Some incident when he was ten years old must have marked a change in some people's attitude towards him and his mother. Maybe the boy stood up to them after ten years of cruelty. Maybe it was because of changing times, or because their neighbours ultimately had to admire and accept the young woman's courage. He did not want to elaborate. Eileen never married. Tom looked after her when she grew old and he himself 'never found the right woman'. I would think his valiant mother would have been a hard act to follow.

But recently something momentous had happened – and that was why he wanted to talk to me. He had received a letter from America, from a grandson of the man who was Tom's father, who had been exploring his family history and come across Tom. Presumably the GI Joe must have told someone about his love affair during the war, maybe even his wife. Or maybe someone discovered a letter from Eileen. Both of them were now dead. Tom had never really talked about his father with his mother, although she had told him that he was a fine man. Did he know about Tom? If so, why did he not help? Maybe he did. How did his mother afford to buy him a bicycle? There were so many questions, which Tom was happy to leave unanswered.

I could tell that receiving this letter had turned Tom's life upside down. He was obviously well liked in the pub and I suspect after all these years most of the younger residents did not know about his childhood. He had certainly told no one about this new chain of events. He told me that he had replied to the letter, confirming that they had his mother's name right, and that he almost certainly was their grandfather's son. Tom thought, indeed hoped, that would be the end of it.

But the previous week he had received another letter. The grandchildren were planning a party for their father, Tom's half-brother, a celebration for his eightieth birthday, and would like him to come over, all expenses paid. I grasped his hand as he told me, and my heart sank when he said, 'What would you do, Sheila?'

My first thought was that of course he should go. The bastards owe him something. It sounds as though Joe's descendants have had a good life, while Tom and Eileen's lives were a poverty-stricken struggle. Maybe he would enjoy the adventure of going on an aeroplane for the first time, and a whole new country. He has never been outside Cornwall. The young relatives who made the effort to trace him would probably treat him lovingly. A new generation, not blighted by those bigoted, cruel values of old, would welcome him into their family. What an adventure. That would be my reaction as an endlessly curious woman.

Then I saw the fear in his eyes. It could go horribly wrong. He has a version of his childhood that he has accepted as the truth, the one his mother gave him. What if he discovered that Joe wanted her to take his son out to the US and she, like him now, was afraid to go? What if the grandchildren thought it would be a jolly party jape to bring over their father's brother but, having maybe had charmed lives themselves, would not understand the sort of unworldly man Tom is? What would these presumably relatively rich Americans make of an old fish-poacher wearing clothes from the charity shop? He had never been to a big lavish party in his life. He was seventy-four. His bitterly hard young life is long forgotten, and his routine, which revolves around catching the odd illicit salmon, and holding court from his seat in the pub, is comfortably set. The wounds of his childhood are buried deep and I saw the danger of digging them up. We talked for a long time and had a good few jars. I helped him weigh up all the options, but told him it had to be his decision.

I held him in my arms as I said goodbye, and he whispered, 'I don't need to go there. Tonight has been the best night of my life – meeting you.'

It broke my heart.

That his life should be so low on loveliness that meeting me was a high spot. That the opportunity for betterment in his damaged existence came too late.

Tom has led a good life. He can look back in pride at his survival and defeat of prejudice, at his loving care of his mother. He doesn't, because he is not aware that they are a reason for pride. Maybe that is why meeting me was important to him. I am probably the only person who has ever told him he is special and, like Eileen said of his father – fine.

December 2016

I had to go to France to join my neighbours in fighting the destructive building directive. I girded my loins and marched up to the mairie to confront the mayor. He once attended one of our parties in the barn, and left in the small hours having supped deep of our local wine, so I hoped he might have a soft spot for our beautiful hameau. True to form he was sweetness and light.

I don't trust him an inch.

2017

My first job of 2017 is an odd fish. It is about a supposed meeting between Salvador Dalí and Alice Cooper in which I play the intriguing Gala Dalí, muse of her husband and several other artists. It is a bizarre script but with David Suchet made up to look surprisingly like Dalí, and Noel Fielding, in a rare acting performance, having no trouble getting under the skin of Alice Cooper, it is great fun. The directors are artists and completely taken up with the suitably surrealistic appearance of the film, so we are left to our own devices as to the interpretation of the roles.

The three of us have worked well together, taking it all very seriously, whilst not being altogether au fait with what is going on. My favourite moment was when David, for some reason half-naked standing in a boxing ring, asked me to help him decide what sort of chicken voice the script required he should use. 'What do you think, Sheila – should it be "squawk, squawk", or "cluck cluck cluck"?'

I reminded him that the last time we worked together had been an erudite programme for the RSC analysing the syntax of Shakespeare's sonnets.

February 2017

My work and play are proving varied and fun this year. I have visited several towns in my role as patron of DigiSmart, a method of learning to read and write in schools for children who are falling behind. So, lots of exciting engaging with kids.

I was thrilled to take part in my very favourite TV quiz programme, Would I Lie to You? Just as I find when I appear on Just a Minute, I was lost in admiration for the other team members, most of whom were comedy players. David Mitchell, Lee Mack and Rob Brydon in the chair have a superb rapport. No one tries to dominate, they feed each other generously and their personalities, whether just for the screen or maybe in reality, are perfect foils to each other – square Mitchell, smooth Brydon and slightly mad Mack seem to relish their differences. I forgot that I was being paid to entertain rather than enjoy myself.

I have also taken to attending stand-up comedy shows in the Leicester Square Theatre, usually with one of my grown-up grandchildren. One of my favourites is Bridget Christie, who talks about family life, and children, and politics, with a dangerous edge of hysteria. Her husband, Stewart Lee, is regarded by other stand-ups as the Master. He doesn't appear very much on the television as his material is probably too esoteric. His rage consumes himself and the audience, and I find it very cathartic. He sometimes lapses into a fantasy world of his own, in what seems an unplanned way, but it is probably meticulously prepared.

One evening I did not enjoy. I am a great admirer of Russell Brand. He too has an edge of mad recklessness. He is his own person, with seemingly no regard to what is acceptable. He shocks and angers many people, which I find laudable, but when I went to see him at the Apollo in Hammersmith it was too much for me. I did something I rarely do: I left at the interval. Not as a demonstration of disapproval, but just because I personally could not take it. And was disturbed by those who could.

We were told before the event that there would be audience participation. That used to be in a song sheet, with everyone joining together singing silly songs. In Brand's case it was asking the audience, amongst other loaded questions, what was their most embarrassing sexual experience. The audience roared their approval at someone recounting in detail an occasion when his mother slipped on the 'results' of his 'sneaky wank in the bedroom'. The audience were shrieking with delight as the stories topped each other in excess, culminating in a girl with a lovely face like the Mona Lisa graphically describing her first experience of anal sex, which involved defecation. In answer to the question 'What are you most proud of?' a young girl in glasses told us, 'People say I give good head', and bowed courteously in response to her standing ovation.

The mob – for that to me is what they had become – demonstrated the power of a personality like Brand to stir people into extreme behaviour, in a highly charged atmosphere. I suspect a lot of that audience woke up the next day disbelieving what they had said and done, as they prepared to go to work in the office. I'm sure the racist Bernard Manning had a similar hold over a crowd. As did Billy Graham, with perhaps better motives, at his religious rallies. And that American who made his disciples drink poison. And Hitler at the Nuremberg Rallies. Now, of course, Brand means no harm. In actual fact, he did no harm that night – perhaps it was liberating for those young women to declare their sexuality proudly in public. But this old bird found it ugly and hoped they wouldn't regret it when they sobered up and, maybe later in life, learned to equate sex more with love.

Even Brand seemed a bit concerned about the excesses that he had stirred up, saying as we left for the interval, 'Be kind to our perverts.' My grandson Jack told me he was much more restrained in the second half so it may be the demon that possessed him was exorcised over a nice cup of tea in the interval break.

October 2017

Decided to buy myself some silk bed linen. Felt in need of a bit of a treat.

I am slightly obsessive about beds. I blame the war. Of course I do. In the air-raid shelter I was on a narrow bunk with no mattress, and all hell going on outside. When I was evacuated, in my billet, I slept on an ancient cracked leatherette couch and the toilet was down the garden, a wooden seat with a hole in the middle over the entrance to Pluto's underworld. You even had to pass a savage dog to get to it. No wonder I wet the bed.

The night before I sat my exam for a scholarship to grammar school, there was a particularly noisy air raid, and when we heard the German bombers retreating my worried mother decided that, to prepare my brain, we should leave the shelter and try to sleep in the house. As Dad was on ARP duty, tending to the wounded and clearing up the debris from the raid, she said I could even sleep in their bed with her.

My parents' bedroom was a sacred place to which I was not allowed access, maybe because they might have to explain to me what went on there – something they never could bring themselves to do, preferring to leave it to hygiene lessons at school. Of course, I crept in when they were at work. It was the height of luxury to me. There was an unused silver-backed hairbrush and mirror, a cut-glass powder jar and a mysterious ivory object which, I discovered years later, was a glove-stretcher, all set out neatly on a lace mat on the large ornate dressing table, and presumably all inherited from someone. My mother had made what she called a 'dusty-pink' satinette eiderdown for the super-comfortable bed. On that night she had to shake off some plaster dislodged from the ceiling by a nearby landmine before we could nestle under it. Not usually given to physical expressions of love, she gently stroked my forehead, hoping to quell all fears of the coming ordeal the next day which would allow me to 'better myself'.

Later, in theatrical digs, I have shared beds with fleas, bedbugs and the occasional cockroach.

One of the first things John, who had a similar bad bed history, did when we fell in love was to buy a beautiful brass bed that had belonged to the handsome matinee idol Ivor Novello, who by all accounts had as much fun in it as we did. I sleep in it to this day. Now under silk sheets. Bliss. I would like to end my life in its sensuous embrace, as did John.

November 2017

I was in France gathering black figs from the garden when the phone rang.

'Mum, I'm afraid I have some bad news.'

It was Ellie Jane, my eldest daughter.

'What? Tell me?' My whole being cringes with fear.

'Okay. I have breast cancer. Sorry.'

No one dead, then. That's good. Then – foolishly, frantically, 'Oh dear. Well, darling, they have made enormous headway since I had it. It's a nuisance, but they can deal with it nowadays.'

Nuisance? Deal with it? They? I'm talking nonsense.

'Unfortunately it's rather an aggressive one. Grade three. But don't worry, I'll be all right.'

'Of course you will. I'll get the next flight to London.'

I put the phone down and went into the newly installed downstairs toilet and vomited into its pristine lavatory. Then, clinging to the table, I said out loud, quite calmly, 'Okay, so, yes, now I want to die.'

I genuinely meant it. How could I go on without my beloved eldest daughter? How obscene if she, at fifty, should die, and I who had already lived for eighty-four years should continue. A child dying before her parent is unnatural. Not to be endured. Not by me.

Back in England I have watched as Ellie Jane is swallowed into the vortex of endless tests, scans and agonising waiting for results. It is a rare type of cancer that necessitates drastic treatment. I am desperate to 'kiss and make it better', make it go away, but I don't know how.

When your daughter is married with children, you are demoted to the nana of her primary family. My instinct with problems is always to charge in fighting, but now I realise I have to take a ringside seat and watch and support. Her immediate family is shocked and frightened but coping as people always seem to. Her partner, Matt, a highly successful producer, has put all his work on hold and never leaves her side during the gruelling treatment. A marked contrast to my dear husband, who coped with my cancer by denying it was happening and not getting involved. From the day John's mother deserted him when he was seven, that was how he dealt with people threatening to leave him. I understood completely, but it was lonely. Something my daughter certainly isn't. She has myriad friends who shower her with love. At one point she had to be reminded that the chemotherapy ward at the Marsden was not designed to hold parties. But sometimes we all need a mum and I try to be there when she does.

She has to give herself injections. Having nursed several people, it is a skill I have acquired. She sat on a stool in the bathroom like a little girl, frightened, white, silent. I showed her what to do. She did it. I cuddled her.

My child.

'Well done, you did it, clever girl, clever girl.'

The rest of the time I sit in the corner making notes at doctors' meetings, bring cakes into the chemo ward, search the web for the latest research and sort out wigs and headgear for the inevitable hair loss. Ellie Jane somehow continues to work, however ill she is. The dedication and love she feels towards the disadvantaged kids she supports with her special brand of drama therapy made her determined not to let them down. I could not be more proud of the way she has dealt with the torture of chemotherapy, radiotherapy and the prospect of two operations. I do my best not to show my horror at the chemical bombardment on her beautiful body, but when I get home, alone, I howl with grief.

I am racked with anguish that this is happening to my daughter and I am powerless.

Throughout the treatment she is unfailingly cheerful. Certainly, in front of me. Never for one moment do I see a sign of fear. Any bad news about the progress of the treatment is kept from me. I always get any information after it has been mulled over with her sisters. 'We didn't want to worry you.'

My three daughters are in constant contact with one another, something that pleases me because I know they will be there for one another when I'm gone. They came together as a family very suddenly. When I married John, he had a little girl, Abigail, and I had Ellie Jane. They were both thrilled to go from being only children to having a sister, and very soon along came another one, Joanna. As a threesome they have supported one another through some fairly hairy times and do so now they are women with children of their own. I just wish they would still let me support them a bit more. Maybe it would be different were I the sort of woman who looks after her grandchildren on a regular basis while their parents work, as many do, but the irregular nature of my job makes that impossible, and, let's face it, after a large chunk of my life being dominated by mothering because of the big age difference in my children, I am not that keen to go back to it in old age. I have no right to expect them to need me only when it is convenient for me. I can't have it both ways. So, instead, I seem to have turned into the person that they look after: 'Don't tell Mum, it will only upset her.' 'Mum, I'm a grown woman' is the usual rejoinder to any advice I might venture to offer.

I'm not sure when the role of mother changes from being in control to taking a back seat. As a self-reliant, proactive person, it is not a situation I relish. It coincides with being ignored by waiters and bartenders, and not being expected to join the cast and crew for a drink after a day's shooting. Anyway, my anxiety, despite my efforts to conceal it, is not helpful to Ellie Jane during her treatment, and she is better able to discuss her worries with friends and her sisters. They have more in common. Looking back, I realise I was exactly the same with my mother.

When my father died in 1965, I moved my mother from her mobile home in Sussex to a tiny flat near me in Hammersmith. She yearned to be an intimate part of my life and Ellie Jane's upbringing, but there was a yawning gap between her disciplined approach and my Swinging Sixties lifestyle. How Ellie Jane was 'turned out', with clean white socks and shiny shoes, was a top priority. It was way down my list of things to cope with when bringing up my wayward daughter. Ironically, with my grandchildren, I have turned into my mother. I insist on good table manners, especially in restaurants, and putting away books and toys at bedtime – rules happily abided by when I have them on my own, but when my daughters are there I have to bite my lip till it bleeds. My mother did not speak the same language as my colourful friends, and despite, or maybe because of, having been a barmaid was wary of alcoholic excess – and there was a lot of that about. Having weathered two world wars, losing a fiancé in the first and enduring bombing and separation from her children (my sister away touring the world with ENSA and I evacuated) in the second, as well as dealing with an erratic and somewhat unstable husband, she was a sober presence. I seldom remember her laughing.

The gap of understanding between my mother and me was, I think, bigger than happens nowadays. I was a snotty grammar-school-educated girl, as my parents had strived for me to be, by then earning reasonable money and living in some style; she left school at fourteen, her education coming from library books and the radio, ending up living in a mobile home on a caravan site, which she seemed to like. I look back with huge regret that I did not make more effort to find out how she really felt about life. You just didn't have those sorts of conversations with your parents in those days. When my father was alive, she could seldom get a word in edgeways anyway. Her only utterance usually was a wry 'Oh, Rick' as Daddy held the floor. She was always busy doing something, and no fan of idle chit-chat. Maybe most daughters never do know their mothers as anything other than a mother.

I am discovering now that the relationship often ends with this strange role reversal as the mother ages. I ended up bed-bathing my mother and carrying out intimate care in the last weeks of her life, something that mortified her but seemed just repayment for all the years she had nurtured me. As I combed her hair, I would tell her she was beautiful. It was obvious no one had ever done that before. In fact, she shyly told me that she had always been worried about her looks. She was, in old age and, judging by photos, when she was young, dazzlingly lovely. How tragic that in those austere days no one made her feel attractive, except maybe my dad in a jokey, awkward way, although he would protect her from difficult customers in the pub, and once slapped me hard for being rude to her. My mother was a successful worker behind the bar in hotels and pubs, and on the counters of shops, but she always saw her most important job as being a wife and mother. Which is all very well if you're a good one, which I wasn't.

Two weeks before Ellie Jane was born I was doing a broadcast, and two weeks after I was giving my all as Senna, wife of Hengist Pod, in Carry On Cleo. I was proud to be part of a film in which my friend Kenneth Williams as Julius Caesar had the deathless phrase 'Infamy! Infamy! They've all got it in for me!' but it was not a comfortable engagement. I was still breastfeeding Ellie Jane, so my mother was in the dressing room waiting to thrust her at me whenever I could escape from the set. The Carry Ons didn't hang around. Only one take was expected and then quickly on to the next. Time off to feed a baby was not an option. So there was none of that lovely quiet bonding that is intended to take place between mother and child. It was a salutary lesson for baby Ellie Jane, perhaps a forewarning of a childhood being pushed from pillar to post by my job. All of my girls have spent much time in tatty dressing rooms, digs and neighbours' houses, looked after by my mother and, after her death, by dressers, fellow cast members, various wonderful au pairs and friends. My youngest daughter, Joanna, sat in a box at Drury Lane on matinee days of Sweeney Todd. I thought it was a treat. Only recently did she explain that she was completely traumatised by seeing her mother regularly thrown into a red-hot oven.

We seldom had holidays. Neither of my husbands nor I did holidays as children. John occasionally stayed in a relative's caravan in Wales and I remember a pub outing to Ramsgate when I was about six, mainly for being groped by one of Dad's customers whilst crushed next to him on a fairground ride. My girls' children have several holidays a year.

In my defence I did spend absolutely all the time that I was not working with my children, and turned down any jobs that would interfere with their schoolwork. When she was a baby, I dragged Ellie Jane, along with my mother, to New York, when I was doing Entertaining Mr Sloane on Broadway, for which I was nominated for a Tony Award, but once she and Jo were school age I would not leave them, thereby vetoing a possible career in America. Mrs Brigstocke, the high mistress of St Paul's Girls' School, said I was unusual amongst all the high-flying parents in that I would always respond to her request for a meeting to discuss Ellie Jane's latest misdemeanour, once rushing to the school wearing full stage make-up and wig between the matinee and evening performances of Annie to cope with the latest drama.

I may not have taken them on holiday much, but I provided them with lovely homes. When Ellie Jane was born I was living in a rented basement flat in which the kitchen was combined with the bathroom. Then I daringly bought a cottage with an outside lavatory, which I did up, paying for it one job at a time, eventually selling it for a tidy profit. I was on the property ladder, which gave me and my family a bit of security, so that even in out-of-work periods we had a roof over our heads.

Despite my absences due to work, I loved my girls with all my heart and soul, which may have contributed a bit to them turning out to be splendid women. But there is no doubt that their childhoods lacked stability. Joanna probably suffered the most; being the youngest by ten years, she became the peacemaker. I realise the toll this took every Christmas when I receive a DVD from her husband, another son-in-law called Matt, of the year's events. Their three children go on wonderful adventures and holidays and there in the middle, shrieking with delight, is Joanna, belatedly living the fun childhood she didn't have enough of.

My only comfort is that, despite their rackety childhoods, all three of my daughters are wonderful mothers. They have demanding jobs yet manage to be there for their offspring much more than I ever was for them. They are considerably helped by partners who totally share the burdens and delights of running a home and bringing up children. I was married to men from old-fashioned working-class backgrounds who, with the best will in the world, and despite efforts to acknowledge the feminist revolution, were brought up in times when men wouldn't be seen pushing a pram, let alone changing a nappy.

As far as mothering skills go, maybe my daughters have benefited from my example of how not to do it, just as my disorderly approach was probably a reaction to my mother's rigidity and her disquiet when our lives became chaotic through circumstance. The one behaviour I did inherit from her is allowing the household to revolve around the moods of the paterfamilias. 'You just wait till your dad gets home' became my 'Don't upset Daddy, he's in a bit of a mood.'

We all smile now at the memory of the first visits home of my sons-in-law, who were greeted by a grunt or snarl from John, then frantic, compensatory prattle from me. John didn't like people invading his space, even potential sons-in-law. All this changed towards the end of his life, when he found sobriety, and I am anguished to think how much he would have enjoyed his eight grandchildren had he met them. The three that he did meet remember him with pleasure. The others are very proud that Mister Tom was their grandad. Lola and Molly-Mae are at Manchester University and secretly took a photo of themselves outside the John Thaw Studio. Not bad, I told them, for a boy who only got one O level.

When life gets hard for my girls it is gut-wrenching to just be an onlooker. To relinquish my front-line duty of leading them not into temptation and delivering them from evil, and letting them take the responsibility themselves with the help of their immediate loved ones, as befits my age and status, is not natural to me. What John used to call my Messiah complex is still deep in my psyche, and he was right that oftentimes it takes away people's own power and ability to look after themselves. Right and proper, but this back seat is uncomfortable.

Why can't I relax and enjoy my daughters' solicitude? Contentment and wisdom have not come to me in old age. I am a grumpy old woman. It is true, particularly in the last two years, that I have become more aware of pain than pleasure. Grenfell Tower, immigrants drowning and reviled, food banks, appalling crimes against children, bloody Brexit, have tortured my mind. Ludicrously and unhealthily out-of-proportion misery has swamped my brain.

November 2017

My mental pain has suddenly become physical.

I went to see the stage show of An American in Paris, in which my friend Julie was appearing, and planned a lovely supper after the show, trying to cheer my miserable self up.

The road on which I parked my car had an incline and it was an effort to push open my car door. As I did so I had a sudden searing pain in my right hand. The show was a delight, but could not distract me from the continuing acute pain. I made some excuse about missing supper.

The next day I had to fly to Antibes, where my sister was seriously ill, and, convinced I had broken a bone, I went to the chemist at Heathrow and bought a hand splint. Over the next few days, distracted by trying to make Billie comfortable, and swallowing massive analgesic doses, I gradually subdued the pain. I flew back and forth over a period of two weeks, torn between the needs of my sister and those of my ailing daughter. Then my left hand suddenly developed an agonising pain too, rendering it useless. I tried to ignore my body's erratic behaviour until one day, after sitting for an hour studying a script, I stood up and found I could not walk. My right leg was hurting more than anything I can remember, except perhaps childbirth. In fact the groans, yelps and foul language that came out of me were similar to that experience. I threw down yet another handful of painkillers, and covered my knee with frozen peas. I tried but couldn't move it without terrible pain.

The next day it had recovered just enough for me to drag myself to my GP, who took a blood test. My inflammation levels were sky-high and I was dispatched to a specialist. He gave me a massive steroid injection, which had a very quick effect, and he then went through a series of tests to find a diagnosis. At one point, when he surmised that it might be something that would go away as suddenly as it arrived, my lovely GP said, 'Oh well, thank goodness it's not rheumatoid arthritis.'

'Why?'

Her face said it all. 'Don't let's go there.'

December 2017

Unfortunately, that was exactly where we did go.

But the painful business of diagnosing what was happening to my body had to wait. Billie had been moved into a hospital and was apparently fading fast.

An age gap of eight years, the war and Billie's adventurous nature meant I saw little of my sister as I grew up. If she appeared in a theatre in London I went to see the show, but when she moved to Paris after the death of variety theatre in England, we seldom met. I did admire, nay worship, her as a child, especially in her raffish ENSA uniform during the war, and when I researched her life for the book Just Me I was flabbergasted at her adventures, which she thought were just normal life. We were there for each other in times of trouble. So, with splints on my two hands, and knee, and a bagful of painkillers, I hobbled over to Antibes.

Billie had fought tooth and nail to stay in her flat after her fall, but despite having huge support from the health services – she was particularly impressed by the flowers sent to all old people at Christmas, and wielded her pass to go to the front of a queue with fierce zeal – I could see what a burden it was becoming for her devoted friends to look after her. She took a lot of persuading to go as a resident to the home she had attended for the physiotherapy on her hip fracture.

In no time she was practically running the place. She took to sitting in the entrance hall vetting visitors and playing with visiting children. In the dining room she took it upon herself to feed some of the badly disabled inmates. She would introduce me to them in her appalling French, and sometimes a smile would cross their impassive faces. 'Poor old buggers,' she would say loudly to me.

Her friends made her room homely with all the photos of her early career, looking stunning in her tights and satin corselette, which greatly impressed the staff. She was forever complaining. Her independent spirit was never really happy in an institution. As time went on she was becoming visibly troubled, clinging to a notebook which she constantly referred to or scribbled in but wouldn't let anyone take from her.

Now I was shocked to find her in bed in a hospital, looking wizened and fearful. She had multiple ailments that she had always kept at bay with the usual French over-medication and sheer willpower. It appeared she was letting go, her energy ebbing. In the hospital I sat by her bedside day and night, talking to her and holding her hand. She was in a ward on her own, so I sang some of the songs Mum and Dad used to sing in the pubs: 'The Riff Song' – 'Ho! So we sing as we are riding. Ho!' – and for Mum 'Just a song at twilight, when the lights are low'. I started their duet 'If you were the only girl in the world . . .', and her lips mouthed, '. . . and I were the only boy.'

I put earphones at her head and played show selections. I sneaked in some Elgar, which made her frown, but eventually, amazingly, nod approval.

The hospital let me sleep on the other bed in her ward but it was difficult with the pain I was suffering, and I was exhausted. Eventually they suggested I went back to the hotel for a sleep and they would phone me if necessary. For some reason, before I left, I said our childhood prayer to her:

Jesus, tender shepherd, hear me,
Bless thy little lamb tonight.
Through the darkness be thou near me,
Keep me safe till morning light.

All this day thy hand hast led me,
And I thank thee for thy care.
Thou hast warmed and clothed and fed me;
Listen to my evening prayer.

Let my sins be all forgiven,
Bless the friends I love so well.
Take me when I die to heaven,
Happy there with thee to dwell.

And I left her.

There was no phone call, so I went in the next morning very early. There was no one around. Billie was lying sleeping peacefully. Then I noticed rose petals spread around her pillow. I touched her and she was cold. The night nurse had not rung me. She died alone. As, ultimately, we all do, I suppose.

By the bedside was the notebook she always clung to. I was devastated when I looked through it to see how desperately she had tried to bring order to her chaotic thoughts.

Written in blue and crossed out in red are mundane entries like:

1 o'clock lunch

2.30 walk round grounds

Do big toilet

Sheila coming

What today???

Every now and then, amidst the obsessive diary-keeping, are repeated plaintive cries in capital letters, sometimes the paper perforated with the pen so fiercely has she written them.

Me 91 years old

Me

Me young woman

Who me

It was as though she was trying to cling on to her identity, her past, her presence. And she succeeded, until, at ninety-three, on 18 December 2017, she quietly let go her grasp.

December 2017

Billie's friends and I organised a small funeral for her in Antibes. As Ellie Jane was flattened by ongoing gruelling cancer treatment, my granddaughter Lola came with me and read out her mother's eulogy for her beloved aunt. It captures the spirit of my colourful sister.

'My extraordinary, exotic, extravagant, energetic, eccentric, exasperating Auntie Billie.

'Right from early primary-school days, Aunt Bill was a legend amongst my peers. Who was this blue-haired woman with a man's name that I would spend school holidays in Paris with? I would come back full of stories, lapped up by my friends, of strip clubs and topless girls, and visits to the ballet, and stilt acts.

'"What does she do?" they would ask. Well, Uncle Roy used to be on stilts, and she pretended to be his puppet, but now they both put their heads on top of small puppet bodies, and do the cancan in between the strip acts. They would be open-mouthed with amazement at such tales.

'I spent some of the happiest days of my childhood in Auntie Bill and Uncle Roy's minuscule flat on the Rue d'Amsterdam. Right from when I was very small, when a visit to the ballet would become central to the trip. She would make me my outfit, and there was such a build-up you would have thought we were going to Prince Charming's ball, and I did end up walking up the steps of the Opéra de Paris feeling like Cinderella, expecting everyone to turn and look at me. She did the same again many years later, for the first night of Miss Saigon in London, spending hours making me feel wonderful and special, with huge attention to detail. Which reminds me of the most incredible gift I think I ever received from anyone. Four shoeboxes converted into wardrobes for an exquisite set of clothes for my Barbie. Some she had hand-sewn and some were vintage. All with matching shoes and handbags. She must have worked so hard making that for me; I just hope I was grateful enough.

'Just going about everyday business with Auntie Bill was fun. She was such a well-known figure in the area and everyone loved her, as she barked out greetings to them in her best Franglais. How she managed to spend so much time in a country without learning the language still remains a mystery, but it didn't stop her being friends with everyone.

'There was always some major drama going on, every time I visited. Either a new act that needed rehearsing, or more usually something to do with "Papers", e.g. Uncle Roy's tax affairs. We often had to go early in the morning to strange offices to do paperwork, and poor old Uncle Roy would be shouted at, and brow-beaten by a stressed-out Billie. But then her "paperwork" was always a cause for stress, until very recently, as I'm sure Stella, Nicky, Juliana and Mum will verify.

'There were always lovely people around, who clearly adored her. Madame Gérard, Giselle the dancer downstairs, Stella, who we visited with her chimp (another thing my friends would be agog at), Bert and Marianne. Life was always colourful and fun.

'I was lucky to have an aunt who didn't have her own children who took more than a passing interest in her niece. When I went back to live in Paris after I finished school, it was a great comfort to have her there. I would visit her from my grim hostel, for hot dinners and some home comforts. She would have me parade around her front room, semi-naked, with books on my head, and then invite the neighbours in to have a look, and see if I might be eligible for a topless job at the Moulin Rouge. I can't believe I agreed to that. But she was very persuasive, was Auntie Billie.

'She could also be exasperating, as we all know. She never listened, she talked for England, forcing even her strong-willed sister into silent submission, she was full of deeply dubious and ill-informed political opinions – i.e. she read the Daily Mail. But if you forgave her these things, she was a ferocious whirlwind of energy, a positive force for life, and a loving aunt.

'I shall miss her so much. I was quite peeved when she decided a little while after Uncle Roy died to move back to France. I selfishly hoped she might want to be near her family in London, and I would have loved Jack and Lola to have grown up around her. But I am so glad she made the choice she did. Her quality of life here in the sun has been so good, and the love, friendship and support of her wonderful friends has been unmatchable. Thank you, Stella, Nicky and Juliana.

'Bon voyage, my beautiful Aunt Bill.'

In the chapel in Antibes that day, retired showgirls, a juggler, circus acts and people Billie had accosted in cafés, or on park benches, and those who supported her in her final months, laughed and cried at the memory of a genuine free spirit.

2018

When I got back to England I had to sort out the – by then – crippling pain I was experiencing all over my body. I was put under the care of Professor Mackworth-Young and his rheumatology team at Charing Cross Hospital in Hammersmith. The professor, a highly respected consultant, deals with the many varieties of autoimmune disease that seem to obey no set rules and therefore need each patient to be treated for their individual manifestation, which he does with painstaking care. Mine was loosely labelled the dreaded-by-my-GP rheumatoid arthritis.

Rheumatoid arthritis is an autoimmune disease which in laywoman's terms means that your body has turned against itself. The mechanism that is supposed to protect you – your immune system – is attacking you. If my body had heard my desire for death when I learned about my daughter's cancer, I wish it had chosen a less agonising method of achieving it. Not all that long ago a diagnosis of RA had a hideous prognosis of increasing disability, gross deformity and terrible pain, leading often to death from either the disease itself or complications arising from it. It's best to avoid the web on the subject. It is still incurable, but brilliant medical science has come up with modern drugs that make it quite possible to go into long, and even permanent, remission.

On one occasion during my treatment I was moaning about a pain in my foot, and the chief nurse, Antonia, who has become a good friend, pointed out that when she started over twenty years ago the waiting room would have been full of wheelchairs and crutches, whereas now, thanks to the new drugs, everyone was walking. Or, at worst, limping.

My immediate problem about commencing the treatment journey was that I was about to start rehearsals for a stage version of the film Harold and Maude. It was a project that the brilliant young director Thom Southerland and I had discussed for some time, and considerable effort had gone into making it happen. The cast and band, designer, composer were all in place and rehearsals were due to start in January 2018, so I could not let them down.

As I rather simplistically understand it, the new biologic drugs work by killing off the part of the immune system that has run amok, with the risk that they thereby lower your resistance to other illnesses. This presents two problems. In different people the bit of the immune system that needs eliminating varies. It is a long process to discover which part has gone wrong, and therefore which is the most suitable drug, each one having to be taken for at least three months to see if it works, before, if it doesn't, trying another. And some of them can affect you badly. The second problem was that the theatre we would be performing in was atmospheric and charming, but below ground, airless and somewhat overcrowded with actors, stage staff and a large resident population of beetles and mice. Not ideal for anyone with a vulnerable immune system. So, I decided to postpone the drug trials until the show finished and meantime survive on large doses of steroids.

These had a dramatic effect. They gave me frenetic energy. With no trace of my usual stage fright, I ricocheted about the stage, climbing ladders, dancing, and spouting long speeches not always completely accurately, causing some muffled mirth amongst the brilliant actor-musicians who were on stage throughout. In the wings it was a different story. My wonderful dresser and friend Ruth struggled to keep me still for changes, and had to negotiate pulling dresses off and on with me being unable to raise my arms above my head because of the pain. The cast were endlessly patient with me and, despite the problems, we all loved the play and what it says about relationships between young and old, reaching out to people and respect for difference. The standing ovations every night indicated that the audience agreed. I was aware that it might well be my last venture on stage and it felt right that I was finishing up in a fringe theatre, slightly tatty like me, but surrounded by some of the most brilliant actors and creatives I have ever worked with.

May 2018

When I eventually left the cast of Harold and Maude, having miraculously never missed a performance, I set to work to get the better of this illness that was in danger of taking over my life. I tried a punishingly spartan regime of beans and seeds – I didn't know there were so many – and horrible vegetables like bok choy. And endless bloody sweet potatoes with everything. I lost two stone, which I could ill afford, ending up a skeletal eight stone. I eventually settled for a simple vegan diet and was quite pleased – although admittedly it was not my first motivation – that I could finally look gambolling lambs in the face.

I exercised at the gym, working through my pain and not allowing the fatigue, which is an added ingredient of the RA package, to deter me. One of the nasty traits of the illness is that you desperately want to curl up and sleep, but I find that just intensifies the pain. You have to keep moving. Alternate boiling-hot and freezing-cold showers also helped, I discovered.

The medical team at Charing Cross and I focused on getting me off the steroids before they utterly destroyed my liver, gut and bones, and onto drugs with less toxic side effects. This has to be done very slowly and I felt pretty ill in the process. I was at that time doing publicity for Edie. I sat in a hotel room, chatting to journalists about what a miracle I was at my age to make such a film. Climbing a mountain at eighty-three! What was my secret? What was my advice to other old people? Little did they know that, when they left, I could barely walk across the room to the toilet. Being 'an inspiration' can be a liability.

It is not vanity on my part that has wanted to conceal my illness, but my old credo, dinned into me by my father, of not letting people down.

Pull yourself together.

Stiff upper lip.

Don't be a burden.

I often heard him, working behind the bar even when he was struggling with relative poverty and TB, reply to a customer asking, 'How are you, Rick?' with, 'Mustn't grumble.'

Why the hell not?

There's a programme on the radio at the moment about the joys of old age, asking people to phone in with their 'uplifting' stories. It's the sort of programme I get asked to go on. These days I am all too aware that there are some people listening who are wretched, and in pain, and don't want some idiot like me wittering on about how lovely it all is. Especially if, as I now confess, it's a lie.

October 2018

I have taken part in a gala performance of Harold Pinter's work to celebrate what would have been his eighty-eighth birthday. It started badly, with gridlocked traffic in London forcing me to abandon my car. It was only when I got out to set off on the long walk to the theatre that I remembered I can now no longer impetuously take a decision like that, as my body has ceased to obey my intentions. However, I eventually made it to the rehearsal, albeit late, drained and in pain, and wishing I had not agreed to appear.

The cast was to stay on stage during all the other readings, and for the duration of the rehearsal and the ensuing show my fatigue and pain were transcended by the sheer genius of Harold's work. The show covered excerpts from his haunting plays, political polemics, love poems, dark and light, tragedy and exquisite comedy. Felicity Kendal and I did a perfect little revue sketch called That's All. It is merely a series of repetitive, vacuous comments with many scripted pauses, yet the simplicity of the sentences and the silences creates a hilarious yet tragic picture of two lost souls disturbed by a break in their mundane routine.

Mrs A: I always put the kettle on about that time.

Mrs B: Yes.

           (pause)

Mrs A: Then she comes round.

Mrs B: Yes.

           (pause)

Mrs A: Only on Thursdays.

Mrs B: Yes.

           (pause)

Mrs A: On Wednesdays I used to put it on. When she used to come round. Then she changed it to Thursdays.

Mrs B: Oh yes.

Felicity and I had next to no rehearsal, and we had never actually worked together before although, both performing largely in comedy, our paths had crossed, but the sketch virtually plays itself if you just say the lines and observe the pauses. We discover that the She that they are puzzled about has started coming on another day, without telling Mrs A. These last four lines, as in much of Pinter, can mean many things.

Mrs B: She doesn't come in no more, does she?

           (pause)

Mrs A: She does come in. She doesn't come in so much, but she comes in.

           (pause)

Mrs B: I thought she didn't come in.

           (pause)

Mrs A: She comes in. (pause) She just doesn't come in so much. That's all.

Is Mrs B being cruel? Is Mrs A coming to the hurtful conclusion that She is avoiding her? We certainly know that this trivial event, despite our laughter, is a confusing near-tragedy in their banal lives.

What came over clearly that night, hearing a lot of Pinter's work gathered together, was the compassion of his writing. The empathy. The anger at the cruelty towards and neglect of the outsiders in our society. His lethal mockery of the manipulators and dominators, the exposure of bullies. As I sat surrounded by some of the finest actors in the country, lovingly performing Harold's work in the theatre named after him, I was full of wonder at the situation I found myself in.

For both Harold and me it was a far cry from When Knights Were Bold at the Palace Court Theatre, Bournemouth. Or Ten Little N******, as it was then shockingly named, at the Pavilion Theatre, Torquay. (Strange that Harold and I were happy to appear in a play with that title back then, whereas now I cannot bring myself to write the word.) I and David Baron, as he was known at the time, spent many months in the 1950s touring these moribund seaside resorts with the Barry O'Brien Company, adding to the dreariness of the joyless English holiday in those days, of which the highlight was eating a Wall's ice cream whilst wandering along a concrete esplanade. Or, when it was wet, a daring outing to the penny arcade to gamble on a fruit machine. You weren't allowed back into your boarding house during the day, so, rain or shine, mainly the former, holidaymakers had to trudge round in macs and plastic pixie hoods trying to convince themselves that the change was doing them good. Some families opted for the frenetic Butlin's camps, where out-of-work actors in red coats shouted 'Hi-de-hi' and urged you to desperately call back 'Ho-de-ho', and enter into talent and hairy-leg contests. This was before people ventured abroad to cheaper, sunnier climes, something my parents nervously did only once in their lives. Bournemouth and Torquay seemed to be peopled by old folk sitting glumly on deckchairs staring at a steel-grey sea. I cannot think we cheered them up a lot with our seasons of second-rate plays in shaky, ill-painted sets.

David did not hide his disdain. He seldom joined us for a drink after the show in the hotel that we persuaded to let us drink after time, and I thought he was a bit pretentious when he claimed he was too busy writing. He was darkly handsome, but a rather over-the-top actor, giving it his all as Mr Rochester in Jane Eyre, and the wicked husband in Gaslight. He was very definitely not available, as he was obviously obsessed with his wife, my rival for good parts in the company, Vivien Merchant. An actress of sphinx-like subtlety, her superficial respectability covered a seething sensuality. She is recognisably portrayed in several of Harold's plays.

As we struggled through our schedule of doing a new play every week, rehearsing one during the day whilst performing another at night, we were all kept going by dreaming of the rosier lives we hoped were in store for us in the future. After our stint with the Barry O'Brien Company we continued to drudge on in various weekly repertory companies and tatty tours, and I lost touch with David and Vivien.

In 1958 I read the reviews of a disastrous flop at my local theatre, the Lyric Hammersmith, and photos in the paper revealed that the writer, Harold Pinter, was my erstwhile colleague David Baron. In a half-empty auditorium I watched what I realised was a revolutionary piece of theatre. I couldn't pretend to understand it fully, but it moved and frightened me. Thankfully one of the Sunday critics, Harold Hobson, went against the grain and raved about The Birthday Party. Too late to save its truncated run at the Lyric, but enough to set his namesake Harold on the road to deserved serious consideration.

The following year, 1959, I was amazed to be invited to be in a revue with Beryl Reid at the Lyric Hammersmith, having been spotted playing principal boy in a pantomime in Bromley. Maybe Eleanor Fazan and Disley Jones, the two creators of the show, took a risk on this unknown, with her CV of concert party, second-rate rep and touring roles, because the established people they approached first were alarmed by the offbeat nature of the material by N. F. Simpson, John Mortimer and, yes, Harold Pinter.

So, we met up again. The sketch of Harold's that I did with Beryl was about two old-lady tramps sitting in a café talking about buses, bread and soup. Plus, pauses. Harold took us through the piece, insisting on those pauses being long. Beryl, who had done years in stand-up, and I, who had had lessons in timing from Cyril Fletcher on the end of Sandown Pier, and Frankie Howerd, on tour in one of his out-of-favour periods, were appalled. 'Don't drag', 'Keep up the pace' and even on some scary occasions 'Don't leave any pauses that allow the audience to heckle or boo' were our customary rules. With fearful misgiving we did as Harold said, even observing the pause that he demanded should last for a count of fifteen. And of course he was right. It was the same premise as That's All. The audience hung on our words, or rather our silences, and then hooted with laughter when the line we gave them was another version of the one before, or something completely inconsequential. It also drew the audience into the world of these rejected women, who had no apposite words to express their condition. I confess, once having realised the laugh potential of an extended pause, Beryl and I became drunk with power and the sketch tripled its running time. Perhaps that's when Harold began to disown his trademark of the Pinter Pause.

I lost touch with him again as he stratosphered into Nobel Prize country, whilst I – well, stayed earthbound but busy. Of course, I read about his seemingly glamorous life. He met and fell deeply in love with Antonia Fraser. She was the perfect woman for him, intellectually and politically, and has proved a loyal guardian of his legacy of work. It was obvious that they were very happy together.

I did read in the papers that Vivien was deeply hurt and angry. In 1978 I was appearing in the musical Annie at the Victoria Palace when my wig designer on the show asked if I would see a good friend of his who was in a bad way. At first I did not recognise the bloated, dishevelled drunk who reeled into my dressing room ranting incoherently about Harold. In this wreckage, the husky voice survived. That the elegant, reticent Vivien should descend into this hell broke my heart. I couldn't help her. I was to learn later, from personal experience, that alcoholism cannot be assuaged by anyone other than the sufferer themselves. This is what Vivien herself had chosen. I understood her despair; I too am apt to have obsessive relationships, and the thought of someone taking my place is unthinkable – even if that relationship is wrong and destructive. Harold and she were married for twenty-four by all accounts tempestuous years. They had a son, and latterly wealth. Who knows how it all went wrong? The strong can recover from the wounds of life, but some never find the way to heal. Vivien died four years after our meeting. She was fifty-three.

In 2008 I got a phone call from Harold asking me to appear in the revival of The Birthday Party at the Lyric Hammersmith, fifty years after its first disastrous showing. I found when working on it that there was something about the play that reminded me of the ones we did in Torquay and Bournemouth – three acts with good curtain lines. The crosstalk sections were like the vaudeville acts most actors in the provinces used to relish, when we visited the variety shows in which artistes staying in our theatrical digs were appearing. I no longer found the play confusing. Like Harold, I lived through the Blitz and evacuation, so the random terror and bullying in the writing were no puzzle for me.

After the gala night party Harold was looking tired so I offered to go out to the car with him, sheltering him from the rain with my umbrella. The car was late arriving and we clung supporting each other, me the worse for drink, he mortally ill. We laughed about our past experience as colleagues in tatty theatre, and talked about the state of the world. Suddenly he said, 'Are you still angry, Sheila?'

'More than ever,' I said.

'Good girl.' And he kissed my forehead.

He died a few months later.

November 2018

This year the annual remembrance service at the Cenotaph is marking the hundredth anniversary of the end of the First World War.

The night before, stuck in traffic, I was irritated by the roads being closed around the Albert Hall for a big commemoration with all of the royal family present. Shame on me. I was even cross that the police stopped me for ten minutes outside the Palace to allow this ninety-two-year-old woman past, to grace yet another event with her unyieldingly sad presence. She doesn't seem to care that her solemn face can be read as grumpiness. No false smiles for her. She is what she is. She does her duty, quietly and efficiently – all that standing around, and walking backwards down Cenotaph steps, and trying to make conversation once a week with Theresa May. Her hair is the same old-fashioned style, lacquered into the same neat curls and waves that it was in the sixties, the style of her coats and hats unchanged over the years. A frumpy, tiny, stalwart figure that fills me with love. A good woman. This Remembrance Sunday, for the first time attending without Prince Philip at her side, he having retired from public service, I have a sense of foreboding that she herself will not be with us in the foreseeable future. Though, with her family history of longevity, she may well see me out.

With her on the balcony watching were, as the television compère described them, 'the two leading royal women': the seemingly rather jolly Camilla, animatedly trying, unsuccessfully, to chat with the Queen, and the Duchess of Cambridge, coiffed immaculately, and demurely dressed in what looked like a run-up to her Queen role. In the middle, sombre, watchful, stolid, was the real thing. I will feel less safe when she goes.

She seems to be gently guiding her son into his onerous future role. A recent television programme, and his gravitas at the Cenotaph, showed Prince Charles to be a well-trained successor. I have only met him briefly, but I know him to be kind and thoughtful. When John died in our house in Wiltshire, the next morning on our doorstep were some flowers and a handwritten note from the prince, who lived up the road at Highgrove. In the occasional meetings I have with him at charity events, I find him to be surprisingly knowledgeable about his less privileged subjects, and he has done many imaginative things to help them. He is well informed and, like his mother, utterly dedicated to his job. He can also be self-deprecating and very funny.

I suppose, if I think it through rationally, with my hatred of the class system of which our aristocratic royal family is the apex, I should be a republican. When it comes to something like Remembrance Day, I only know that I am comforted by the royal presence. I wallow in the ceremony and tradition. The bands, the uniforms and costumes, daft rituals with bowler hats, saluting hands and bowed heads, and old men and women, chins up, arms swinging, marching as they did when young. In the chaotic year of 2018, I need the images, the music, the feeling of unity that the royal family inspires. Whether it is real or not.

As I watched the ceremony on television I wept, as I always do, at the thousands of graves in France; I gasped when the commentator reminded us that, of the 720 troops of the Accrington Pals regiment, 584 were killed or wounded in one half-hour of the Battle of the Somme. A swamp of blood and guts in the mud. I found myself walking alone around the room shouting 'No, no, no' at the idiocy of war. Just as, when I was a child, I was comforted during the Blitz by the King and our Queen's mother visiting the bombsites, and the little princesses sending messages on the radio to us frightened children, I wanted to hug that tiny, crouched figure, because she represents something unaffected, and real, in the world of PR and image.

She is not one of the ludicrous cartoon figures that dominate our world now. She is not the disgusting Trump, the gadfly Boris Johnson, the determined toff Rees-Mogg, the shambolic David Davis, the pompous Dr Liam Fox or the guffawing Farage. Nor the scruffy Jeremy Corbyn, in his shabby anorak, and a tiny, miserly poppy brooch, as he laid his wreath at the Cenotaph, when everyone else had on their Sunday best to honour the dead. What kind of message was that? Michael Foot, in his notorious duffel coat, was obviously trying to keep warm; Corbyn's dishevelled outfit seemed like some grotesquely misplaced gesture of defiance.

Dishevelled seems to be the order of the day now. The two men behind the scenes promoting the populist movements on either side of the Atlantic, Steve Bannon and Dominic Cummings, look like tramps, and one wonders if they actually smell as grubby as they appear. If they do, no one would dare tell them. Boris Johnson has worked hard on his boyish messiness. He ruffles his ill-cut hair, and unstraightens his tie, before he goes on camera. I suspect, when he is off-duty with his kith and kin, he wears bespoke Savile Row tweeds, and hides his slicked-back hair in a felt trilby from Lock's, the hatter in St James, as befits his upper-class background.

The solemn ceremonies of remembrance in 2018 contain much more emphasis on the pity of war. In Paris, President Macron made a brave speech about the similarities of what is happening now to events in Europe in the thirties. Could this event be the start of the fightback against the dangerous rise of populism? Trump chose not to attend the French president's peace conference, but in both France and the UK a German head of state was present at the ceremonies. I admit that, when I heard the Bible reading spoken in German at the ceremony, my heart fluttered a bit. I was shocked that I momentarily felt resentment, fear, anger. My moment of discomfort was replaced by reason, and relief that the German president's presence was possible this year. We were able, albeit hesitantly, to accept that in war everyone suffers, friend and foe, foot soldiers and officers.

Whilst working in Wales on a small film, I arrived back to my hotel room late one night after filming to find my room freezing cold because the radiator had packed up. A caretaker came up to fix it. Seeing the white poppy that was lying on the bed, having been sent to me ready for Remembrance Day, he asked me why I wore it. He told me he had been a marine serving in Africa, Ireland, Afghanistan, Syria and Iraq. He came from a military family. His father had been injured on D-Day. I felt pretty uncomfortable and tried to explain that I was grateful for his dedication to the service of our country. Then he suddenly said, 'I've changed my mind about war', and I saw that there were tears in his eyes.

I sat him down with a drink and he told me that Remembrance Day was always difficult for him. He used to spend it with a mate he served with who was blown up by a roadside bomb and has no legs and only one arm. They had a ritual of remembering and drinking to every comrade in turn who had died or been badly injured. When he retired from the forces my new friend believed that, as a professional soldier, he had done his duty. He managed to squash any unreasonable survivor's guilt until four years after his retirement at fifty. He was going through his Remembrance Day ritual with his friend when he could not remember the name of one young man who had been killed. He could recreate a clear vision of the youth's mangled body but could not put a name to it, identify it, honour it.

'For the first time I wept. And I wept non-stop for six months.'

He was diagnosed with post-traumatic stress disorder and given desultory treatment; his marriage broke up and his plumbing business collapsed, leading him to his current caretaking job. Pity more care had not been taken of him.

He asked if he could have my white poppy.

November 2018

I can't stop thinking about the caretaker. I aspire to be a pacifist. It is one of the things you sign up to when you become a Quaker, as I did in 1993. Along with Churchill, I do firmly believe that 'to jaw-jaw is always better than to war-war'. Although there is some doubt that he really did say that.

The Quakers try to abide by the Peace Testimony but it provokes troubled discussion even amongst Quakers themselves. The original Quaker Peace Testimony stemmed from Charles II trying to stamp out radical religious groups, like the Quakers, after his return from exile. In 1660 the Quakers sent a declaration to the King that included lines that became the basis of the Peace Testimony:

'All bloody principles and practices we do utterly deny, with all outward wars, and strife, and fighting with outward weapons, for any end, or under any pretence whatsoever, and this is our testimony to the whole world.'

Well, that's pretty clear, Charlie, and has landed us Quakers with an almost impossible responsibility. We are to oppose all war, for any reason 'whatsoever'.

But what about a Just War?

No such thing.

What about Hitler? Should we have just stood by and done nothing?

Because I experienced the Second World War first-hand, and saw the suffering it caused, leaving images that are gouged into my brain, these are hard questions for me to consider.

What else could we have done to combat the savagery of Hitler's Nazi regime? Well, here goes . . .

Maybe the world could have intervened in the rise of Hitler as soon as we realised, in 1933, that he and his gang were madmen? Book-burning, persecution of Jews and other vulnerable groups, had all started by then, and the first prison camp, Dachau, was opened that year. Assistance could have been given to the people in Germany, and the countries Hitler later invaded, to oppose him by political intervention, and support provided for resistance groups, like those that saw off Oswald Mosley and his gang of fascists, which included influential aristocrats, in England in 1936.

Instead, we had the Treaty of Versailles, less a treaty – more a punishment of Germany for the First World War. We could instead have given or lent money to help the Germans reconstruct the wreckage of their country, which was left fertile ground for the rise of tyrannical leaders promising better things.

The bitter truth is that the war we waged did not prevent the Holocaust, and it added other atrocities as well, like our own devastating firebombing of Germany and Tokyo, the dropping of the first nuclear bombs, and the deaths of 70 million people. As a Just War it was not an exemplary success.

The Quakers proffer another possibility. Isn't it worth looking more seriously at taking action to avert 'the occasion of war'? Like the Marshall Plan after the Second World War, perhaps, when a generous and worried United States, which did not then believe in building walls around itself, poured money into repairing war-torn Europe, including Germany. The Americans' involvement was not entirely altruistic, as at that time communism was thought to be a big threat to the future, and they deemed it less likely to take hold in countries that were thriving. Could not the same have been done in Germany to prevent the rise of fascism? Might that not have helped?

Maybe not, but the new surge of activity to save the environment, such as by Extinction Rebellion, shows that it is possible to rally people worldwide to a cause. That cause could be peacekeeping.

Quakers have mediators in most war zones trying to bring people together, in Palestine, Israel, the Middle East. They were also active in Ireland during the Troubles. So, it is an active pacifism. It is not smiling acceptance. Quakers work in prisons and schools sharing mediation skills.

I try my best to do the same in my own life, aware that conflict resolution starts with the individual. I do try, but it is a hard challenge for me. Possibly as a result of a wartime childhood, I am by nature aggressive. My metaphorical fists are always at the ready; if I think I see injustice, or cruelty, I can react too hastily. I am frightened of bullies but find the best course is to stand up to them. When I was young I developed a certain rash fearlessness in the face of antagonism. I always have to stick my oar in. (Why do I keep using phrases thrown out at me by my parents?) Whereas I hesitate at verbal intervention, when it gets physical I will usually 'have a go, Joe' (there is my father again). Following Quaker practice, if I see a parent shouting at, or even walloping, a child in the supermarket queue, I force myself not to belt the adults, but to offer help: 'Oh poor you – it's stressful, isn't it? Can I take your kid while you pay?' I then try some of the distraction techniques on the child that I use with tricky schoolkids I sometimes teach, and with my grandchildren and, in the old days, with my errant offspring. Parent and child are usually so flabbergasted that someone is understanding, rather than being silently or even vocally critical, that the situation calms down. Anyway, the batty old lady won't let them get a word in edgeways. I once intervened in a quite violent altercation between a man and a frightened woman in the dead of night on Hammersmith riverside. After a bit of a struggle, vocal and physical, I managed to stop the large attacker. Sadly, not with my Quakerly anger-management approach, but because he recognised me off Gogglebox.

I am far from sure that I would have intervened had he been wielding a gun or knife. In the latest type of war, manifesting as terrorism, it is not clear how the power of persuasion can be effective. Had I chanced to be in Woolwich with a gun in my pocket when Lee Rigby was being hacked to death, would I have refrained from using it? I don't know. I only hope I would have had the courage of Ingrid Loyau-Kennett, who kept talking to the two killers, one with bloody hands holding a knife, until the police arrived, thereby possibly avoiding further carnage. Or, when Jo Cox was slaughtered by a deluded far-right fanatic, would I have intervened like seventy-seven-year-old Bernard Kenny, despite being wounded?

Very often these assailants have given clues as to the dangerous journeys that lead to their deranged violence. We must be better at detecting them and making early effective interventions against the polluting of their minds by misinformation and neglect. Khalid Masood, formerly Adrian Elms, who drove a car killing four people on Westminster Bridge and stabbed to death a policeman, had already come to the attention of the police for earlier petty crimes. He was a classic example of a man constantly in trouble who should have been more closely monitored. I remember seeing a school photo of him, the only boy of colour in his class. One wonders how difficult it was for a black lad whose mother had been an unmarried, white, seventeen-year-old girl, in respectable Kent in the sixties. Of course, a difficult childhood is no justification for the enormity of his ultimate crime, but it could provide clues as to how his path might have been changed – and hopefully in future the paths of others.

As wars are proven to create in their wake terrorist groups and individuals, how valid is Britain's involvement in the arms trade? In July 2016 the Unite union issued a statement saying that it firmly believed in 'beating swords into ploughshares', but it had to think first and foremost of 'the protection and advancement of its members' interests at work', and this included the renewal of Trident. One is sympathetic with the union's predicament, but would the billions expended on this outdated nuclear programme not be better spent developing good alternatives to the jobs it provides in the Barrow-in-Furness area, and, above all, waging an all-out war, through education and improved opportunities, on the radicalisation that leads to extremism?

The mayhem of war promotes some complex moral choices. It was us and the Americans who exploded the first nuclear bombs. We were told that our appalling destruction of civilian lives and homes in Nagasaki and Hiroshima would shorten the war. I read that an airman who watched the mushroom-cloud explosion commented, 'I think they have saved our lives at the expense of our children.'

November 2018

I know one should not attribute cliché labels to people, so let us say that it is just a coincidence that all my gay friends have enormous style and know how to enjoy themselves. Like Martin. He is king of the make-up artists, especially good with the old and raddled. He has made a wonderful job of transforming me for glamorous events, and Joan Rivers on her shows, as well as being her and my loyal friend. He has virtually retired, but now uses his expertise to transform women who are suffering the ravages of chemotherapy, all of whom adore him.

He lives in an estate in Devon that he and his partner turned into a shrine of British craftsmanship and super luxury. There I am cossetted and spoiled, and sleep in one of the most comfortable beds in the world, with its fragrant sheets, special squidgy mattress cover, and, when I sit up drinking my early-morning fragrant tea, a wonderful view over rolling hills and a lake.

After my diagnosis with rheumatoid arthritis, Martin organised a confidence-giving trip to the Edinburgh Festival for me. I was daunted at the prospect of negotiating a crowded city as usual overfull of people trying to create funny, sad, informative, beautiful work. Martin dragged me over the cobbles and up and down the hills, making me laugh at my pain and incapacity, and managed to discover all the best vegan restaurants in Edinburgh.

He is great at planning treats. When he invited me to what seemed a fairly everyday outing of a pizza in Chelsea he did not realise quite how special it was. I was astonished to discover that Pizza Express was the old Pheasantry Club. Whilst at RADA I lived a Withnail and I-type existence in one room with two other girls in St John's Wood. We had left the Young Women's Christian Association because they locked the doors at 9 p.m. and climbing through a window after some fellow students and I had done a cabaret at the Wishing Well Club was beginning to pall. In my efforts to supplement my RADA subsistence grant I found myself in situations where I could have had a Christine Keeler-like lifestyle. In the fifties The Pheasantry was a club where some of the members paid good money to spend the evening with young girls. Hostesses, we were called. One of the agencies used needy students as a source of supply. Mostly they were chaste evenings to provide company for lonely men, maybe in London on business. Unofficially, however, more could be earned from extra services. I always found the possible meal tickets so unattractive, and anyway my respectable working-class upbringing inhibited me from employing this more lucrative adjunct to a famous old actor luvvie's acting classes, where we were not paid for the groping that went on.

Whilst a student I was also nearly offered a job as a Bluebell Girl. These tall showgirls worked at the Lido in Paris, where my sister Billie performed as a dancer, and often married well. Unfortunately, Sir Kenneth Barnes, the principal of RADA, got wind of my successful audition and intervened, thus condemning me to eight years of underpaid weekly rep and third-rate tours instead of who knows what glamorous life. Although it didn't turn out very glamorous for poor Christine and many other badly used young women.

Later, in an out-of-work period, I started the training to be a Bunny Girl at the Playboy Club, but found the corseted leotard, fishnet tights and teetering heels agony, and I was thrown out. I still have the ears which I stole as a memento of the humiliating, uncomfortable depths we were called upon to plumb whilst sexily serving all the nice rich gentlemen. Sadly, I have lost the fluffy pom-pom tail that decorated our bums, which the titillated men were strictly forbidden to touch.

What a weird world it was. I didn't really look the part. I had a good figure but my face didn't fit the pretty Bunny mode and I have never been good at smiley simpering, which in those days was deemed attractive to the sort of men who frequented these clubs. I say 'was' but in January this year there was a report about a similar use of young girls at a function in one of our posh hotels. A male-only dinner organised by a set-up called The Presidents Club, purporting to raise money for charity but actually, as reported by an undercover journalist, an excuse for some men to behave like delinquent boys, treating the girls who were enlisted to keep them happy like dirt. The organisation was closed down when looked at through modern, more enlightened Me-Too eyes and seen for the debasing of relationships between men and women it represented. The sadness was that the businessmen involved could not understand the objections to their sleazy night out. So what if a few breasts got squeezed and bottoms pinched and lewd remarks made? It was just a bit of fun, and the girls were paid and they collected a lot of money for charity, after all. For them money changing hands overrides any moral compass.

Speaking of moral compasses, over my vegan pizza I regaled Martin with slightly embellished stories of my Pheasantry days that left him open-mouthed.

November 2018

I was reminded of another dear gay friend the other day when I was visiting the Building Centre in Store Street, and I discovered the enduring restaurant Olivelli's was still open. I used to visit Olivelli's in my 1949 student days at RADA, just round the corner on Gower Street. I usually went with my friend Tony Beckley, classically handsome and camp as a row of tents when it was dangerous to be so. We would have fantasies of being stars, and becoming colleagues in wonderful shows, living together in a Mayfair house, plus a mansion in Brighton, like the one owned by Terence Rattigan, where Tony attended daring parties. His enchanting good looks and ready wit gave Tony entrance to many glamorous star-studded events, which were held in secret locations in that furtive time for gay men. He would delight me with the details over a free meal, given to us and other students by the ever-generous Signor Olivelli. We promised each other that, in the highly unlikely event of us ever getting old and infirm, we would share a room and raise hell at Denville Hall, a retirement home for old actors. It was not to be.

Tony went to Hollywood with one of his lovers, Barry Krost, did some films and tellies, the most notable of which was playing Camp Freddie in The Italian Job. I treasure the out-takes of a scene he played in Revenge of the Pink Panther, in a small lift with three other actors, one of whom was Peter Sellers. Sellers proposed that it would be funny if he farted. The resultant uncontrollable giggling is Tony as I knew him. I watch an interview with Sellers about it on the web, with clips of the struggling actors trying to be professional, whenever I want to remember him.

Tony loved LA and had many adventures, but then became ill. Barry having become successful, and rich, organised and paid for me, who hadn't, to fly over to see Tony, and he died aged fifty not long after my visit, of what we later deduced was the dreadful, then mystery, illness AIDS. I have tried to depict the profound love there can be between a straight woman and a gay man in my novel Miss Carter's War. This old age of mine would be richer if I could have shared it, as we planned, with Tone.

November 2018

Saw a film of some of the wonderful commemoration artwork for the 2018 Remembrance Day tribute, devised by Danny Boyle, who caught the mood of the country in 2012 with his Olympic opening ceremony. Danny commissioned sand artists, a discipline I admit that I did not even know existed, to sculpt portraits on many beaches around Britain, of people who fell in the war. They were stunning works of art, which made it deeply upsetting to watch them being washed away by the tide, leaving not a trace, as the ex-marine I met in Wales felt he had allowed to happen to his unnamed young comrade in arms. Particularly moving was the portrait of the poet Wilfred Owen on Folkestone beach, where apparently he swam the day before embarking from that beach to fight in France. He was killed one week before the armistice was signed.

In the days of the First World War there were not embedded journalists reporting from the thick of battle, telling the truth of what was going on, as so valiantly they do nowadays. We owe our knowledge of the appalling carnage of the First World War to poets like Wilfred Owen and Siegfried Sassoon, as their poetry gave an insight into what it was really like, as opposed to the romanticised version of the war being spun to the people back home.

Photographers and artists who went to the front have had the same effect. In the First World War, Paul Nash said he was not an artist but a messenger who wanted to 'bring back word from the men who are fighting to those who want the war to go on for ever'. His painting, ironically titled We Are Making a New World, of a devastated landscape of shell holes, trenches and leafless burned tree trunks, said it all.

Searing photos of the effect and reality of battle can shock us. Who can forget the naked child, her back burned by napalm, running away with her terrified friends during the Vietnam War? Or the tiny mite washed up dead on the shore near Bodrum, in an attempt to escape another vicious war? Film too can be affecting – the little boy dug out of a bombed building in Syria, sitting stunned, coated in dust, his face blank, even when he looked at the blood on his hand that had come from his forehead. His childish guilt as he tried to wipe it on the seat of his chair is unbearable. Conflicts fade from our memories but the work of artists bear witness to them for future generations. 'Lest we forget.'

There is no more potent picture of the destruction of war than Picasso's portrayal of the bombing of Guernica. Picasso was in occupied Paris during the war when a German officer saw a photo of the painting and asked him, 'Did you do that?'

Picasso replied, 'No, you did.'

2019

January 2019

Went to another funeral. I have reached the age where my friends are more likely to be buried than wed. When he was very old, John Gielgud was reputed to have said, after yet another ceremony, 'It's hardly worth going home.' This was a happy do, which John Thompson, the dear friend we were celebrating, would have thoroughly enjoyed.

My first husband, Alec, died just before Christmas in 1971, when Ellie Jane was seven. A year beforehand, she had also lost her beloved grandma. My dear friends John Dalby and his partner John Thompson came to our rescue. They invited us to stay with them in their colourful flat in Earl's Court, which had been the scene of many louche goings-on throughout the sixties. There we played gentle games, and ate delicious food, and relaxed into their comforting arms. Dalby was a composer and performer and Thompson a nurse. Theirs was a profound love affair with no rules, which lasted till they died, Dalby in 2017 and Little John, as we called him, following a period of bereft confusion, now in 2019.

They met in 1959 and lived, along with many of my friends, through the AIDS epidemic, and times when their love was illegal. Often, with one singing class, Dalby would restore my lost voice to perform in a musical that night. A cuddle and a pep talk were part of the treatment. Throughout the fifties and sixties we had enormous fun together and right to the end they were experts at friendship.

Little John's funeral was held in the beautiful St Mary's Church in Twickenham, with the sun shining on the nearby River Thames. Like all theatrical funerals, it was good-humoured, with beautifully read poems, and his Actors Centre choir singing one of John's songs. The vicar who conducted the service, Father Jeff Hopkin Williams, had been to the same epic parties in Earl's Court, so he expressed perfectly what I think we all felt that day, that the departure of the two Johns was the end of an era. An era of some pain, prejudice overcome, loving companionship. And such terrific fun.

I sat in a pew with a plaque saying:

Lawrence Gaskell 19

Died in France of wounds received on the 27th of February 1918

Buried near Arras

So, I shed a tear for Lawrence too, and thought of him in his grave so far away. I hope his spirit, if it was present, enjoyed the lovely ceremony of which he and his family were deprived by another bloody war. Nineteen. My God.

February 2019

For over a year I have omitted to visit Gwynne, my sparky Welsh neighbour with whom I have, in the past, spent time drinking good wine and talking politics. Overcome by my depressing illness, the worry of my daughter and the state of the country, when I have reached home during these last two years I have wanted to shut up and watch telly or listen to music. Or just cry. Now, with a few days free to catch up with friends, I went round to call on him and found he had moved upstairs. There he spends the day in a wheelchair reading his Guardian and the Oldie magazine until retiring to his special hospital bed at seven, where he lies watching television, playing music or reading a book until he goes to sleep about twelve. In other words, he has settled for a bedridden, invalid status. Were he to do something about his knees, probably even now, with physio and determination, he could be mobile. Or even install a chairlift so he could go out and sit by the river, or I could wheel him up to our lovely Italian deli for a coffee. But he doesn't want to.

'I'm fine, I sit by the open window from 2 p.m. onwards and keep an eye on you all. And people come and visit and we have a nice glass or two and a chat.'

Had he tackled his knee problem earlier when it was first around, it could've been remedied, but I suspect that after the death of his wife, who lovingly tended the roses in our square, he couldn't see the point. I tried to give him a pep talk – Messiah Hancock – but it was clear he is satisfied with his life as it is. He tells me that the carers who come in every day originate from all over the world, and he is thrilled by their company and by that of a gentle saint of a man who spends the day with my friend taking care of all his needs. Struggling, as I was when I visited, with a flare-up of pain, I ended up almost envying Gwynne. At ninety-one or ninety-four – he has lost count – he can't be bothered to fight any more; he has worked out a way of life that suits him and he is enjoying it.

The next day I went to Hampstead to visit another of my friends. Her whole life revolved around her husband

and family. Much like my neighbour, when her partner died her life lost direction, and not long afterwards she was diagnosed with Alzheimer's disease. Thankfully her daughter has organised things in such a way that she can stay in her home, where she feels safe. My girlfriend is in the early stages of this horrific disease. She is often consumed by terror but this was a good day. She went through a stage of being alarmed by her mind's waywardness, but on this occasion she seems quite calm as she wanders from subject to subject, sometimes mid-sentence, struggling for words, and finding odd, often rather good, substitutes. I try to accompany her along the wild paths of her mind, pretending that her long-dead husband will come home soon, and repeating the same information about my family several times over. Then she suddenly blurts out that she is furious with her husband.

'Why?' I ask cautiously.

'He simply will not finish decorating the bedroom.'

Memories of a difficult patch in their marriage, and the pain it caused, are completely forgotten. I can't help thinking that, despite my sadness at her decline, and my fear for her future, she herself was happier for a little while than many times in our shared history. Forgetfulness in old age is sometimes merciful.

For myself, I am trying to organise my affairs to deal with infirmity and dependence, should they occur. I have installed a lift and made all my cupboards more accessible. I will try to accept graciously the decay of my body. It has always been unreliable anyway. When my specialist explained that my immune system had turned against me, I was not in the least surprised. It has never been particularly friendly. Acne afflicted my youth, cancer my middle years, and nerves have always affected my bowels and bladder so that proximity to a toilet is a lifelong fixation. No change there. I can predict that cold sores will disfigure my lips the day before I am due to film some close-ups, and laryngitis has threatened the first night of every musical I have done. In other words, I don't think I have ever felt 100 per cent fit, so the ailments of old age are all part of the pattern.

As, of course, is death.

Death is a reality. I still haven't quite accepted that it is going to happen to me, but from what I have observed in others I will know when to let go. Nicholas Parsons and I had worked together since the beginning of Just a Minute in 1965. I loved his old-fashioned cravat-and-blazer-type charm. Kindly, courteous, utterly professional, reliable and loving. In the last few months of his life, his strong physical and mental persona began to fracture. Obviously loathing this disintegration, with his usual impeccable timing, he took his exit.

I find some people want to cling to life even though to observers it seems to have become intolerable. But what if you want to die? I once sat next to that stalwart man of the theatre Brian Rix, comforting him as he explained tearfully how he longed for his life to end.

Like many comics, Brian was an intensely serious man. All his life he campaigned for people with learning difficulties, like his daughter. When his beloved wife, Elspet Gray, died after sixty-four years together, he was distraught. That, together with a painful terminal illness, made him write to the speaker of the House of Lords, of which he was an active member, saying: 'Unhappily my body seems to be constructed in such a way that it keeps me alive in great discomfort, when all

I want is to be allowed to slip into a sleep, peacefully, legally, and without any threat to the medical or nursing profession. I am sure there are many others like me, who, having finished with life, wish their life to finish.'

Years ago I did a TV monologue written by Hugo Blick, depicting a woman going to Zurich to die. The reality of the bleak procedure and commercial killing machine that the character went through, based on fact, shocked me. When I went on a television programme to discuss it with MP Diane Abbott, at the time shadow minister for public health, she was so adamant that legal euthanasia would lead to people being coerced into dying, to get them out of the way and steal their money, that she could barely bother to engage with me, making it clear a silly actor did not understand these things. When I pointed out that it was her job to frame a law that encompassed any possible danger, she could not be bothered to reply.

I have reached the age when I do consider the manner of my death. I hope it will be, with the help of medical science, relatively peaceful, but if that is not possible, then, like Brian, I want the right to manage my own departure, when I choose, where I choose. Even though I am a vice president of St Christopher's Hospice, dedicated to aiding people to die with dignity, I would like to end my life at home, as John did, with my loved ones in the house – though maybe not standing round the bed waiting for me to deliver a good exit line. 'Bugger Brexit'?

When I have a bout of pain and fatigue, with the accompanying depression, or I despair of 'the great' and 'the tyrants' in the world, I find the idea of there eventually being an ending quietly comforting. As Will said in Cymbeline:

Fear no more the heat o' the Sun,
Nor the furious winter's rages;
Thou thy worldly task hast done,
Home art gone and ta'en thy wages:
Golden lads and girls all must,
As chimney-sweepers, come to dust.

Fear no more the frown o' the great,
Thou art past the tyrant's stroke:
Care no more to clothe and eat;
To thee the reed is as the oak:
The sceptre, learning, physic, must
All follow this, and come to dust.

I am making practical arrangements for my departure –
will, power of attorney, legal set-up for the management
of my charity, the John Thaw Foundation, after my death.
I am erasing my human animal tracks, gradually destroying
diaries and letters, offloading belongings and refusing any
more gifts, trying to make it as easy as possible for my
daughters to tidy up after my death.

Then, when all that is done and dusted, I will settle down,
like Gwynne, with the help of my friends, to bloody well
enjoy my decline.

March 2019

One of my grandchildren asked me, 'What is the difference
between the classes?'

I hate the class system, having been a victim of it myself.
I have always felt a profound gut reaction against its

manifestations in our country. I classify myself as working class, because I believe that is what my family was, but now I am floating about leading a middle-class life, with working-class attitudes. A phony, in fact.

Three of my grandchildren have the odd situation of having grandparents on one side who are upper middle class, verging on aristocratic, whilst on the other side there is me, at least originally working class.

Not long after this conversation, in an ill-advised revelation of his true colours, Jacob Rees-Mogg, when discussing on a radio programme the burning to death of seventy-two people in a tower block called Grenfell, said to the interviewer, 'I think if either of us were in a fire, whatever the fire brigade said, we would leave the burning building. It just seems the common-sense thing to do.'

So, on reflection, my answer to this question from my grandchildren is that the working class obey orders, often to their cost, and the upper class do what they choose. The upper class know they can get away with a certain moral laxity, legal tax-dodging, that sort of thing, whereas the working class know that if they do not sign on for their benefit at the right time they won't get the money, and if they are caught shoplifting they will be sent to prison, rather than for a course of psychotherapy. The upper class are confident that they are right.

In this instance, Rees-Mogg was right. Patronising, insensitive, condescending and appallingly derisive of what he would probably call the lower classes, or maybe, like Farage, 'the little people', but right. Those people obeyed the advice they had been given by supposed fire experts, and didn't dream that the council and builders would have saved money by putting flammable cladding on their homes. They trusted and obeyed. Rees-Mogg was doubtless also right to open an investment fund in Dublin, to join others he had in the Cayman Islands and Singapore, whilst pontificating about the glories of Brexit. He will doubtless find it easier to organise his wealth when Britain becomes a tax haven. I am sure in all his business activities he obeys the law – as he interprets it. Just as in his political activities, anti-same-sex marriage, anti-abortion, he has chosen to obey his Roman Catholic Church. Like Boris Johnson, he has cultivated the jokey posh-boy image, lying with his legs up lounging on the bench during parliamentary debates, wearing and dressing his children in old-fashioned suits, and the public seem to love it. The upper and middle classes still have their hunting, their gentlemen's clubs, their dinner and cocktail parties. Plus, let me not forget, their support of opera, ballet and paying my wages in the theatre.

It is less easy to explain to my grandchildren what working class actually is. The arrival of high-rise flats and decimated industries has changed the working-class culture of my childhood. In the old days, when I was young, there was a vivid lifestyle attached to many workers' jobs. The unions ran educational events, the pits had the brass bands. The Welsh had their choirs. There were even traditional dances. In Scotland the Highland Fling, in Wales and the Northern mill areas clog-dancing, and in Ireland the intricate energetic step-dancing. There was Wakes Week, and May Day with its beauty queens, and Butlin's holiday camp, and hop-picking. The church of different denominations was still important, with its Girl Guides and Boys' Brigades. Most of those things have gone into decline. Morris dancing survives at some events. It may look faintly ludicrous to our modern eyes, but that, and dancing round a maypole, is probably all the tradition we have left in England if, as I fear, Wales, Northern Ireland and Scotland decide to leave us.

Time off from work used to be spent having one or two pints in the local pub or working men's club on a Saturday night, playing darts, billiards and dominoes, or at whist drives or bingo. During the week you were too knackered to go out so you listened to the radio at home. Nowadays, abuse of alcohol is regarded as a badge of honour; getting excessively drunk counts as a good night out. Even better, also getting laid by someone you chose on a dating app. (I really am in old-fart country now.)

March 2019

I have spent a lovely two days visiting my youngest daughter's elegant new house in Exeter, and my grandchildren's new schools, one alongside the cathedral, the other a beautiful building set in spacious sports fields. I met dedicated teachers and eager, shiny-eyed, bushy-tailed students.

When Ellie Jane was eleven it had not occurred to me to send her to a private school. My mother, who left school at fourteen with only a rudimentary education – although her ability to recite all the kings and queens of England meant she had a much firmer grip on history than I did for all my grammar-school education – had somehow heard tell of St Paul's, a venerable public school for girls near where we lived in Hammersmith. By that time I was earning a reasonable amount and she was incensed that I did not want to 'do the best' for my daughter by sending her there.

She pointed out that, despite my scholarship, she and my father had worked their arses off to support me through school, with all its uniforms, clubs, books and hockey sticks. They had the working-class ethos of wanting a child to 'better herself'. She declared that 'anyone who was anyone' in the world had been to a posh school. That I would be stunting a bright child's growth by sending her to the local comprehensive, which was at that time notoriously badly run. Eventually I succumbed and two of my daughters went to posh schools, Bedales, Westminster and St Paul's. Abigail, guided by her much more principled biological mother Sally, went to one of the best schools in London at that time, Pimlico Comprehensive.

I have always felt hypocritical about it. I try to assuage my guilt by now working in state schools with a scheme to help kids who are falling behind, but people like me, middle class now whether I admit it or not, who take our children out of the state system are doing it harm. Now I see my daughters are facing the same dilemma with their children. Abigail's two girls went to state schools in North London, because they are excellent. My other two daughters do not pursue that route, not because they want their kids to go to a posh school, but because they judge the state schools in their area to be up against impossible odds of overcrowding and understaffing. The standard of your local school is the luck of the draw, largely dependent on the endurance and dedication of the teachers. I have visited many schools, mainly primaries, all over England, and the best, in every way, were often in deprived areas, but driven to excellence by the head and their staff, as well as some local board members.

Primary education in this country seems better than secondary. All my children and grandchildren went to excellent state primaries; indeed Joanna was chairperson of the governors of their St Ives school. My grandson Jack, to my enormous pride, has started training to be a primary teacher.

It would be foolish to deny that the mere 7 per cent of the population who go to private schools do better than state alumni – if your definition of 'better' is in terms of career prospects rather than experiencing diversity. Many more of them go to Russell Group universities, get top jobs in government, journalism, the BBC, the city – you name it, they've cracked it. They have a confidence, bordering on arrogance, that opens doors. They do not have the lack of belief in themselves that meant that I, even with a grammar-school education, did not believe that people like me wrote books, until I was eventually persuaded to try when I was seventy. They are led to appreciate and regard as their right the beautiful surroundings of their schools, whereas most state schools are ugly. State-school playing fields were sold off by Margaret Thatcher, and at present I see in the schools I visit a shameful dilapidation. The independent schools put an emphasis on the arts and music, usually having purpose-built theatres and studios, whereas in state schools anything not likely to lead to a job is being cut from the curriculum. No mind is being paid to a future where jobs will be taken over by robots and culture can fill the chasm that will be caused by the inactivity of brain and body that this revolution will provoke. There is a huge divide in our country, which Brexit has exposed, and the education system has contributed to it.

I am involved in Gallions, a state primary in London's Tower Hamlets that uses music as the basis of its work. It has battled to survive against the authorities' suspicion of its approach and lack of finance. Every child has an instrument and plays in one of the several orchestras and sings in a choir, and many lessons bring music into the learning process. Attainment and behaviour have improved radically across the board. It is a deprived area and many of the children have difficult home lives, not least the refugees and the other 67 per cent for whom English is not their first language, but the school bursts with energy and invention inspired by its grossly underpaid and overworked staff.

For some reason Eton decided to send a few of its pupils to Gallions, to see how the other half – or, actually, the other 93 per cent – live, and they in turn invited the Gallions children to visit the college. The coach ride to Windsor was exciting enough for the kids, most of whom had never left their neighbourhood, and the ancient splendours of Eton reduced them to silent disbelief. This was Wonderland. I was moved to tears as the children, resplendent in new red jumpers, walked nervously onto the stage of the majestic concert hall, where their pink-haired teacher led them into their performance. Those tears were at the desperate injustice of their lives compared to those of their hosts. The well-meaning wife of one of the Eton staff said to me, 'Isn't it wonderful for these children to be shown something to aspire to?'

She got the full blast of my despair.

'Do you seriously think that any of these kids stand a hope in hell of achieving any of the privileges of your boys?'

'Well, we have bursaries.'

'And where would the money come from for the tutors needed to get them up to your entrance standards?'

Eton and my grandchildren's schools in Exeter are wonderful. I would not want them abolished. I just want everyone to have access to that quality of education. It is a pity that the reforming Labour government of 1945 didn't take them over when they saw the country was open to radical change; if they had done, the comprehensive system would have worked better – everyone educated together, no matter what their background, with the child learning to be a brilliant plumber valued as much as the one doing classics, all eating in the same canteen and playing the same sports, learning to respect and understand each other. The present proliferation of different types of schools – church, free school, academy, whatever – do nothing to unite us.

I get a little tired of the sneering about the middle class, the metropolitan elite. I am guilty of this too when I bang on about my working-class roots. In every primary school in which I have been involved, it is the middle-class parents who do most of the organising of activities like fetes, sports days, storytelling and nowadays, shamefully, raising money for books and other basics that the schools can't afford. Sadly, many of these proactive people, if they can afford it, transfer to the private sector when the children are older, if the choice of good schools in their areas is limited.

I want governments of all colours to consult teachers at the coalface as to how our education should operate, rather than teachers having new systems frequently imposed on them by people who do not know the problems. Teachers are too often called upon to be social workers as well. Many believe that schools should have a qualified staff member on the team specifically to deal with the complex family and mental health problems with which the teaching staff are increasingly burdened.

I was once bewailing my lack of educated, intellectual prowess to a high-flying lover, and he replied that I was streetwise, and that was better. At the time I thought that he, with his private-school/Oxbridge credentials, was being condescending, and probably referring to my sexual lack of propriety. But he had a point. Maybe the supreme self-confidence that I see in those who have attended private schools, usually leading also to a Russell Group university education, has its drawbacks. Was it perhaps the hubris that comes from an Eton education that led David Cameron to believe the referendum would go his way? He is, I think, not a bad man. Much as I dislike their views and attitudes, neither, I suppose, are Rees-Mogg and Boris Johnson. Even Farage, that poseur as a man of the people, who actually went to the distinguished Dulwich College and worked in the City, must, I suppose, sincerely believe in his mission to restore us to a mythical bygone age of beer-drinking and Little England. They have all been taught in their excellent schools to believe in public service, duty and compassion for lesser mortals. What they disastrously lack is a real, gut, first-hand understanding of what it is like to be poor, ignored and excluded. The teacher's wife at Eton really believed that, if you want something enough, you can work hard and get it. She had no conception of the desperate isolation of poverty.

On the drive home from Eton, my grandchild, Lola, who came with me on the trip, took me to task about my behaviour with the teacher's wife. She pointed out that the Eton boys had been kind and solicitous towards the East End youngsters, providing a delicious cream tea and lots of fun. The music scholars had not been snooty when the youngsters started to clap and stomp along with their exquisite rendering of Vivaldi.

'Yes,' I snarled, 'they are probably now all having a nice drink feeling well pleased that they have done something to merit their school's charity status.'

This painful ambiguity that I feel about the education of my family as opposed to the elimination of privilege in our society troubled me as I travelled back from Exeter. My grandchildren will enjoy the swimming pool, library, sports facilities and, above all, well-paid, enthusiastic teachers, one of whom explained that she had deserted the state sector as she no longer found it possible to teach properly in it. Charlie and Alfie were already experiencing the joy of learning new things, and I am so pleased that they will have this excellent start in life. But what of the rest? The ones who live where the local schools are failing – overcrowded, lacking facilities, with disillusioned staff. Whose parents can't afford to send them anywhere else and maybe are not well enough educated themselves to help them with their homework.

If the Tories have their way they will bring back more grammar schools for the academically gifted. But all children are gifted in some way and should have their particular skills recognised and valued. I well remember when my headmistress read out the names of the five girls, I think it was, out of a class of fifty, who had obtained scholarships to the grammar school. (This was just before the 1944 Education Act that made it free for everyone.)

The rest knew that they were condemned to attend the awful secondary modern, or the inferior technical school. I met a girl from my old school at a book festival recently, who told me that her whole life had been blighted by that eleven-year-old branding of her as a failure. I know from the work I do with young people that one of the most important things they need is respect. For others and, above all, themselves.

I had booked my return ticket to Exeter online but omitted to reserve a seat, so I phoned to do so. I was told that there were no seats.

'But I have a ticket.'

'Yes.'

'Are you telling me that I will have to stand?'

'Well, there may be one or two seats not booked.'

Not wishing to probe the mysteries of the running of our railways, I decided to change to a later train on which I could still book a seat. As instructed, I picked up a ticket for the seat reservation and was assured that this was all I needed. Oh no. Travelling by train is not that simple. When I arrived at Paddington, my ticket would not open the barrier, so I asked a crumpled official to help me and he said it wasn't a ticket, just a seat reservation, and he couldn't let me through. I tried to explain the saga of my booking experience but he was convinced that I was cheating the railways: how could he be sure I hadn't travelled back the day before too, as my original booking said? He would not accept that this would have been quite a lot of travelling for an old girl, or that it was unlikely that they would have issued me a seat reservation if I had no ticket. By now a crowd was watching my efforts to persuade this obstinate jobsworth. That was when I heard myself turn into a supercilious grande dame, despite my lack of public-school education.

'Oh, come on, darling. Don't be silly.'

'I'm not your darling. And I'm not silly,' he quite rightly snarled, detecting my lack of respect.

My exasperation was at his bloody obstinacy, his mindless sticking to the rules rather than listening to reason, his power to impose his misguided judgement on me. I nearly said (but thank goodness didn't), 'I bet you voted Leave.'

By this time the crowd was hoping that I would be arrested. After a long altercation he summoned two colleagues and another official in a less crumpled uniform came along, as it happened a woman of colour, heard my tale and opened the barrier.

My rude awakening from the joys of academe I had enjoyed in Exeter was not over. My taxi driver turned out to be a black-cab cartoon character.

'We want our country back.'

'Er . . .'

'We are a great country.'

'Yes, but . . .'

'Why don't they get on with it?'

'It's not that easy.'

'They should get that Trump over here. He'd sort out the bloody Germans. And get rid of all these bloody foreigners. Send them back where they come from.'

I tried to reason with him but he was in his own world of fury and disillusion.

When we arrived at my house, I offered him an over-large tip. Was I asserting some kind of superiority, some condescension?

For a minute he hesitated. Then he took it. A Brechtian moment.

We were both diminished.

May 2019

The delightful musical by Tim Firth I am appearing in in Chichester has been a huge success and everyone was convinced it would 'go in', as we say, meaning transfer to the West End of London. It won't and the young cast – well, younger than me, everyone is – are desolate. Particularly because, when you are away from home, the company becomes even closer. The show is called This Is My Family and we really have been for a time, together at night, and on day trips, eating and drinking, mainly drinking, ensemble. They have been hugely supportive of this old bird, especially after I had what could have been a disastrous accident.

I woke up in my digs one night and, probably confused by the unfamiliar layout of the new flat I was staying in, fell in the bathroom and hit my head on the edge of the shower. Stunned, I found myself sitting on the floor, blood pouring from my head. I tried to stem the flow with towels but eventually rang 999. I can't remember much about what followed, except that the paramedics were super-efficient and in no time I was in the local hospital having ten stitches put into my scalp. I insisted on leaving as I had a matinee that day, and we had no understudies.

When I got back to the flat my bathroom looked like a crime scene, with blood everywhere, handprints up the wall and bloody towels soaking in the bath. Our director, Daniel

Evans, came round, took one look, gulped and said, 'We've got to cancel the performance.'

I knew the season was sold out so if we cancelled the audience would not be able to rebook. In the past I have performed with broken bones and broken heart, and so, to the alarm of my fellow actors, on I went, blood still dripping down my forehead from under my wig. Their faces were ashen, and I am sure they would have much preferred an afternoon off. Absurd behaviour on my part, when nowadays you can get a matinee off to attend a friend's wedding. Once I remember a John Lewis salesperson thinking I was being obstructive when I told him I could not receive a delivery on a matinee day. 'Take an afternoon off, that's what people do,' he said. I asked what he would think if he went to the theatre and the tannoy announced, 'Ms Hancock will not be appearing today as she is awaiting the delivery of a new oven.' His shrug showed that he would not give a damn. Fair enough. But old habits die hard.

The youngsters in the company find it difficult to accept the unexpected and brutal end to such a highly praised, convivial venture. Sourpuss me is not in the least surprised. I have learned, as they will, that disappointment is all part of the job. 'On to pastures new' is my motto. In work and life.

When directing a play, Neil Bartlett, playwright, novelist, artist, actor and wondrous cook, always addresses his company as 'dear colleagues'. One dictionary definition of 'colleague' is fellow worker, which has a comradely, like-minded ring that appeals to me. It is difficult to define this close, albeit usually temporary, allegiance that binds actors, musicians and dancers to one another, but it is probably the thing I value most about my job. In all my long career I can only remember one show where the discord was so great that I dreaded going to work, but that painful experience is submerged by all the pleasure before and since.

A relationship with a colleague is less enduring than that with a friend; it demands little of one, a lovely flash in the pan – a saying that refers to the flash caused in a musket when the ball doesn't go off. Colourful, but not drastic, and not really harmful. Never mind artistic integrity, critical acclaim, message – all are meaningless without the mates I work with. It is why I have always rejected offers of a one-woman show. The thought of eight times a week going through a stage door to an echoey theatre with no one to gossip or moan with, except an equally depressed small stage management, does not appeal to me. And it is why I prefer long runs of a musical to a straight play, because the sound of yet more colleagues, the musicians, tuning up and playing an overture never fails to lift my spirits.

The first day of rehearsals, when everyone is on their best behaviour and nervous about saying the lines out loud for the first time, is always a bit stiff and formal, but almost immediately we are in the rehearsal room, or in front of the camera, inhibitions are abandoned. When I was young I inevitably fell in love with the best-looking actor, or the director (always male in those days), and longing looks and furtive caresses were exchanged, but sadly not consummated, as in those days a well-brought-up working-class girl was taught that you did not have sex outside marriage and, more importantly, had no access to birth control. I must have been, and latter-day laughing discussions with old colleagues has confirmed indeed I was, a source of considerable frustration with my innocent romantic obsessions.

Love lives and sex are much less complicated these days. There are often flirtations, sometimes leading to more committed relationships, in companies, which now, in my old age, I observe with remembered pleasure. When first John astonished me by inappropriately telling me he loved me, I gently explained to the ardent nine-years-younger suitor that I was already married, and what he was feeling was caused by propinquity. Little did I know then how resolute he could be. Later, 'It's propinquity' became a catchphrase between us when we suspected any romances, or perhaps if he was feeling bored at some grand event, when he would whisper in my ear, 'Fancy a bit of propinquity?'

Affairs are relatively rare, but many less emotional friendships grow during the run of a show or television. If the piece of work flops, the cast cling together even more. The relationships are close and supportive. For the run of the show. Then suddenly everything is over. The set is destroyed, the clothes sent back to the costumiers, and the cast say weeping goodbyes. Promising to keep in touch. Mostly they don't. This can be heartbreaking for some. Which is why Clive Swift asked me to join him in setting up a place for actors which could be a club to meet up in and do class and hear about auditions. It took years of begging, borrowing and stealing funds and making plans, but together with a few other theatre colleagues we set up what is now the thriving Actors Centre, which comforts and inspires people who have chosen this often difficult and strangely lonely career.

After seventy years in the profession, I never do a show or telly without several people reminding me that they worked with me, as an artist or member of the crew, on such-and-such a piece, this many years ago. Sadly, I often don't remember either the person or the work. The other night I listened to a whole play on Radio 4 Extra in the small hours of the morning, only to hear my name given in the cast list at the end as having played the lead. I have absolutely no memory of doing it, though it must have been so important to me at the time – I always took my work very seriously then. All that wasted angst. Ah me!

May 2019

So, Theresa May has resigned as prime minister. It's difficult not to feel sorry for her.

I have done a lot of cringing while she has been in office. The sad sight of her standing in the European Parliament, before the start of proceedings, looking for someone to talk to, shy, awkward and completely ignored by the mainly men bustling around her happily greeting each other. Then there was the pathetic failure of her speech at the party conference, when a tickle in the throat could not be controlled, and the set disintegrated behind her. Even worse, another speech when she unrhythmically and gawkily attempted to dance onto the platform.

She is a vicar's daughter, goes to church every week and talks about loving her neighbour, yet as home secretary she promoted the 'hostile environment' policy to deter immigrants, including sending vans out warning people to 'go home or face arrest'. Another cowering-behind-your-hands moment was when, on a TV programme, she was asked what she had done that she was ashamed of. She looked nonplussed, and made herself a laughing stock again by saying that as a child she naughtily ran through fields of wheat. Presumably she had forgotten those vans.

She has clung to her post for three years, trying the magic three-word-slogan technique until the public too has flinched every – numerous – time she parroted 'strong and stable' or 'Brexit means Brexit'.

She is a disastrous campaigner, which I wouldn't hold against her as those who are good often make lousy ministers, but she seems unable to communicate. The glaring example being her inability to visit the survivors of the dreadful Grenfell fire, even though I am sure she too was devastated by what happened.

She is a poor judge of the public mood. On a hike with her husband one weekend (she is a serious walker) she decided to hold a snap election. Another faux pas. It resulted in her losing her majority. It is hard to tell whether, during her time in office, she was appallingly badly advised, cripplingly shy, or just stupid. But I suspect rather nice.

Since the decision to leave the EU, the country has had three years in limbo trying to ratify an agreement while Theresa May secretively led us into chaos. Maybe it is her notorious inability to communicate that has made it impossible to understand what is going on. Theresa May, and her acolyte men designated to lead us out of Europe (where are they now, those brilliant deal-makers David Davis and Dr Liam Fox?), have struggled to make Brexit work, because, her other much-repeated phrase, 'it is the will of the people'. They, in compliance with Farage, promoted, as their main objectives in leaving, stopping immigration and making our own laws. 'To get our country back.' The disgusting Auschwitz-like poster which was plastered on buses and walls by the Leave campaigners, threatening invasion by millions of Turks and other unsavoury foreigners, certainly seems to have done its job. Racist crime increased during the referendum and has continued to do so during this negotiating period. My grandson's mixed-race girlfriend is constantly harassed.

I sometimes feel we are a country that is prone to self-pity – we have been put upon by the nasty foreigners, coming here stealing our jobs, using our NHS, making us obey their laws. The next step from self-pity is blame. Migrants and Europeans, Jews, Muslims – it is everybody's fault but ours. 'We didn't ask to join,' whined a man on the television. Er, yes, actually, we did, and we were turned down to begin with, mainly by Charles de Gaulle. In the seventies we were 'the sick man of Europe', our economy was in a mess, and we were desperate to join the thriving, young European Union. A few diehards never got over the fact that we needed Europe, and drip-fed their opposition over the years through the right-wing press. With Jeremy Corbyn catastrophically sitting on the fence, so that no one really knew what Labour stood for, the argument for staying in Europe was never properly heard.

The Remoaners' useless pitch was a lot of bleating about the financial disadvantages of leaving, but the sense of loss felt by those who voted Leave was more profound than that. That posh boy David Cameron was telling them to stay; he's been no help, so let's kick him in the teeth as well. That man with the beer seems to understand, so let's do what he says. The expenses scandal, years of austerity, have led to a country losing faith in its Parliament. Mind you, this is nothing new. In 1934, J. B. Priestley said in his English Journey:

'People are beginning to believe that the government is a mysterious process with which they have no real concern. This is the soil in which autocrats flourish and liberty dies. Alongside that apathetic majority, there will soon be a minority that is tired of seeing nothing vital happen and will adapt any cause that promises decisive action.'

How right he was. It took Europe a war to bring it to its senses last time. So, God help us.

May 2019

Our leaders worldwide are not the most dependable at the moment: Putin, Erdoğan, Netanyahu, Kim Jong-un – the lunatics have taken over the asylum. But what can one say about Mr President, the Leader of the Western World, Donald Trump? Luckily, I have already said it. Twelve years ago. There was recently a message on my website from a reader of my books, suggesting I must be a prophet and suggesting I look at page sixty-six of Just Me, which was published in 2008, a passage I had completely forgotten. Often when I dare to look back at previous writing I find my opinion has changed and I disagree with myself. This time I felt exactly the same. Only more so.

I am discussing the horror of reality television:

'Almost more sickening was a programme where Donald Trump set about testing young people for the honour of being employed by him. This nasty, tacky man, with his silly blow-dried hair and slack mouth, was treated like a god. I suppose he is an idol of the modern religion of materialism, with its tenets of greed and determination, never mind who or what ever needs to be trampled on, to get to the top rung of a rather dubious ladder. If they were lucky, they too could live in a palace of bad taste, and update their partners regularly to the latest Barbie doll. I wanted to punch his vacuous, lifted, pampered face. Instead, I took it out on a poor chap who made the mistake of climbing up on my balcony, and had the nerve to try and force his way into my house. I leaped up and screamed, "Fuck off, fuck off, fuck off." I think even the all-powerful Trump would have backed off and slunk away from this raging old dervish, leaping about shaking her fists. I wasn't in the least afraid, just very angry with the nasty Mr Trump, and all the trashy new values foisted upon us, including this young man at my window, who was opting out with his drugs. I was incandescent with fury not just with him, sad, scared creature that he turned out to be, but the whole Trumpery of our values, at least as shown on reality television . . .'

Our moral compass has gone awry. We seem to be choosing personalities, celebrities, madmen to lead us.

Let's see who the Tories choose to replace Theresa.

June 2019

Fascinating watching May dealing with the end of her lifetime dream of being prime minister. Whilst the Goves and Johnsons and other slimy customers stab each other in the back, she glides around with a grim half-smile, her back just a bit more stooped, but with a vicar's-daughter dignity. 'Nothing became her like the leaving of it.' Her slightly silly leaning walk doesn't seem to match her rather good fashion sense, especially for cheeky shoes.

Observation is a constant practice in my day-to-day existence. I am always looking at how people walk, use their hands, pitch their voices, avert or hold my gaze, laugh, and I even cold-heartedly consider their and my own various ways of weeping, or, more potent in my opinion, trying not to weep. The empathy comes in when you put yourself into your character's mind and often discover, in the rehearsal process, why they committed that murder, or abandoned that child, or fell in love with that scoundrel. In the Chichester musical I was playing a woman in the early stages of dementia and I shamelessly studied my dear friend, who is struggling with her new bewildering world, and when I then put what I observed into my own head to show to an audience I found it deeply disturbing.

Getting inside the mind of a character you are playing is a basic essential of acting. Empathy is an essential tool of our trade. Which is why I get riled when people, mainly journalists and politicians, who seem to overlook their own rarefied existences, talk dismissively of actors as luvvies, telling us we should keep our mouths shut as we know nothing about real life. My colleagues, proper actors as opposed to TV personalities, are mostly serious, hard-working, well-informed people and I like them very much. I would suggest that our practice of empathy, and the research we carry out into the varied worlds of the characters we play, make us better equipped to understand people's needs and troubles than those who inhabit the Westminster Bubble or Grub Street. No matter if the character you are portraying is repugnant to you, somehow you have to experience their thoughts and motives, as well as using some equivalent feeling from your own emotional store cupboard. I may not have actually committed a murder, but I've often felt like it. That is a step in the right direction, but the final leap is to actually 'be' a murderer for the duration of the play. John's frequent note, to himself as well as to me, is always in my head: 'Don't demonstrate – be.'

Some actors brilliantly convey a character by technically looking and sounding like them, and sticking to a set pattern. I am of the school that tries to keep everything fluid, not set in stone, but the other, planned, approach is just as effective, and much easier to sustain for eight performances a week in a long run. The master of it was Laurence Olivier. His spider-with-a-hump appearance and scuttling walk as Richard III was chilling. Sliding down the proscenium arch, singing the blues, he broke hearts in The Entertainer, and who is not fired up by his vocal acrobatics at the end of the Agincourt speech in Henry V?

'And gentlemen in England now a-bed
Shall think themselves a'cursed they were not here,
And hold their manhoods cheap whiles any speaks
That fought with us [wait for it – here it comes – roaring yell] upon Saint Crispin's DAAAAY'.

All technique, and brilliant.

I, a generation later, have tried to emulate the Marlon Brando approach practised at the Actors Studio, which I attended in New York when I was over there doing Entertaining Mr Sloane in 1965. Although Brando later denied that Lee Strasberg had taught him anything, he along with many later stars did attend class there. Brando's acting of the sensual, desperate Stanley in A Streetcar Named Desire, and the taxi scene in On the Waterfront, which seem to be improvised sheer emotion throughout, were revolutionary. Olivier's approach was thrilling in the theatre, but less successful on film. He met his comeuppance when he worked with Marilyn Monroe in The Prince and the Showgirl. She had, like Brando, studied the Method with Strasberg. She drove Olivier mad with her approach, but in my opinion acted him off the screen. Her little improvised dance whilst alone in a grand room waiting to meet the prince is one of my favourite film moments. Olivier apparently would insensitively tell her to 'just be sexy'. She was delightfully sexy, but for all her wiggles and giggles she is not demonstrating sexiness; it comes, bless her heart, from the core of her tortured being. She just is. She is 'being' – truthfully. It just so happens that her true self is heartbreakingly beautiful. Many blonde, attractive actors have tried to emulate her, with the same sexy movements and breathy voice, but none have ever matched Monroe's potency.

July 2019

Very good interview with David Tennant in The Times. No mention of his role in a dreary Gorky drama called Vassa that we did together in 1998. Much best forgotten. He was wonderful, though, playing a badly deformed man, for which he diligently contorted his body and face. Can't remember much about the play, except that it was very gloomy and the audience hated it. Next time I saw him was when he came backstage after a show I was in. He had accepted the role of Doctor Who, and expressed some concern that it could lead his career astray. No way. He is a remarkable talent. Not just an incredibly versatile actor, but also charismatic.

What makes a star? By that I mean not just a superb actor but the sort who plays leading roles and can put bums on seats. The critic Ken Tynan maintained that they had to have an ambiguous sexuality. Not necessarily in practice, but just in their performing persona. Many male stars do have a feminine streak. In Tynan's days Olivier certainly did, John Gielgud too. And of course Noël Coward, but also Cary Grant, Ralph Richardson, Alec Guinness, Peter O'Toole, and the man I loved as a child, Danny Kaye. Nowadays Benedict Cumberbatch, David and their contemporaries are not belligerently butch, being unafraid to show gentle sensitivity. The women stars of an earlier period, Katharine Hepburn, Greta Garbo, Marlene Dietrich and certainly the comedians Mae West, Lucille Ball and Jean Harlow, had a strength in their presentation. Nowadays Glenda Jackson, Helen Mirren, Clare Foy, Nicola Walker and Olivia Colman and their starry ilk are feminine, but also have a straight, no-nonsense side to their work, which could be deemed a masculine trait. Maxine Peake brought an effective ambiguity to her portrayal of Hamlet, and a staging of an all-female Julius Caesar at the Donmar was revelatory. Maybe it is because they appeal to all genders in the audience if as actors they have a mixture of masculine and feminine in their make-up. Monroe alone seemed all woman, and that, alas, is probably what destroyed her. Yet she is loved by a wide variety of filmgoers. Maybe in her case it is her potent vulnerability that makes her universally loved. Vulnerability seems to be another trait that audiences warm to – the beloved Judy Garland being the prime example.

Although I confess I really have no idea what makes a star, I do pride myself on being able to spot that special quality in colleagues, like David, that I've worked with.

The company I carefully chose when I was artistic director of the Royal Shakespeare Company small-scale tour (which led to my first book, Ramblings of an Actress), have all gone on to have successful careers. Roger Allam, whom I drove insane with my constant notes, has become the versatile, brilliant star I knew he would be. His voice and body are very male but when he laughs or shows emotion Ken Tynan's ambivalence can be glimpsed. The shy young man in my company who played both Romeo and Flute the bellows-mender in A Midsummer Night's Dream, had a mysterious, fragile intensity that made it impossible to take your eyes off him. Daniel Day-Lewis portraying Flute trying to act Thisbe in the ridiculous amateur dramatics the mechanicals put on for the toffs in the Dream captured the fear, the excitement and the embarrassment of a working man forced to play a woman, at one point dissolving into suppressed giggles, that every night had me and the audience aching with laughter. He just simply *was* that man – in a part that can become a comedy cliché. The complete immersion in his varied roles that has characterised his meteoric career was there then, and is how I knew, without a shadow of doubt, despite disagreement from the other RSC directors (his Romeo was unconventional), that he would eventually be a huge star. He has now decided to retire and, although I am sad that I will see no more of his work, I am glad he is conducting his life as he chooses. Our profession can be cruel in its discarding of artists, if they begin to weaken, in favour of the new. Dan has made sure he will never suffer that. He has always thrown himself 100 per cent into the parts he is playing, and for him, I suspect, that has been sometimes damagingly demanding. Certainly it leaves little room for a private life. It is understandable that he should now wish to cherish his time, his privacy, his family, and all the other interests he has.

I believe performances like those of David, Roger and Dan will not date because they are unmannered and utterly truthful, but, alas, even huge success is soon forgotten, certainly in theatre, although films too can date and disappear. These days we do not hear much of James Mason, Kenneth More, Eric Portman, Margaret Lockwood, Gracie Fields or my particular heart-throb Stewart Granger, all of whom were huge stars in their day. When I was young we got our gallery stools and queued all day to see the latest performances of Dames Edith Evans and Sybil Thorndike, Wendy Hillier, Peggy Ashcroft and the elegant Margaret Leighton. Young actors nowadays, let alone the public, do not know their names, but they were venerated in their day. *Sic transit gloria.*

July 2019

In old age I see more of my friends than my family. My two grannies lived with my mum and dad until the day they died, squashed together in one room – they fought like cat and dog and must have driven my parents insane. I am independent, and my daughters have busy family units to which I am an occasional visitor. They, especially Ellie Jane, are there if I need them, but up till now I seldom have. It is part of Nature that animals leave the nest when they are mature and set up new nests, but the deserted parent birds still fly or float around with their mates. As do I.

During my marriages I neglected my friends. I had needy husbands, the first because of the damage wrought on a very young man by active war service, and the other because of a difficult childhood. John was not a very social animal anyway – and nor indeed was I. Being on display in our work made us almost reclusive in our private lives. For me, my work, the family and keeping John happy in our all-consuming relationship was a full-time occupation that left little time for friends.

When we both had time off, we did not want to share it with others. We were not good hosts. As children, neither of us came from backgrounds that understood the concept of dinner or cocktail parties. 'Dinner' was what we called lunch anyway, and parties were just rather spartan dos for children's birthdays – junket and pass the parcel, with the prize being a gobstopper, quite a bonanza during sweet rationing. I never remember my parents entertaining guests. So, as grown-ups, for John and me the idea of inviting people in for a meal was a scary enterprise. John was a good basic cook but didn't feel confident about cooking for anyone other than the family. After his mother left them when he was seven, his father was often away, so he had to provide food for his little brother. He would rustle up something usually involving jam, bread and baked beans. HP Sauce remained an essential ingredient. My mother had neither the time, doing a nine-to-five, six-day-a-week job, nor the means, with scant ingredients during and for a long while after the war, to teach me to cook. I did domestic science at school during rationing, so potatoes in their jackets are still my speciality, and I am good at beating butter, margarine and milk together to make them spread thinly and go further.

To this day entertaining guests is an ordeal for me, taking days of planning and near nervous breakdown when cooking the meal. I am a member of a lovely book club where we take it in turns to host the meeting. The others conjure up gastronomic feasts whilst I sneakily spend a fortune at Ottolenghi's. I so envy the women and men who make holding a dinner party into an art form. To visit the home of my friend and neighbour Delena is sheer delight. Ellie Jane often stayed with her and her husband, Gary, when I was working away, and when she returned home she would tell me, awestruck, of sit-down teas with tablecloths and serviettes and home-made cake and jam.

Delena's table, with mixed antique plates and dishes, and garden flowers, is a feast for the eyes, and one's taste buds are blessed with flavoursome invented dishes and a perfect cheese from the little shop in Chiswick. Even as a vegan, eating at Gary and Delena's is a joy. It all seems to go so smoothly but must have taken painstaking effort to present such a gift to their friends. What amazes me is that she actually seems to enjoy it, always perfectly coiffed and clad. I would be sweaty and anxious that the vegetables didn't go cold because the meat took longer to cook than the recipe said. Always a recipe for me – God bless Delia – whereas my good cook friends spurn such plebeian aids. It is all creative artistry for them. Over the dinner table they discuss what special process or ingredient they have used, and I sit there like Banquo's ghost, saying nothing, trying to follow a complicated foreign language.

My friend Helen has the hostess gene as well. She has never married and has now abandoned her colourful love life to concentrate on enjoying herself, writing and painting. Part of that pleasure is from sharing her skill at making the most of life with others. She has a perfect small house and an adored pug dog, she chooses her guests for dinner carefully so that they will maybe make new friends, and her food and wine is perfect. She inherited money and uses it generously to take friends on treats and imaginative trips abroad. Just after John died we had a family holiday booked in Barcelona; we decided to still go, and Helen agreed to take his place. She is an inveterate traveller, and rallied us into excursions and restaurants. Whenever we go away together, she has a tradition of bringing some corny self-help book, from which she reads out improving advice at bedtime. Even as a distraught new widow she had me howling with laughter. She makes every aspect of life as enjoyable as she can. Even when on her own, she cooks a proper meal, sets the table and changes her frock. When she stayed with me in France I was horrified when she came down in the evening, elegantly dressed, to eat my pathetic broken omelette and salad. It is not affectation or conformity; she likes dressing up. She relishes the small details. No wonder so many men fell in love with her. Still do at eighty, but they would get in the way of her idyllic lifestyle. And they say spinsters are sad.

When I first went on a diet for my rheumatoid arthritis, which meant no gluten, no dairy, no meat or fish and very little oil, my dear friend Neil and his husband James asked me round for dinner one night. When I explained my regime and suggested we just have a drink, he paused a mere nanosecond before saying, 'No, it'll be a wonderful challenge' – and of course concocted a banquet of buckwheat, quinoa, seaweed, spices, exotic vegetables and God knows what other fabulous exotic ingredients.

Entertaining well is a generous and loving act, and with all my heart I wish I could do it. I've done courses, watched television programmes, practised on my own – the kitchen always ends up looking like the Somme and I bitterly fail to produce anything really tasty. I just about manage my weekly delivery from Mindful Chef of measured-out ingredients for a simple vegan recipe, but it takes me much longer than they say it will, and in the end I don't enjoy it much because I know I'm cheating. I so want to entertain my friends as they do me, with love and care.

July 2019

Boris Johnson has become prime minister. The world's gone mad. Trump? Johnson? I have got to get out of here. I need to calm down or I will have a heart attack.

August 2019

For nearly thirty years my home in France has been a place of refuge from the turmoil of my life in London. My normally ricocheting blood pressure steadies here, as life slows down to a peaceful calm. I feel at ease. But now, with the government edict about residential expansion in our commune still being fiercely contested, even here I can't relax properly.

The decision by some bureaucrat in Paris has jettisoned me, and my neighbours, into a whirlpool of confusion about the future of our hameau. That, and not knowing the outcome of negotiations regarding movement around Europe, and shared healthcare, in this Brexit transition time, has left me in limbo.

Limbo in the Catholic Church, which is not renowned for its protection of children, was where babies who died before being baptised were condemned to stay, forbidden entry to heaven. Only in 2007 did the Pope decide to abolish that ruling. Good old him. Pity he didn't look at what some of his supposedly celibate priests and nuns were up to at the same time. My very first school was a convent in King's Cross, where threats of hellfire and the cane had me screaming in terror every morning as my father dragged me up the hill towards the malign Mother Superior. In fact, come to think of it, maybe my lifetime battle with fear and rage stems from those few months I spent at that school, not the war, which I normally blame. It could be argued, on the other hand, that those malevolent crows taught me to deal with threat.

I remember limbo dancing being all the rage in the fifties. Brought over by the Windrush generation from the Caribbean, it was a painful competition to dance under an increasingly lowered stick, or in our case skipping rope, in a backbend, legs doubled under us, in a way that did not suit our rigid English bodies.

Limbo, as it has now come to be known in the secular world, is not a comfortable place to be. I know it well. Most actors do. The between-jobs, when you doubt you will ever work again. The almost worse situation, when you are offered two parts at the same time, and can't decide which you should do. In the old days, for me, the decisions depended on which paid best, which might give me a contact for future work, and which might improve my pathetic curriculum vitae. Nowadays the criterion for me is a project I believe in, regardless of the size of my part – in fact, preferably small. Or a new challenge, like climbing the mountain in Edie, or one I have just been offered, to manage a canal boat.

I spend most of my life in a state of indecision. One of the big advantages of being a vegan is the limited availability in most restaurants. I used to drive waiters and fellow eaters mad with my shilly-shallying over the menu, and then my tasting of everyone else's choices, and deciding I'd made the wrong one.

When I have a flare-up of pain from my RA, it is made worse by my mithering about which of my numerous medications I should take, or should I force myself to exercise, or just give up and go to bed? I have started using a UCLA app about mindfulness, and when I make up my mind to do that it seems to help. Until I find something else to dither about. You only realise how damaging indecision – being in limbo – is when you finally decide something, and the sense of relief is tremendous.

The limbo situation that I am in now in France does not promise any imminent resolution. That our mairie, in its lack of wisdom, designated our perfect little haven for expansion beggars belief. It is an ancient mountain village of six dwellings utterly unspoiled by any modern development. It is ramshackle and primitive with some Palaeolithic remains, ruins, and vestiges of Roman and medieval history both in the village and in the fields around the houses. No swimming pools, no geraniums, no concrete roads – just broken stone, and cobbled paths, and a patch of earth used for generations as a boules pitch. There is a working barn where we celebrate the gathering of the grape harvest with aioli and wine, and the fields around provide a cornucopia of cherries, lavender and sunflowers.

My stone house is dilapidated by generations of sun and mistral storms, and my neglect, but it continues to protect and bring me joy. It was built centuries ago, with only two tiny windows as lookouts on the wall turning its back to the violent wind, while the other side basks in the beneficent, healing sun. When it is too hot, the shutters and windows are kept closed, providing a welcome shady retreat. In the winter I light the wooden stove, and watch the flames flicker around the logs. At night, a million stars cover the skies, silence, apart from the white barn owl floating around, occasionally piercing the stillness with an eerie shriek.

We have formed ourselves into an association to defend our ancient home, which, being French, has involved a lot of wine and despairing shrugs. Despite a few changes over time, the community has remained tightly knit. After John's death, I came back to find a rose bush planted by my door, and each one of my neighbours held me in their arms, no words, just the conventional three kisses on the cheek, and some tears. When we were all gathered round André's tomb up on the hilltop town of Saignon, Monsieur Le Cros made a speech about how pleased André's parents would have been, after the travails of war, to see round their son's grave neighbours from Germany, Sweden, England and France.

My dilemma is: Do I leave this place that has provided ease for the last thirty years, or remain and face the inevitable upheaval of change? In the meantime: limbo.

August 2019

Back in London, every time I turn on the radio or TV at the moment I am incensed by a manic, garbled Boris Johnson telling us how wonderful it is going to be under his leadership/dictatorship. His guru, Dominic Cummings, has obviously held training sessions for the prime minister's dazed acolytes in how to walk confidently, talk positively, smile all the time, making sure that you hide the fear in your eyes, and when in doubt promise large sums of money or a title. The most incompetent recruits are not allowed to do interviews that might expose their stupidity under expert scrutiny. This especially applies to Boris – as we have been brainwashed into chummily calling him – who might bring the whole house of cards down with the irresistible temptation of a cheap laugh or a clever bon mot. It's been like a toned-down version of those alarming pictures from North Korea, where huge crowds smile and laugh and clap when the dear, murderous leader appears. Optimism is the flavour of the month. For my part, 2016, 2017, 2018 and what we've had so far of 2019 have been shit whichever way I look.

Before all these things happened, when I was chancellor of Portsmouth University, I often used to warn students that life is not always a bowl of cherries, but the empowering thing to remember is that it's entirely up to you what you make of it, and how you deal with it. Grab and cherish the good bits. Rheumatoid arthritis and the drugs I'm on, plus my age, make death imminent. That's just a fact. With that in mind, wouldn't it be sensible, not to mention more enjoyable, to heed Dominic Cummings's message of relentless positivity myself? No, even as portrayed by Benedict Cumberbatch, that is too big an ask.

There is a poem by Walter de la Mare called 'Fare Well' that I might fare well-er if I observed. The last verse says:

> Look thy last on all things lovely,
> Every hour. Let no night
> Seal thy sense in deathly slumber
> Till to delight
> Thou have paid thy utmost blessing;
> Since that all things thou wouldst praise
> Beauty took from those who loved them
> In other days.

Should I not look around and try to realise what an extraordinary planet I live on? (And how we are destroying it.) Remember my faith in my fellow man. (Farage, Trump, Ann Widdecombe.) Feel grateful for my life so far?

Should I not to delight pay the utmost blessing?

Okay. Yes. The last two. I will resist the urge to snarl, 'Sentimental bullshit.' I will drop the 'rage rage', and I'll try gratitude and delight. That is what I will do.

I'll try. I'll really try.

August 2019

My new passport has arrived. The royal blue that Farage insisted on actually looks a nasty black. I deliberately scowled when I sat for my new photo and look suitably old and tragic. I will use my European one until the last possible moment.

Stop it – I must dig around for a bit of 'delight'.

Life for everyone demands constant, sometimes unexpected, change and adaptation. Those who desperately try to avoid anything that will jeopardise their security are doomed to fail. Illness strikes, villages expand, jobs are lost, people die or leave, politics change, people called Dominic dominate.

Friends and journalists sometimes comment on how I have managed to reinvent myself since John's death. They said the same thing after Alec died in 1971. It is true that since 2002 I have done several theatre shows and films and larked about in Just a Minute and Celebrity Gogglebox, but they do not know how my heart lurches when I see an old couple walking down the street hand-in-hand as we used to. I do not allow myself to dwell on how it would have been to share my old age with the man I loved. I manage. No, more than that. I have freedom. I can live a totally selfish life, eat when I like, or not at all if I can't be bothered, go where I like, when I like, without having to fit in with someone else's life. I have always put husbands and children first. Now I don't have to. So, there are bonuses. Or should that be 'boni'?

Contentment is not a goal I seek. It seems a bit 'I'm all right, Jack' and to hell with anyone else. A tad dull too. It has pleased me that, whenever I do question-and-answer sessions after a showing of Edie, many people tell me that they realise they are in a rut and after watching the woman in the film, who has merely existed for most of her life, suddenly undertaking a huge challenge, they are resolved to do something similar.

When John died I was in agony. Eventually I realised I had two choices. I could spend the rest of my life with my memories, filling his absence with imagining what he would have said or done in any situation that arises. A valid choice that many – especially old people – make. Or I could make up for the fact that all the splendours of living had been taken from 'one who loved them in other days' and ensure I did not waste the life I was privileged to still have. I should put it to good use. This seemed to necessitate a flurry of activity. I had written one book while he was alive, struggling to fit it round work and family. I have completed three since he died, and with a bit of luck this will make it five, in total, before I too pop off.

But I have been struggling to write this book for three years. Along with doing plays and tellies, working in schools, patroning and vice-presidenting a few charities that I'm deeply involved with, especially the John Thaw Foundation, trying to get my head around Brexit, keeping an eye on the grandchildren, saving my French village from urbanisation and supporting increasingly ageing friends. Plus anything else anyone asks me to do. My life is and always has been full of 'I shoulds' and 'I musts'. The Quaker Advices and Queries suggests that you should 'Attend to what love requires of you which may not be great busyness.' I have always found that difficult. All my life I have, as my father used to say, 'rushed around like a blue-arsed fly'. Taking on too much and, when I look back now, achieving relatively little. I never do things by halves, when in fact half would be sufficient. I keep promising myself I will slow down and relish life more tomorrow – well, there aren't many tomorrows left. So, I'd better slow down now and pause for thought.

I do that occasionally, especially now my body won't always do what I want it to, but it always makes me feel guilty; even reading a book feels like slacking if it is not for research. The city excites and speeds me up, but every now and then Nature pulls me up short, not on the revelatory scale that I experienced on Suilven, but in a pleasant and comforting way. So, let's give it a bit of my 'utmost blessing'.

It surprises me, city-lover that I am, to realise the pleasure I find in Nature. The sun is a constant joy. When I am in France I watch the dawn most mornings from my bedroom window and, before it gets too hot, I lie naked on my bed feeling the sun's healing power soothing my rheumaticky old joints. Later I sit in a tree-dappled shade in our local café with my book and a bowl of chocolate, and in the season of the cutting of the lavender, drowse in its heady aroma.

The smells of Nature are potent and evocative. The sea, the rain on earth after a drought, a red rose, freshly cut grass. In the sixties I had a tiny caravan parked in complete isolation on the downs by the sea at Cuckmere Haven near Seaford in Sussex. Most Saturdays after the show I would ride down on my Lambretta, my cat in a basket on the back, to get away from the pressure of the blinding spotlight of sudden TV sitcom and theatre fame. In high summer the sea air was suffused with the sweet perfume of wild honeysuckle drifting over the Seven Sisters cliffs, more headily potent than any of the then fashionable drugs.

The scent of bluebells.

My parents gave me a bicycle for passing my scholarship to grammar school and I started going on cycle rides. From Bexleyheath I would cycle many miles to bring back bluebells to put in jam jars and fill the house with perfume and colour. I was drawn time and again to Shoreham, an exquisite village in Kent. If I could not have the city, I preferred the countryside to suburbia.

On one trip there I met a boy of eighteen who amused and fascinated me. He seemed very sophisticated. A city boy, not a country bumpkin. He too had cycled there from somewhere, and we got on like a house on fire. We arranged to meet up the following week. This time he told me he wanted to be a film director. He was clever and witty. Probably middle class. I'd certainly never met anyone like him before. He showed me the house where the artist Samuel Palmer had lived, explaining why his paintings were good, and gave me a book about him. I have always been bewitched by educated men, and probably this encounter was where it started. We made yet another assignation.

It was a perfect summer's day and we picked bluebells in the woods. We had a picnic, which he had brought in a basket with china plates and cups, and serviettes. Then we lay down in the grass. Suddenly he kissed me. A fierce kiss. My pubescent hormones roared. I was ready for more, not really knowing, in that age of innocence, what more was. He stared at me for a long time, then stroked my face and said, 'You're lovely, you know.' Then he quickly got up, packed up the picnic basket, got on his bike and left.

I do not remember his name or where he came from, but he was a special young man. Maybe he did become a film director. Maybe he remembers the girl that fell in love with him, and whom he treated so honourably. Despite riding to Shoreham several times and searching, I never saw him again. He presumably realised a twelve-year-old girl was dangerous territory and retreated.

My favourite perfume is Penhaligon's Bluebell, as a reminder of the mysterious young man who thought I was lovely, something I rarely think of myself.

September 2019

Gyles Brandreth and I, having raised a few laughs on Celebrity Gogglebox, were asked to take over from our friends Tim West and Prunella Scales, who wanted to leave the beautiful programme they filmed travelling canals in a narrowboat. They made handling the boat look so easy that we were shocked to discover it is fiendishly difficult. I gradually got the hang of it but Gyles seems irresistibly drawn to walls of bridges, lock gates and other boats, many of which bear the scars of his early efforts. We found it hard to see why Tim and Prue loved it so much. Then, on our second trip, we have experienced a change of perspective.

Both sceptical of the countryside, we found ourselves oddly fascinated by the wildlife that has taken over the ruins of a gunpowder mill that we visited on the Lee Navigation. We became aware of the myriad birds and insects and wildflowers that had taken over the wreckage of the buildings around us. Blades of grass were growing through slabs of stone, Nature had gently triumphed over the violent ugliness of the place and its original purpose, replacing it with Beauty. Gyles and I were stirred by the power of this natural life that we were inclined to overlook.

Slowly coasting along the canal, I have made a vow to open my eyes and mind to this whole new world. I will start by learning the different species of birds. Years ago, I spent some time doing events with Dr Cicely Saunders, the main founder of the hospice movement, who would become very excited if she saw some new bird that she could add to her album. It was a marvellous contrast to her dedicated mission and, I suspect, contributed to her well-being.

I will also revise the names of wildflowers. I say 'revise' because that is one of the good memories of the forbidding school I went to when I was evacuated: no talking; sit with your arms folded unless spoken to by a teacher; the cane if you step out of line; weekly nit parade for vaccies. We did learn the names of the wildflowers and made albums of any we found. Mine was pretty empty but I remember being enchanted by their names. Apparently, according to Gyles, everything you have learned is still in your brain but the means of retrieving it becomes weak if it's not used in old age. So that will be my task to fend off senile forgetfulness. I will record, from the fading memories of my brain, evocative flowers. I have no idea what they look like but that can come later.

Cornflower, yarrow, vetch, teasel, bird's foot trefoil, snake's head fritillary, ragwort, deadly nightshade, forget-me-not . . .

September 2019

I was paying my utmost blessing to the view from my window in London of the morning mist over the river, when there was a sudden piercing shriek. From a duck, which was being methodically stabbed by a cormorant's stiletto beak, as it struggled towards the water. I tried throwing things but nothing would divert the cormorant from its murderous task. I did eventually manage to distract the assassin and the duck escaped. Hopefully she knew a good duck doctor. I shamefully quite enjoyed the drama. The humdrum everyday events are apt to pass me by, or I pass them unregarding in my busyness – flowers, insects, pesky urban foxes. But what does it say about me that I am more intrigued by an avian murder on the riverbank than by how many species of aquatic birds there are?

September 2019

Had a phone call from my dear oldest school friend who is ill in America. Brenda represents something profound in my life. Our shared wartime experiences were deep and lasting. I don't want her to leave before me.

There is one event we shared that I have written about repeatedly, used in two documentaries, bored people rigid about all my life – and here I go again.

During the time I was evacuated I stayed a week with Brenda in Dorset. The how and why of this visit are lost in the fog of time, but the where is still as clear as the radiance of the days that I spent there. Brenda and her two sisters were living in a primitive cottage called Sea Spray, in the middle of fields, some distance from a village called Langton Matravers. It was lit by paraffin lamps and water was drawn from the deep well in the garden. Her sisters told tales of smugglers and pirates and for a few days we lived an Enid Blyton odyssey. The focus of our smuggler-spotting was the magic Dancing Ledge. As a result of ancient quarrying of the Purbeck stone, there was indeed underneath the high cliffs a shelf of rock, and in it a roughly rectangular hole that the tide flowed over, receding to leave a perfect swimming pool. I learned later that it had been dynamited by a teacher at a local school in order to make a pool for his pupils to exercise in. He sounds a bit eccentric but it worked. To get to the pool you had to descend a hair-raising iron ladder attached to the cliff. Brenda's sisters allowed us complete freedom, probably sensing that our pent-up emotion from trying not to cry at all the fear and chaos in our young lives needed release. We ran down the fields to the sea, laughing and shouting and dancing with the joy of being together. We splashed about in the pool and stood on the edge of the ledge when the tide was out, getting drenched with spray as the sea crashed against the rock. We were the only people there, but should someone walk along the top of the cliff we hid and tracked them, convinced that their dog and respectable clothing were a cover for nefarious goings-on.

The event that is forever cradled in my memory happened one night when we were allowed to go to the ledge after dark. Looking back, I suspect one of the sisters was lurking in the shadows. We only slightly nervously went down the moonlit fields. With no ARP warden around to shout 'Put that light out', we flashed a large torch around the hedges. In the dark we descended the iron ladder. The tide was out and the pool was full. We stripped off our clothes and plunged naked into its still water, warmed by the day's hot sun. We floated on our backs, holding hands, looking at a million stars and listening to the sound of the waves. No searchlights, no explosions, just the sky, the sea, and the love of a dear friend. In that moment I experienced one of those sensations of trembling total happiness that I have spent my life trying to repeat. I have been lucky enough to have versions of it in loving sex and childbirth and reaching the top of Suilven but, doubtless enriched by memory, never anything quite as extraordinary as Dancing Ledge. Brenda's hand in mine, the laughter, my overwhelming love for her, is what is imprinted on my soul. This is the Brenda who is ill in America, but she is still a daring young girl to me. That will remain unscathed by time.

These moments happen unexpectedly and cannot be manufactured. If I climbed Suilven again, which sobering thought reminds me that I no longer could, I doubt that I could recall my previous experience. Revisiting Dancing Ledge has been a disappointment. Sea Spray is now a nicely restored house with a high wall. The ledge is part of a National Trust walk; some steps have been carved to give easy access and lots of people share in its delight. Part of the iron ladder still hangs rusting on the cliff, and I wonder at the courage of those two small girls – but the mystique has gone.

At the end of 2017 an incident was reported in the newspapers that disturbed me. For days local people had searched the Dorset area for the enigmatically named Gaia Pope. She was nineteen and, judging by her photo, very beautiful; the tributes to her said that she was 'a wise, magnificent soul'. Finally her body was found – in the fields above Dancing Ledge. She was deemed to have died of natural causes. At first, I felt this tragedy would blight my memory of the place. Then I gleaned from newspaper stories that she had for various reasons been troubled, and that the place where she was found was somewhere she went to a lot and loved. I hope with all my heart that she, like two little girls many years ago, found some solace there.

Sharing Nature at its most primitive and wild, allowing myself to dissolve into the elements, accepting the inexplicable. Is this what the nun teachers at my convent school in Holborn felt when they radiantly took part in the Eucharist? Is this faith? Did I for that moment in my life experience God? The word 'God' jars but it is just shorthand for the inexplicable. It can be called anything – a Higher Power, the Infinite, the Spirit. You can call it Fred. That night at Dancing Ledge with Brenda, I was in touch with something Other and it was wonderful.

October 2019

Went to eighty-year-old Ian McKellen's one-man show. Apart from being open-mouthed at the range of his work, and the sheer loveliness of the man up there on the stage, bewitching the audience, I felt he belonged to a different profession to me. His background was not very illustrious, but his Cambridge scholarship took him into the right circles. His CV includes all the great classical roles, working with a pantheon of celebrated directors, and once, as a joke, appearing in pantomime, something I did five times in all rent-paying seriousness. As part of my wildly eclectic career I appeared in concert party with Cyril Fletcher on the end of Sandown Pier, did comedy shows with Frankie Howerd, Tommy Cooper, Brian Rix and Norman Wisdom, worked with elephants in the Bertram Mills Circus, and did lots of television sitcoms. All a bit 'common', as my mother would say. Going backstage to see Sir Ian, I felt like a faintly ridiculous poor relation. A feeling soon dispelled by one of Ian's bear hugs.

When I entered the profession, it was ruled by an impresario called Binkie Beaumont, and the sophisticated world round him that my friend Tony Beckley successfully gatecrashed. It was less easy for a gawky, rather plain actress, who was not obvious casting for his elegant West End plays. So, I didn't fit in with that, hence my years of tatty weekly repertory and touring. Until the likes of a young impresario called Michael Codron came along and broke up the West End mafia, giving me the part of a call girl in Rattle of a Simple Man.

Then, in the sixties, out of Oxford and Cambridge came a whole new wave of actors, writers and directors: Peter Hall, Trevor Nunn, Terry Hands, Jonathan Miller, Toby Robertson, Peter Cook, Richard Eyre, and Uncle Alan Bennett and all. I didn't fit in with them either. Some of them became my friends, but I was not part of the clique of artists that they cast, although I did do some sketches by Peter Cook and other Oxbridge types. When, a few years ago, I worked with the esteemed Richard Eyre, he said, 'You're so good. Why have I never worked with you before?'

My instinctive reaction was that I may be 'good', but obviously not good enough, serious enough, respected enough. The truth was, I was never part of the 'in-crowd' when it came to casting classical roles for serious plays in grand theatres. I was unknown to the National mafia until Ian invited me to join his company there, and be the first woman to direct in the Olivier Theatre, as well as playing juicy parts. But by then I was fifty-two years old: much too late for all the Violas and Rosalinds which, as an absolute devotee of Shakespeare's work, I would earlier have willingly given my then quite attractive body to play. I am grateful for the changes these men, and they were only men, wrought in the great companies. I just wish I had been born later and met them at university and been part of it.

By the time I got to the Royal Shakespeare Company in 1985, I was virtually the only member of the company who had not been to university, or a posh school, and felt at a distinct disadvantage when they discussed Jan Kott and other noted Shakespeare scholars. My ignorance is painfully obvious in Playing Shakespeare, a wonderful documentary on interpreting Shakespeare's work using forensic study of the text, which I took part in, and which is still used by students today. It is led by one of the most eminent of those scholars, John Barton. John was my greatest ally whilst I was in Stratford, and helped me gently to overcome my embarrassment. I watched it again recently with a grandchild, and his sweetness towards me is touching.

I am frequently asked what regrets I have in my life. Regret is an emotion I try to suppress. I regard it as a pointless waste of time. The one that won't go away, though, is my lack of a university education. My teachers tried to persuade me to enter for a state scholarship to Oxford, one even coming to visit my parents at home, but unbelievably, in this day and age, none of us knew what university was. None of our acquaintances or family had been to one, except my teachers, and at sixteen I didn't want to be like them. With no television, we didn't even know what university looked like; Brideshead Revisited in the eighties had me frothing at the mouth at my stupidity in the forties. The ignoble reason I decided to go on the stage was that, after playing Saint Joan in the school play, I had some success with a particularly handsome blond boy at school, so I thought, acne and mousey hair notwithstanding, life in the theatre would be a succession of Greek gods.

But I wanted to be what we called a 'straight actress', as opposed to my sister, and in an amateur sense my parents, who would be categorised as 'variety', and in 1949 the recognised route for that was through drama school. I first obtained a year's scholarship to Blackheath Conservatoire for elocution lessons to tackle my London accent, and then tried for, and obtained, a scholarship to RADA, where I spent another two years with a tooth prop between my teeth, to open up my vowels, and learned to say 'door' as opposed to 'daw-ah'. That is about all I did learn there. Little did I know that, a few years later, all that would change, and the best route into all areas of the media would become university.

November 2019

I bumped into Alvin Rakoff at the gym the other day, an odd place for one slightly disabled person and another in a wheelchair to meet, but we both struggle to preserve what muscles we have left. Alvin was one of the remarkable group of directors in the fifties and sixties who revolutionised television, using it as a tool to inform and change attitudes. It stopped TV drama being polite, anyone-for-tennis stuff and made it more gritty and truthful about all classes of society. Though it is never mentioned in serious assessments of that period, my contribution to those changes was a situation comedy I appeared in by Ronnies Chesney and Wolfe called The Rag Trade, which was, I would claim, in its small, knockabout way, game-changing. It was about women at work in a factory, rather than the customary cute wives or secretaries that were the usual bosomy brunt of sexist gags in comedies of that period. The women in the show always defeated the male protagonists, and it had juicy leading roles for Esma Cannon, Miriam Karlin and me. It was watched by huge audiences and 'Everybody out' became a universal catchphrase. At ninety-two, Alvin is still razor-sharp and as productive as ever. Writing a novel and absolutely up to date with the latest trends in film and theatre. And me? Well, I am limping on.

The rigour of theatre and film work becomes more difficult as you get older. A recent example of this happened when filming in the series A Discovery of Witches. I had had a heavy week, admittedly. My first day as the chief witch, Goody Alsop, was a night shoot involving cameras on cranes, and lots of supporting players. There was a real storm, with torrential rain and thunder and lightning. We huddled in a tent, in corseted costumes, for four hours waiting for the break in the weather that had been promised by the Met Office on the phone to a frantic producer. When it came, there was what John would have called 'a kick, bollock and scramble' to get the scene done. A huge bonfire blew sparks into my and my fellow witches' wigs. The crane swayed about dangerously in the wind, and the extras, not having had a tent to shelter from the rain, were cowering in their sodden costumes, trying to act as though it was a beautiful midsummer's night. When the first assistant bellowed 'Action', I nearly fell flat on my face in the mud. I was terrified I would forget the words before the rain started again. Somehow I managed to get out my lines, but it was not my finest performance. A couple of days later we all had to rush up a hill to the buses when a river overflowed. It was Wales, after all.

A few twelve-hour days after that, I had a tricky scene in which Goody Alsop says a lot of witchy things, this time in a freezing-cold set constructed inside an unheated barn. On about the fifth take, I dried stone-dead. I took a prompt and then dried again. And again, and again. And again. The crew, the gentle woman director and fellow actors were cringing with embarrassment. I could not remember why I was there, what I should say, who I was. It was terrifying. It was my first scene with Matthew Goode, the leading man of the show, and I could see he was upset. Then he suddenly took over the situation, saying, I suspect untruthfully, that he had the same thing happen a few weeks earlier. He helped me do it line by line, held up the script for me to read, and just laughed when I addressed his character by a variety of names, none of them his. After many retakes and chopping the scene into small bits, and with Matthew and the director's tender help, we got through the day.

I went back to the hotel that night convinced that I must retire as soon as possible. I forgot that this is something that all actors of all ages experience and spend a lot of the time dreading. You can be in the run of a play for six months and suddenly find yourself not remembering lines you have said perfectly well over and over again. It's a blank,

A heart-stopping, stomach-dissolving blank. That night I had a drink, and studied my script for the next day. Thankfully, next morning, after gentle treatment by my make-up artist, and a cuddle from my dresser, to everyone's – not least my – relief, I was miraculously word-perfect.

2020

January 2020

On 27 January we remembered the Holocaust, on the date that Auschwitz was liberated and the world discovered the worst crime in human history – a factory for genocide, the largest of many camps set up to methodically strip, gas and cremate fellow human beings identified only by numbers tattooed on their arms. I still try to get my head around the fact that this happened in my lifetime. Recent surveys reveal that many people worldwide do not know what Auschwitz, or even the Holocaust, is. I have twice taken part in ceremonies of commemoration and met survivors. Their testimonies are horrific. One said that, when the Nazis knew of the advancing Allies, they gave up bothering to put the gas pellets down the tube in the so-called shower room and just hurled them through the windows, and when they ran out of gas they herded the victims towards prepared mass graves, shooting or kicking them into the lime, still alive. One woman who survived remembers, as a child, putting out a trusting hand, expecting an adult to hold it as she tottered along, only to be violently pushed over into the pit by the guard.

As the witnesses die off, our memory of this evidence of man's ability to descend into bestial behaviour will fade even more. For me, it clarifies the reason for my visceral fear about what is happening now, all round the world. Walls, metaphorical and real, are going up, borders closed, refugees reviled, prejudice expressed proudly as patriotism, heads down, take care of number one.

Our youngsters have never been more aware of the world at large as they travel around visa-less, and study in European universities, in a way unthinkable when I was young. We are about to put a stop to all that. Why is it that so many of my fellow countrymen consider this idea something to celebrate? Why do they continually trumpet a pride in being an island race that 'stood alone'? Actually, we didn't. We had a lot of help. The Poles, for instance, were much-admired airmen during the Battle of Britain, people from the Commonwealth served in the forces, millions of Russians died, and the Americans, albeit to begin with reluctantly, joined us. The war is long over, but jokes about Germany being super-militant, and France cowardly, still get a laugh. We are stuck in some mythical past. I, too, am obsessed with the past, but the one that has haunted my life is hideously real.

January 2020

I have spent 31 January, the actual day of our departure from Europe, on my own, unable to face the wakes organised by my like-minded friends. I ventured to watch the television only to see the triumphant Farage making a hate-filled speech in the European Parliament, and leading out his ludicrous army of supporters, headed by Ann Widdecombe, that cheap travesty of a politician, waving tiny paper Union Jacks. The rest of the Parliament looked on in dignified sadness, and gently sang, 'Should auld acquaintance be forgot', although I would imagine many were thinking, 'Good riddance.' In merciful contrast to the loutish behaviour of Farage and his tribe, Led By Donkeys, a protest group that has bravely tried to drive home proven facts with its poster campaigns, organised a video that was projected onto the White Cliffs of Dover – a potent symbol for our island during the war – of two veterans telling the Europeans on the other side of the Channel how sad they were to leave them. It ended with a picture of one star falling from the European flag, with the message 'This is our star. Look after it for us.'

I eventually switched off the television, and listened to some Beethoven into the small hours to remind myself that cultural ties can never be destroyed by fanatical idiots. The following day Hammersmith and Fulham council sent out an email to the 70 per cent who voted Remain in the area, telling us that the town hall will still fly the European flag, we will twin with every capital city in Europe, and have a European Fair every year. A lovely, futile gesture that made me chuckle.

Arguments about the validity of the referendum vote are over; we must move on. There have been upheavals all through our history, not least the Troubles in Ireland. The wounds I witnessed there were precariously healed, and we must make sure that Brexit doesn't open them up again. We have an enormous task to see our country through this change and make it into something as good as the Leavers have promised.

Me, I feel weary. The thought of a new start is daunting. The political party that I have supported and been proud of all my life is in ruins. I believe our political system is redundant. It is out of date and has failed us. I no longer trust it to function on behalf of everyone. I need to gather my strength to work out what to do next. What to believe in.

February 2020

I was privileged to open a new wing of St Luke's primary in Rochdale. The young headteacher, Kim Farrall, supported by the local bishop, Mark Davies, the mayor and mayoress of Rochdale, Billy and Lynn Sheerin, and an inspirational, totally dedicated staff of teachers, caretakers, cleaners and parents, have combined to build the school into an imaginative, happy place where children from all backgrounds thrive. They work a lot outdoors using the Forest School teaching method, which is proving conducive to a good response, and is especially successful with troubled youngsters. The pupils learn about their local history and community, as well as the wider world.

St Luke's is a neighbourhood school, based on knowledge of the needs of the area. Music, drama and art are embedded in the whole curriculum. Their latest Ofsted report was good, but one of the comments reflected the problem innovative teachers are up against when dealing with edicts on methodology from government. The kids read me their recent stories and poems. They were stunningly original. Yet the report said:

'Leaders should ensure that pupils are provided with a more structural curriculum to strengthen their knowledge of spelling, grammar and punctuation. In addition, leaders need to ensure that pupils can apply their knowledge of spelling, punctuation and grammar in all areas of the curriculum.'

Did they not see the brilliant invention of the youngsters' work? The teachers' clever linking of subjects such as a history lesson incorporating art, storytelling, film and music? There was no comment about that. Or about the children's delight in language, even if misspelled, usually because they were bravely using an unfamiliar word. Have the officials not heard about mechanical spelling and grammar checks? I suspect they are old, like me, and stuck in a world where these aids did not exist, making English grammar lessons necessary, but they are less so now, especially if they impede creativity. Just as calculators have lessened the need for all those boring times tables we recited, we have magic tools to help with the basics. Thank God for the spelling and grammar check, I say.

February 2020

With my eighty-seventh birthday done and dusted, I flew off to the haven of my French home. I have decisions to make. Am I getting too old to drive the necessary car, to climb the dangerous stairs? Can I move on from this limbo of indecision and make some plans for the probably-quite-short rest of my life?

When I picked up my newspaper, Karim looked genuinely sorry for me, EU outcast as I now am. Even my mysterious Arab friend shook his head sadly as he passed me.

Walking through Apt, I was drawn into the dark interior of the cathedral by the sounds of the organ. A young man was practising an elaborate bit of Bach with some difficulty, feet and hands going like the clappers. I was attracted by a blaze of light in a side chapel, which was filled with a model of the Nativity. It had been put there for the Christmas celebrations and was now being packed away. Curiously, the setting is a recreation of a Provençal hilltop village with churches, ancient washing pools, fountains and little figures dressed in national costumes – these clay santons being a local tradition made in the area. It depicts people working and sitting in the sun, and in the centre is the stable with a few people standing around idly watching the couple attending to their baby. It was a touching reminder of life continuing for the ordinary folk, despite some kings and shepherds having told them this was a big event that would make their town famous. It was an aspect of that story that I hadn't considered. What did the locals think of this refugee couple taking up space from hard-working animals? Those foreigners causing a stir, bringing weirdos into the town with their gifts for the layabouts of gold and exquisite spices.

I asked a lady packing up the installation why it was set locally when we know the birth took place in Bethlehem. I didn't want to equivocate for some political-correctness-gone-mad stance but I wanted to hear this obviously devout woman's take on it – presuming she might see it as a story for all places and all times. Instead she explained that our cathedral, St Anne's, was named after the Virgin's mother who lived in Apt, so it was possible it happened here. I did not express my scepticism as, over the years I have lived in the region, more and more revelations of prehistoric, medieval and Roman activities have been dug up, so I suppose anything is possible. 'There were no Arab outfits

for the santons. And the white baby Jesus est très joli, non?'
Fair enough. There was no point in letting rationality get in
the way of her shining faith.

For me, listening to music, contemplating a painting or
watching ballet dancers doing superhuman things is when
I get close to the awareness of something that could be called
God. I wish with all my heart I could have a more tangible
access to somebody who will answer my prayers and maybe
even welcome me in heaven when I leave this world. Sadly,
until I have solid evidence to the contrary, I do not believe
there is a life beyond this. Mind you, I also have no evidence
that there isn't. It doesn't worry me a lot anyway – I'll cross
that bridge when I come to it. As far as God is concerned,
I will settle for the feeling of unity and something Other that
can occur in the silence of a gathered Quaker meeting for
worship. Or the ecstasy I feel at the genius of Beethoven,
a man who was stone-deaf yet nearing the end of his life
could write the transcendent 'Cavatina' string quartet. We
are all equal and, as we Quakers say, there is 'that of God in
everyone'. But perhaps there's a little bit more of God in the
likes of Nureyev and Beethoven. Hush my mouth.

I find I am contemplating religion, and especially the life of
Christ, quite often lately. At a time when our moral compass
seems to have gone out of kilter, I yearn for Christianity to
get its act together. That anarchic, wise, gentle, angry, utterly
honest man is such an example of how we could make the
world work for everyone. Christ, we need someone like
Jesus to come and rescue us. Put us straight. Instead of
which we've got Trump, Farage and Boris Johnson.

The seasons, as in England, have gone awry here in
France. Floods, extreme cold and midsummer heat are

running amok. The weather is confusing even Denis. Spring is arriving much too early. There are buds on the fig tree, butterflies and lizards have woken from their sleep too soon, and the sun is providing unseasonable, if welcome, warmth.

As I lie in bed with my morning cup of tea, I can see a fir tree that has, over the years, grown far too tall. I keep expecting it to keel over, but it continues to reach for the sky, although its last spurt of growth is a feeble, unfirlike wisp that whirls around in the wind. The rest of the tree remembers it is a fir, and behaves properly in a dignified, evergreen way. The top bit will have to learn to settle down and conform or it will snap off and die.

March 2020

Well. Deep breath. Here goes. Um – um – er . . .

After suffering several weeks of inability to think coherently, I must write something.

Well. Today I—

Last week we—

No, I don't know where to begin.

For heaven's sake, you asked for this, woman. Moaning about the state of the world – this is what you wanted, isn't it? You wanted a revolution, didn't you? You wanted the world to be united? You wanted the frenetic, mindless way you live your life to change?

As my mum would say, 'Sheila, be careful what you wish for.'

I didn't want this.

In a matter of days, the world has been plunged into a crisis which makes it look as though the end of my life is going to be engulfed in a catastrophe as great as the one that engulfed my childhood.

Here is what happened.

In February and the beginning of March 2020, my diary was the usual kaleidoscope of events.

In February I enjoyed working on a television programme, Unforgotten, with a brilliant cast and crew, relishing playing a thoroughly unpleasant woman. Then I went to Rochdale, to participate with the locals in the joyous celebration of the extension of their primary school. In the same month, I made the decision that, even if they build a housing estate in my hameau in France, and I have to hire taxis when I'm too blind to drive, I'm staying. So, I made the positive step of asking a builder to put in handrails to steady the inevitable encroaching dodderiness. On 3 March I went to the fabulous comprehensive Holland Park School to hear Dame Janet Baker explaining to transfixed schoolkids that exquisite artistry such as hers involves utter dedication and damned hard work. On 5 March Martin and I went to the oddly empty Curzon cinema to see the Oscar-winning film Parasite, which blew our minds, and we discussed it intensely over a wonderful meal in a restaurant where you can't usually get a table – bit strange, but we put it down to the torrential rain. On 12 March I spent a riotous night in Soho with my twenty-two-year-old grandchild, Lola. We drank in a packed gay pub, exchanging warm greetings with the raucous customers, all outlandishly dressed and coiffed for a night out. We then went to a crowded comedy club to hear women stand-ups riffing on masturbation, horrible children, godawful men and incontinence, the event having been sponsored by a firm making special knickers. Lola, who is quite a sophisticated theatregoer, her father being an eminent producer, declared it the best night she had ever spent in the theatre. We did literally cry with mascara-smudging laughter.

Not guessing for a moment that it was probably the last time we would experience such cathartic hilarity for a very long time.

Within a few days of that outing, all theatres, cinemas and restaurants were closed down. As was St Luke's, Holland Park, and every other school in the country. All my future work in television and on stage was cancelled. Airports are now closed and flights suspended, so I cannot go to France or anywhere else for the foreseeable future.

Everything has ground to a halt.

At the beginning of January there was talk of some virus in China, but we had been there before with Ebola and SARS and they hadn't affected us much, so this news created only a minor disquiet. On 10 March the Cheltenham Festival went ahead, and on 11 March 3,000 football fans from Spain, where all matches had already been cancelled, were allowed to pack into Anfield to see Atlético Madrid play Liverpool. On 3 March some committee or other was supposed to have said we should stop shaking hands and hugging one another. But we're British, we won the war, and good old Boris went to a hospital and matily shook hands with everybody, so there. And he was jolly well going to see his mother for Mother's Day the next weekend. Poor Boris Johnson, who needs so desperately to be loved, said that we should just wash our hands while singing 'Happy Birthday' twice, and we would be all right. Three weeks later he went down with the virus himself, and nearly died.

I wonder how many lives were lost as a result of his jokey defiance?

When I came home from my outing with Lola on 12 March, I switched on the late-night news to see Boris Johnson announcing it was 'the worst public health crisis for a generation' and that 'many more families are going to lose loved ones before their time'.

What? Hello? Excuse me?

By 18 March they were trying to rally us with slogans, the same technique used by Johnson's chief adviser, Dominic Svengali Cummings, to win Brexit, including a similar lot of lying, misrepresenting of statistics and invoking the wartime spirit.

Stay home. Protect the NHS. Save lives.

This mantra is dinned in to us day in, day out. Along with 'Get it done', which was first applied to Brexit and is now being invoked to rid the world of a virus even more lethal than the European Union. We are asked to stay indoors, to only commune in person with the people we live with, and only go out for one brief exercise session a day, making sure we keep a distance of two metres from anyone passing.

Stay home. Protect the NHS. Save lives.

This from the government that has done its level best to privatise the NHS, as I discovered from personal experience when my National Health hearing aid was suddenly provided by a private company set up within Charing Cross Hospital, only bog-standard ones now being available free on the NHS. Johnson himself voted against a rise in salary for the nurses he now sanctifies, and actually cheered in the Commons when the vote against them was won.

I look back now at one of the acts Lola and I saw in the
Soho Theatre the day before the world turned upside down,
which at the time was a comic turn but now feels like a
metaphor for what was about to happen. A middle-aged
woman came onto the stage carrying a shopping basket
and wandered about nattering inconsequentially. She was
called Mrs Barbara Nice (actually actor Janice Connolly).
After a few amiable exchanges with people in the audience,
Mrs Nice suddenly told us that she had seen someone called
Iggy Pop throw himself off the stage into the audience
and she was going to do the same. She gave the audience
vague instructions as to how she was going to jump from
the back of the auditorium and how we should catch her
with our hands above our heads, and transport her, in the
air, through the crowd, back onto the stage. Everybody
laughed uncertainly, wondering what the payoff to the gag
was going to be. When she insisted, one or two audience
members jokingly got up and held their hands above their
heads. As Mrs Nice continued to direct them, others joined
in, still thinking it wasn't going to happen and there was
going to be a joke ending. When she took off her green
mac, 'my Apple Mac', and wended her way to the back of
the auditorium to a raised platform, they began to look a
bit nervous, especially as the audience was mainly made up
of women, none of them looking overly strong, and most
having had quite a few drinks. She continued to instruct the
audience as to how they should hold her, and still everybody
laughed. Then suddenly she threw herself off the platform,
into the now panicking crowd, who, shouting and sweating,
man- or rather woman-handled her, legs akimbo, exposing
passion-killer drawers, right across the audience and

dumped her on stage, where she thanked them briefly and wandered off, leaving an exhausted and still-disbelieving crowd wondering what had just happened.

It was a surreal experience. Her obsessional gabbling about Iggy Pop, a name not overly familiar to me or many of the young audience, had all the mystery of the new words now endlessly repeated to us: coronavirus, Covid-19, Wuhan, Rishi Sunak, PPE, social distancing. I had never heard of stage-diving or -surfing, or lockdown, or sheltering-in-place, until this month. The way everyone in the audience rallied and, in a rather rough, amateurish way, actually did come together and evolved a method to protect and guide this dotty woman, who trusted them in a dangerous situation, was strangely empowering and touching. A bit far-fetched, but I do keep remembering it as I watch how, as a country, we are uniting to clumsily deal with a lethal threat, particularly for the old, weak and vulnerable.

23 March 2020

I am scared and appalled by the situation we are in but, strangely, despite being such a cry-baby, I haven't cried yet. I just wander about my empty house doing that thing of going up three flights of stairs and then, when I get there, not knowing what I want. I open cupboards and drawers and stand staring at them, wondering what I am looking for. I perform this old-lady behaviour not occasionally, but all the time. My brain seems to have splintered, incapable of a whole thought. Like dementia, I suppose. It's quite frightening. I can't discuss it with anybody. My medical team are unavailable, several of them having contracted the virus. I can't master social media so I can only speak to people on the phone, and it doesn't seem appropriate, when everyone is in turmoil, to tell friends and family I am going mad. Anyway, I am okay. Despite awful stories about the illness, and ominous predictions about the future, I am fine. Fine. I haven't shed a single tear.

24 March 2020

I am glad my sister went before all this confusion and fear. I would no longer be able to go and see her. Actually, if I think about it, she would have been in her element. Making sure that all the old folk in the home obeyed the rules. Keeping them amused.

When she was sixteen, she toured the wilds of Africa with ENSA, entertaining troops in isolated places. Bright yellow from anti-malaria drugs, she still suffered from malaria, as well as dysentery, sandfly fever and, once, a mild case of smallpox from a vaccination. She also had to have painful injections in her stomach, having come into contact with bubonic plague. So, I don't think Covid-19 would have daunted her.

Rereading her diary:

Me 91 years old

Me

Me young woman

Who me

has given me pause for thought.

It has been troubling to ask myself: 'Who am I?'

But, lucky me, I have now received three letters, one from Boris Johnson and two from the NHS, that have saved me any more agonising, because they tell me they have categorically identified me as 'extremely vulnerable'.

What is more, they have the solution for my existential angst. It is simple.

'The safest course of action is for you to stay at home at all times and avoid all face-to-face contact for at least twelve weeks.'

Yes, that should do the trick. Forget about Brexit. All of that now seems so irrelevant. The despair I felt about leaving Europe is nothing compared with the thought of the thousands of people already dying of a virulent virus, and masses more threatened, as it spreads its evil throughout the whole world. With three months shut up on my own I can worry about something other than populism and Donald Trump. It will make a nice change.

29 March 2020

I still have not shed a tear.

When I was a student, and early in my working career, I found it difficult to cry real tears when a part demanded it. Maybe a childhood spent repressing them was behaviour hard to change, even in pretence. Playing scenes with a married actor whom I lusted after, who led me into tortured temptation, then rejection, first released the flow for me. I brought my private agony into the performance of any scenes I had with him – which made for some inappropriate over-acting in a jolly farce like Ma's Bit o' Brass. I later discovered this cat-and-mouse seduction routine was something he did with all the new ingénue actors, presumably to relieve the boredom of being trapped in weekly repertory, doing dreadful plays to indifferent audiences. Poor disappointed soul that he was, he was a much better actor off-stage than on. But he taught me to cry real tears. And probably lots of other actresses as well. So, his career was not a complete failure.

Strangely, now, as practised by John, I have learned that trying to restrain tears, fighting not to cry, is ten times more moving to an audience than gushing water all over the stage or screen. That is certainly true when watching real-life interviews. Directors and interviewers on news programmes and documentaries don't seem to realise that, so they strive to make people cry: 'Tell me' – sad, sympathetic, face – 'how did you feel when you watched your baby die in agony?'

I was doing some preparation work for my edition of Who Do You Think You Are? when Jeremy Paxman passed by and shouted, 'Be careful, they'll try to make you cry.' As, to his fury, they did him. I swore I wouldn't but, of course, ended up blubbing snot and tears over the grave of a woman I had not even known existed. I was genuinely upset, fortunately. They would have been very let down if I had not been. It was perfectly staged – graveyard, lonely tombstone and even, to their delight, depressing rain. 'A moving interview' is considered a success, and that means people crying, breaking down, suffering.

I once saw a remarkable old Jewish woman telling of her ordeal as a member of one of the orchestras that were forced to play in concentration camps. She recounted her experience with searing calm and restraint, and I was sobbing watching her until the desperate interviewer, obviously frustrated that this dignified woman was not fulfilling the 'moving interview' criteria, actually asked, 'I mean, you're a musician – did you perhaps enjoy playing there?' Only then did the woman's astonished eyes moisten, confronted by such crass ignorance.

In real life I usually have no trouble with tears. If you searched this book for the words 'tears' and 'wept', I dread to think how many times they would come up.

Maybe lachrymosity is inherited. My father wept all the time, even when he laughed. He would bend double, with his eyes streaming, muttering, 'Oh Christ! Don't, that's so funny!' But since the coronavirus appeared on the scene, I have been a model of stoicism.

Like my mother. I only remember seeing her cry twice. The first time was when we all sat round the wireless listening to Neville Chamberlain saying, 'This country is at war with Germany.' Her tears frightened me much more than the air-raid warning that followed the broadcast. The second time was when I received a phone call from the manager of the caravan park where she lived in a mobile home, and I rushed down to find her sitting holding my father's body, on the floor, where he had died of a heart attack. She wept violently as we insisted on taking him away from her. At the funeral and for the next few years, coming to live near me in a flat on her own, she never cried again. At least not in front of anyone. Since the arrival of the virus I have shown the same restraint.

2 April 2020

Last week Ellie Jane left a bunch of flowers on the doorstep, in which were two pink antirrhinums. Because my parents worked in pubs and hotels we lived above the shop, usually in a couple of rooms, and never with a garden. When they stopped this gypsy existence and moved to Bexleyheath in Kent, for the first time we lived in a house with a garden, front and back. The back was mainly vegetables but in the front I aided my father in constructing on this small plot a maverick Italianate concoction of crazy paving, different levels, steps, and an ancient stone birdbath stolen from a bomb-damaged mansion. It caused a sensation amidst our neighbours' neat lawns and hedges. The flower beds were irregular shapes and the blooms of choice, not following the Mediterranean theme, were a joyous mix of English catmint, pinks, cornflowers, daisies, poppies, foxgloves and antirrhinums – or bunny rabbits, as we called them, because if you pinch the blossom it opens like the mouth of a rabbit.

The two antirrhinums in my daughter's bouquet were a bit poncy and cultivated-looking, rather than the sturdy rough-and-ready ones at 58 Latham Road, but they gave me a childish pang of delight. After a couple of days one of them started to wilt. I was out-of-proportionally upset. I snipped off a bit of the stalk and took off two dead flowers to let water and strength go up to the buds above. It worked for a day or two, then the top began to droop. I propped it up against a sturdy iris. It seemed to rally and I rejoiced. Then the next day, as I tenderly took it out of the vase to change the water, the unopened buds gently curled over and hung limply. Again, I cut off some of its stalk and propped it against the iris, telling it, 'Come on, please, open just one more bud before you die, make the effort. There are people surviving a horrid virus – surely you can get better. Look at your sister there, look how she's enjoying the sun.' Out loud. I said it out loud, with serious intensity. Desperation. But the flower gave up the ghost.

As I put it in the bin, the floodgates opened. I sobbed my heart out.

I am on my own, so do not have to hide my tears. I am fine, my tears are not for myself, but for the thousands of people worldwide whom this virus is causing such pain. And a dead flower.

8 April 2020

The deaths in England from this virus have risen to 1,461 in one day.

One of the awful sadnesses is the way the virus has forced us to deal with death. As vice president of St Christopher's Hospice, I have watched many people die feeling genuinely happy, surrounded by their nearest and dearest, hugging and holding hands, and saying their goodbyes and thank yous – laughing, even. Now people are often on ventilators with wires and tubes all over them, alone but for nurses in plastic gowns, masks and visors. Even a thirteen-year-old boy died like that. The ultimate cruelty.

Old people in rest homes are not allowed visitors for fear of bringing in the virus, so they lose touch with the family that they have spent their lives caring for, and are left bewildered and alone. They deserve to be cherished in their last years rather than forced to stay in their rooms, and if they have any form of dementia they must be so frightened to be suddenly surrounded by people whose faces they cannot see properly. In some homes the virus has taken hold and the elderly are dying, cared for only by distraught staff ill-equipped to deal with complicated medical treatment. This is truly a sort of Armageddon. Each day produces yet another horror story of what this virus is causing. How long can we bear it?

10 April 2020

Today I reached my nadir of misery. I always have found Good Friday disturbing. As a very young child, after I left my first horrible school in King's Cross, I found myself at yet another convent school down the road in Ely Place, Holborn, being taught by nuns and attending services in St Etheldreda's Roman Catholic Church. Every year we would go through the ritual of the Stations of the Cross, following the final journey of Jesus towards his crucifixion, stumbling along the Via Dolorosa, carrying his own cross, falling under it three times, being helped for a while by a man in the crowd, Simon of Cyrene, his brow wiped by a saddened woman stranger, seeing his distraught mother in the jeering mob, comforting a group of grieving women, being stripped naked and flogged, a crown of brambles and thorn forced on his head, nails driven through his hands and feet, and hoisted to hang for hours of agony before he died crying, 'My God, my God, why have you forsaken me?' Not exactly the Easter Bunny whimsy that kids associate with the spring bank holiday these days.

Good Friday used to be the only day off in the year for actors, apart from Christmas Day. All theatres, shops and businesses closed down. Now it is scarcely marked, apart from consumption of buns displaying a cross. It has taken a little virus to shut us up for a while and maybe, just maybe, give a passing thought to what the day represents.

This Good Friday evening I sat and listened to Bach's St Matthew Passion on Radio 3. Early in our relationship, John and I had one of the most profound musical experiences of our lives listening to this oratorio performed at the Royal Festival Hall. From the first pounding double-orchestra introduction we were open-mouthed, and when the two choirs joined in, the tears began to flow and seldom stopped for the several hours of the performance. The story of the relentless betrayal and torture of this innocent man had both of us aghast, yet enraptured by Bach's vision of it. John and I had a turbulent relationship, but the one thing over which we were never divided was our love of classical music.

So, there I was on Good Friday 2020, sitting alone, feeling deeply sorrowful as the St Matthew Passion embraced me from the four speakers of my ancient Bang & Olufsen. Eighteen years since his death, I still ache for the pressure of John's hand tightening and his elbow pressing against mine, as it always did at thrilling concerts. There is one phrase in the *Passion* that I think is the most agonising expression of sorrow that I know of in any art form. The Evangelist narrator tells us of the promise that Peter makes to Jesus that he will never desert him. Jesus wryly replies that he will do so three times before the cock crows. Inevitably, in terror for his life, Peter does three times tell people he didn't know Jesus, and when the cock crows, the Evangelist tells us, Peter went out and 'wept bitterly'. I defy anyone hearing what Bach does with that phrase not to join Peter. For me, no one interprets it more heartbreakingly than Peter Pears, probably because, having to conceal his love for Benjamin Britten in those dark days, he knew all about denial.

So, another day of uncontrolled weeping. And it helped. No one sees my tears so I upset no one. But it achieved nothing either. If I really want resurrection, revolution, then I will have to contribute. I must dry my eyes, pull myself together and get on with it.

11 April 2020

I spent most of the day on my laptop. Hurrah for the internet, with its cornucopia of information. Not as lovely an experience as sitting in the stacks of the now closed London Library surrounded by piles of books, but nevertheless full of enthralling knowledge.

My greatest progress during the pandemic has been in my mastery of social media. After several unsatisfactory phone calls, my three daughters and eight grandchildren decided I had to move into the twenty-first century so that we could see each other's faces whilst I was in isolation. We started big, with them talking me through the process of joining a family Zoom meeting. I did just about manage it, but was bewildered by them all shouting instructions at me.

'Unmute! Unmute!'

'What the hell are you talking about?'

'Oh, Nana, for heaven's sake.'

After insisting on one-to-one coaching, rather than them all trying to teach me together, I have gradually mastered WhatsApp, Zoom, FaceTime, YouTube – in fact I will have a go at anything. It takes a bit of time and patience on the part of my instructors but I get there in the end, and it is saving my sanity. I actually went on the television and advised other older isolated folk to do the same.

I have a relationship with a charming young man called Craig, who works for my service provider, and comes into my screen and sorts it out when I get really hysterical.

'Sheila, Sheila, just listen to me. Do what I tell you.'

I've never met him, or even seen him, but I love his masterful approach.

If I have to phone a call centre I always ask the people where they are based and try to have a chat. It must be a soul-destroying job. I've met people in Ireland, Malta, India and all over Britain. When I was trying to sort out a problem with a new phone, I had a long session with a lady in South Carolina who was working from home. We talked for a full hour, with me relishing her perfect Southern accent and both of us having a right go about Trump. We ended up great friends. A young man in India told me of the rapid spread of the virus where he lived long before I read about it in our papers. He was very frightened and I tried to give him advice based on our experience.

It is difficult for youngsters who have grown up with technology to understand someone who was middle-aged before she ever used a keyboard, never mind attempting to understand the mysteries of the Amstrad computer. I remember spending days on end with my then PA, Paulette, trying to decipher a huge, complicated book of directions. It was incomprehensible. We then heard of some geek in Devon who had written a simplified version, and that helped. Since those early attempts I have progressed steadily to having a working knowledge of the web. I have given social media a miss until now for the same reason that I never watch my own films or tellies – I don't want to hear or see things that will lower my self-esteem even further – although I do have a website. A young man called Norbert Bakos, who travels over from Hungary to see every show I appear in, has set up what I am told is a wonderful site about me, delving into the archives to find old photos and programmes. He knows more about me than I do. People leave messages on the site and my PA lets me see the nice ones, which are heart-warming. Norbie always brings me delicious chocolate, and I have watched him progress from a rather shy lad into a successful, artistic, colourful personality.

12 April 2020 – Easter Sunday

This morning a few of us had a Zoomed meeting for worship. Quakers are not meant to observe the Church festivals such as Easter, because every day should be holy and sacred, not just a few inaccurate dates, so there was only one reference to the Easter story in our virtual gathering. It was a bit weird sitting in silence in front of a laptop, but there were several deeply felt ministries of the blessings to be had in our enforced slowing-down, relishing Nature and silence. Easy if you live in a nice house with a balcony, like me, not so good if you are jobless, trapped in a high-rise flat with no access to fresh air, with a couple of bored over-active children. Nevertheless, I find it comforting to see the Hammersmith Friends as we say 'gathered', even if only on a laptop.

I am frequently asked, 'What do Quakers stand for?'

Every Friend will give a different answer. There are no rules. Indeed, some Friends verge on the anarchic. There is a structure, but there is no one in charge, no fierce nun or man in a frock telling us how to behave, or what to believe.

Although most will maintain that 'there is that of God in everyone'.

We will then agonise about the definition of the word 'God'.

We have an insightful book called Quaker Faith & Practice, in which there are wise statements from members of the society since its foundation in the seventeenth century. It is updated regularly to reflect changing times. The nearest to commandments is a section called Advice and Queries. No catechisms or creeds, just more or less: Here is some advice, it is up to you if you take it. And here are some queries, but you have to provide the answers.

I welcome the lack of certainty. I am fearful of people who think they know best.

The downside of this vagueness is the length of time it takes Quakers to make a decision. There are no votes – everyone must be in accord. The discussions go on for ever, interspersed by periods of silence to calm people down if it gets heated. My meeting house is being knocked down and rebuilt elsewhere and it took us months just to decide on the chairs. Not only do we all have to approve the choice, we are also obliged to check that the firm making them is ethically sound. The people involved with us start by thinking our processes are weird, but usually end up agreeing that they are powerfully successful. Witness the businesses set up by the confectioners John Cadbury, Joseph Rowntree and Joseph Fry, as well as shoe manufacturer Clarks, and banks Lloyds and Barclays, all originally based on Quaker values of caring for their workforces and trading honestly, even if it was less profitable.

Our form of worship is a silent meeting in which anyone can say something if they feel moved to speak from the heart, as opposed to a debate, but in the main it is an hour of potent, sometimes ecstatic, silence, 'a gathered stillness'.

I find that silence much more meaningful than the ritualistic hymns and prayer routines in churches, some of it feeling unacceptable to my modern ears. Despite knowing them all by heart from my childhood, I can no longer join in with the passages about being meek and humble and sinful; they seem so paternalistic and undermining. Putting us in our place.

Oh dear. Advice 17:

'Do not allow the strength of your convictions to betray you into making statements or allegations that are unfair or untrue.'

We do take seriously the guidance of what we call our Testimonies of Truth, Equality, Simplicity and Peace. The Truth Testimony has to be handled with subtlety. I try to be honest, even though it is not a quality universally admired, especially in a woman. If I hear it being said that I am 'a strong woman', I know it is because I have been too brutal in my honesty. Quakerism is not an easy path for a loudmouth like me.

As an example, I got a lot of stick in 2014 when I suggested the beautiful poppy installation at the Tower of London commemorating the two world wars was sentimentalising our grief. Making us feel good because we were moved by its beauty. There was a discussion on The Andrew Marr Show about what should happen to the skilfully crafted flowers when the display closed. Should they be sold for charity? Used in exhibitions round the country? I ventured that perhaps a tank should roll through the moat destroying and mutilating all the lovely poppies, as had been the young men and women by the two world wars. That didn't go down well with the Daily Mail and the Telegraph, not to mention the man who tweeted 'Stupid woman.' Not sure what he found more offensive, the fact that I was stupid, or that I was a woman. Still, Advice 38:

'Do not let the desire to be sociable, or the fear of seeming peculiar, determine your decisions.'

That is a recipe for trouble for any luvvie making their voice heard.

'Speak truth to power' is a Quaker saying, and one that they have stood by all through their proud history, at great cost. Sometimes it calls for more courage than I can muster. Minding your own business is much easier. There can be no doubt that it would be infinitely easier for people if our politicians and communicators could tell the Truth and put aside the current fashion for lying.

I am proud of Quaker history and the work that today's Friends are doing to fulfil the Equality Testimony. Since Quakers maintain that 'there is that of God in everyone', it behoves them to treat everyone with equal respect. This duty of respect is regardless of who a person is, or what they have done. The voluntary work that Quakers do is often with the rejected members of society. A classic example of the modern Quakers' work is the mentoring of sex offenders when they leave prison to help them settle into society and not reoffend. Nowadays they also provide support for reviled refugees.

The Simplicity Testimony has particular resonance in this materialistic age. If we all kept our lives simple and fulfilled our needs rather than our wants, the planet – and we ourselves – would, I suggest, be happier. Is a dirt-cheap dress made by an underpaid child in India, worn once and then added to landfill, really worth the few hours of superficial pleasure it gives? I actually relish the bargains I buy in charity shops, and recycling old outfits when they come into fashion again, as they inevitably do. Greed is never ultimately fulfilling. Stuffing myself with food that I barely taste at Christmas does not give me as much satisfaction as a queued-for, unforgettable Crunchie bar, licked very slowly, during wartime sweet rationing.

I was accepted into membership of the Society of Friends in 1993 by 'convincement', as it is called – a certainty that I want to try to follow the Quaker path. It is challenging sometimes. For an angry old woman like me, the Peace Testimony is especially difficult, but Advice 27 – 'Live adventurously' – guides me in my old age. I have tried Catholicism, Buddhism, Congregationalism, Atheism and Humanism, eventually finding a home in Quakerism for which, especially in these troubled times, I am truly grateful.

13 April 2020

Well, that didn't last long. So much for Quaker silence. The rage keeps returning. I find myself yelling at celebrities on television, all being jolly and saying how wonderful it is that we are all united and helping one another. What really irritates me are the comparisons that are being made with the wartime spirit by people who were not there and have no idea what it was really like. I want us to be looking forward, not back to some mythical past.

During the war people were already planning for a better future. The Beveridge Report, proposing reforms for a more equal world, was published in 1942. We wanted, and came out of the war prepared to fight for, change. I feel we should be using this enforced hiatus to envision better ways of handling the environment and inequality in the way that we are finding possible during this emergency. To use the situation for a cleansing of the Brexit toxicity, an Easter resurrection.

People are seeing things differently. There is an impressive feeling of unity. Some have resented the police breaking up their barbecues in the park, but others have public-spiritedly quietened down, and stayed indoors, in an effort to rid the community of the threat that has suddenly engulfed us. On the path beside my house on the river, cycling and running has been banned, so people are walking calmly, two metres apart in the sun, noticing the scent of the blossom and the sound of the birds, as opposed to the usual aeroplanes piling into Heathrow. We have united, partly out of self-preservation, but also through acts of discipline and regard and gratitude towards others, in a mass movement.

Someone sent me this poem, which apparently has been doing the rounds on social media recently.

and then the whole world
walked inside and shut their doors
and said we will stop it all, everything,
to protect our weaker ones
our sicker ones, our older ones,
and nothing, nothing in the history of humankind
ever felt more like love than this.

But I am troubled as to whether we older, weaker ones have the right to ask this of our young.

15 April 2020

Louis, my twelve-year-old grandchild, is struggling with this strange new world. He had just started at a new school when he was forced to study virtually at home, and could not pursue the fledgling friendships he had begun. Suddenly the past looks different, the present insecure, the future completely unpredictable. Not allowed to take part in sport, or meet up with his new pals, his world is encompassed in his iPad. He does his lessons, and then communicates with other children via online gaming and social media. It is no life for a child to be huddled over a screen all day, every day.

I have suggested that he should keep a diary. Get the nasty thoughts out of his head and onto a bit of paper, which he can then tear up or burn if he likes.

He is living through an historic time and it is worth recording it. But in ink, so it won't disappear into the ether. Something that he and maybe one day his grandchildren can hold in their hands. I showed him a battered notebook in which I kept a diary of my first visit to France. It catalogues my teenage attitude to the war that had not long ended, and, more fascinating to Louis, an account of my first proper kiss. I suggested that, if he is feeling upset and doesn't want to discuss it with grown-ups, it helps to scribble it down. Tell it to a diary.

Which is what I appear to be doing.

Despite my recommendation to Louis, I am rather nervous of diaries. Whenever I had a row with Kenneth Williams, which was often, he would mutter darkly, 'I am going to put that in my diary.' I never dared read them when they were published.

I am intending to destroy mine. But how? It is not an easy task burning flame-resistant, bulky, page-a-day booklets – as I discovered in one of my rows with John when I packed my bag to leave him, and on the way out attempted to dramatically destroy all evidence of our life together, in preparation for the new start I told him I was making. He sat chuckling in his armchair as I flung my diaries onto the log fire, only to see them curl and char slightly as they put out the flames.

I must get rid of them, though, in the process of trying to tidy up my life before I die. I have always used diaries to pour out my feelings at the end of each day. As a sort of therapy. After any particularly suicidal entry I would flick back and see if I had ever felt so desolate before. In the course of doing this I incidentally discovered that some of these days of inexplicable blackness recurred annually on the same date, and could be traced back to a genuine traumatic experience: the death of a loved one, serious illness, or a forgotten accident sometime in the past. I know friends that have discovered this too. I wonder if anyone has ever done research into it.

I am appalled by the content of my old diaries. Maybe this vicious, moaning, frightened, lustful, verging-on-insane woman is the real me, but if it is, I don't want my daughters to know. If ever they read the diatribe against them for forgetting to phone me, I would hate them to think I really felt that. So, into the fire the diaries will go. But not till this current nightmare is over.

I need to get my mind in some sort of order. At the moment my thoughts are like the shrapnel fragments I collected as a child after a bomb explosion. They are littered all over the place. I was hoping that writing a book about old age and a long life would lead me to a kind of uplifting, philosophical conclusion. Some neat, positive outcome. That journey is now aborted. No new route is revealing itself. I have no idea where I am going. Take it a day at a time.

5 May 2020

There are a lot of wartime phrases flying about. We are urged to celebrate the anniversary of VE Day this coming weekend with bunting and socially distanced street tea parties. It all feels a bit 'opium for the people' to me, so I have refused two invitations to go on popular television shows that stipulated that I should be 'upbeat'. There is a lot of forcing us to be upbeat going on. I did manage to let rip on one live show, when they could not edit me, saying that it is all very well clapping for the NHS every Thursday, but we need to make sure that they, and all the other public servants that are keeping us going – care workers, dustmen, shopkeepers, postmen, teachers – should not only be respected, but paid properly in future. Even if it means higher taxes for some of us. I pointed out that, after the war with which this pandemic is being constantly compared, the welfare state and the NHS were born – a miracle for families like mine.

In 1945 there were not a lot of parties with cream teas like we are being urged to recreate in our front gardens in 2020 – if we have one. In Latham Road in Bexleyheath we did have a rather sad little street party. The banquet was tinned fruit with evaporated milk. My mother conjured up some blancmanges, made with condensed milk and set in her glass rabbit moulds, one mummy rabbit and one baby, and she daringly put some currants round their bums. Our next-door neighbour's son was still in a Japanese prisoner-of-war camp, so it was hard for everyone to really enjoy ourselves until the war in Japan was over. Everybody's fears about his treatment there were proved horrifyingly true when he eventually returned, his mind and body destroyed.

In those days people did not drink at home, or certainly not people from my background, and even though my family had lived mainly above pubs, excessive drunkenness in public was rare, so we children watched from the bedroom windows that night, fascinated to see our parents getting a bit tipsy and dancing in the street. I remember seeing my mum and dad doing a rather sedate waltz to the thin music coming from the wind-up gramophone balanced on the garden wall. I had never seen them in one another's arms before. I would imagine the grown-ups were feeling hugely relieved, but exhausted. We heard on the radio that crowds were going mad in the West End, which sounded fun, and of course we listened to the King's speech.

10 May 2020

My mother's birthday. Lots of people seem to have enjoyed today, dressing up and putting out flags. I think everyone is desperate for a party and to see, albeit at two metres' distance, another human being. Children, for whom the Second World War is something they learned in a history lesson, must have wondered why we are making such a fuss about this particular event, but they enjoyed the cakes. They are going through such an unnatural experience. No school, no sport, no playing with friends. I worry about the long-term effect of this unnatural episode in their childhood, but I suppose we had five years of massive disruption before the original VE Day, yet we survived. But damaged, I think. Judging by my grandchildren, the biggest harm will be to their eyes, which are glued to iPads and computers for virtual lessons and games. God knows what is happening to the children who cannot afford these technical supports.

The Queen did a broadcast at the same time as her much-beloved father had done seventy-five years earlier, urging us to be strong. It was lovely to see her in her sitting room being her usual unperturbed self. In her speech she quoted from a song by Vera Lynn that was very popular during the war. She finished by saying, 'We'll meet again.' I remembered another song that Vera Lynn sang, supposedly to cheer up us evacuees. It made us all so miserable that it was banned, but the lyric is etched on my brain:

Goodnight, children everywhere
Your mummy thinks of you tonight
Lay your head upon your pillow
Don't be a kid or a weeping willow

So now this eighty-seven-year-old vulnerable old bird must try not to be a weeping willow.

I can hear my mother ('For heaven's sake, Sheila, pull yourself together'), who brought up two girls when polio, smallpox, scarlet fever, diphtheria, TB, German measles, whooping cough and the like were constant threats, and did a lot of pulling-together of herself and her family. I must do the same for mine, in this unfolding worldwide tragedy.

With the increased threat of death to someone of my age, and taking dodgy immunosuppressant drugs, and being stuck at home with no work, no outings, no direct human contact, there never has been a more impossible time to 'look my last on all things lovely', as Walter de la Mare urged. In my personal morass of gloom, I am sick to death of people telling me how much they are enjoying being furloughed in their lovely homes and gardens in this extraordinary sunny spring. I, in contrast, am obsessed with, and riddled with guilt about, the many more people who are suffering terribly from the repercussions of this ghastly plague.

Enough is enough. Moping about is not helping anyone, not least myself. So, I must pay my 'utmost blessing' to things that bring me, if not 'delight', then comfort.

12 May 2020

I live under the flight path to Heathrow, and near a main road to the airport or, in the opposite direction, into central London. The roads are now completely empty, and the airport is closed. No planes, no cars – an uncanny peace. Nature is being kind to us with perfect sunshine in which to bask on the one outing a day that we are allowed to take, as long as we keep moving – no sitting on the grass, no cafés or pubs open in which to pass the time with friends. As a 'highly vulnerable' person I'm not even allowed to do that. I am supposed to be 'sheltered' for three months, not leaving my house at all, but I sometimes sneak out at about 5.30 a.m., before anyone else is about, and never has the air felt so fresh, the sky so clear, the sun so gentle, the honeysuckle so fragrant, the birds so happy to be heard, as in the eerily quiet atmosphere. I stand outside the home of William Morris, just along from my house, and wonder what he would make of a world that finds this calm so remarkable. This must be more or less what it was like when he lived here. Except his home would have been a hive of activity, designing Arts-and-Craftsy things, in his quest that you 'have nothing in your houses that you do not know to be useful or believe to be beautiful', and holding socialist meetings with Rossetti and Burne-Jones, Ruskin and the like. If only we could incorporate their idealistic philosophy in our rebuilding of society after this disaster. The William Morris Society still has meetings in his old home. Perhaps the revolution could be planned here? I cannot stop and think about it for long, though, because of some newcomers to the river path.

Probably because there is less pollution in the Thames, I notice there is a new carpet of green plants on the bank when the tide goes out. It looks quite nice, but it seems to have become home to clouds of small green flies that fortunately don't bite, but do get in your eyes and mouth. That is my theory, having had time to observe them. I have started wearing elegant masks made by my friend Annie, not to defend myself and others from the virus, but to keep out the pesky flies. There are also many more birds around (it could be I have not noticed them before) and I am hoping that the balance of Nature has sent them to eat the bloody flies. If so, I could take some seagulls and whatever the other ones are up to Scotland during the midge season. With my new-found talent for biology I may have rescued the Scottish tourist trade.

13 May 2020

What with the flies, the joggers and the cyclists, the river path has started to become so crowded that social distancing of two metres is impossible. So today I cheekily took a walk inland from the river. I wandered through an area I have used as a back-double in my car but never really noticed. Bedford Park was the first garden suburb, designed in 1875 by Norman Shaw to accommodate the existing mature trees on the twenty-four-acre site, so it is now a verdant, elegant place to live and, as I discovered, to stroll around. Doubtless Norman popped down the road to chat about his plans with William Morris and co. Each house is different – the majestic fences and gates are the only common features – and the gardens now are full of roses and jasmine, making for a walk of sensory delights. The eyes and the nose are sated, as well as the ears. In the unaccustomed quiet I stood transfixed for about quarter of an hour listening to a blackbird, undisturbed by rat-runners, perched on a roof singing complex melodies that would have thrilled Stravinsky. These were then copied by another bird in the distance that I could not see. They were definitely mimicking one another. I did not know they did that. Or care, if I'm honest. But I do now. I rushed home to look up blackbirds on Wikipedia. They are amazing. And I have spent eighty-seven years ignoring them.

14 May 2020

Overdid it yesterday so my body is protesting. Today sat on the balcony in the sun. I am listening to and looking at the world around me more closely than I ever have. I have been blown away by dramatic landscapes like Suilven and Dancing Ledge, but now I am noticing the minutiae.

Every year two swans that live near us have cygnets. They are very much metropolitan birds, and previously when they took the new little ones for an outing they kept very close to the bank, to avoid the trip boats, rowers, yachts and general river business. This year the cygnets were born in April, and because of the virus rules banning rowing and sailing and motorboats, the river is completely unused by human beings. Today I watched the four little fluffy adventurers taking off from the adults and playing in the middle of the river, ignoring their angry parents who were trying to herd them to the side. Like all kids when told not to do something they deem unreasonable, the cygnets were squeaking: 'Why?' I watched this charade for about half an hour, something I would never have done BC. It gave me great pleasure. I will watch the cygnets' development with trepidation. They seldom all survive, and whereas before I only vaguely cared, this time I feel a special new bond with them. If I am not careful it will become an antirrhinum situation. I am new to this naturalist stuff. I am apt to humanise animals and flowers – anthropomorphising, it is called. This is frowned upon by proper country folk. Which is why they can happily kill birds, and foxes, and deer, and cut down forests.

My ornithological discoveries have not been limited to swans. I have not encouraged birds to visit my balcony, as they seem to think of it as a lavatory, but now I am desperate for company of any sort. Two wood pigeons (I looked it up – they have white splodges on their necks) have taken to sitting on my balcony railings. They adore one another, billing and cooing and nuzzling their heads together. I am very jealous. I am touched to see that today they are perched with their bums over the river, after I told them off yesterday for making a mess. I'm slightly less friendly now, as I read that they carry a disease that is very dangerous to old people. Everyone is out to get us.

Just now a crow arrived, gave one squawk, and they flew off. Maybe the crow knows about the virus-carrying pigeons and he was protecting me? Maybe I should make friends with the crow? I've seen him around the area quite a lot. I rather like the way he swaggers around on the road outside, unafraid and cocky. I'm sorry that I don't get more birds visiting. A blue-coloured bird (I didn't have time to look him up) came and perched on my Sky television dish for about ten minutes. I sprinkled seed around, but he never came back. He probably returned to Dover. Despite my very expensive birdseed – or 'world-class', as Boris Johnson says about all his failures: apps, tests, second-rate Cabinet members. Where are the sparrows and robins? Why don't they come and keep me company? Maybe the crow has seen them off too? I see him looking covetously through my French windows at my lounge. Maybe I'll be the next to go? The survival of the fittest – and I am 'extremely vulnerable'.

This is what two months in isolation does to you. I have gone from admiring a blackbird to an Alfred Hitchcock horror film.

15 May 2020

'Stay alert, control the virus, save lives.'

That poses a bit of a mystical challenge to us all. I certainly feel incapable of alertly being so powerfully controlling, especially while stuck in my home forbidden to go out. In his televised press conference one could practically see Dominic Cummings's gun in Boris Johnson's back, as Boris tried to look stern – he had even combed his hair – whilst ordering continuing 'lockdown' and also loosening up. But it is all right because he has a 'road map' to get us back to normal. I wonder if the road map will be on Google Maps for those who have no idea what a road map is.

16 May 2020

Felt desperately lonely today. It is difficult not to slip into a dystopian-nightmare way of thinking when you have no one to use as a sounding board for your thoughts. I like solitude, but not enforced. For an indefinite period. Even in prison you have a release date. I wish John were here. I disapprove of attributing possible opinions and behaviour to dead people, but I can't help thinking John would have quite liked this situation. Driven, as we both were, by the Protestant work ethic, he would have enjoyed an excuse not to do thirteen hours a day on a film set. He did not have friends, apart from those he worked with, so having people round for dinner or drinks never happened anyway. He liked it that way. For my part, I would love to hear his doubtless sardonic take on all the political shenanigans. I would sell my damaged soul to hear his comments on the daily briefings that we are receiving on television. Anxious medical puppets weakly trying to restrain Boris Johnson's desperation to give good news, even when people are dying and our economy is collapsing. They want us to take it deeply seriously, but his apparent inability to resist a lie, especially if it gets a laugh, has forced many a U-turn or retraction, for which he tries to blame The Science – those helpless experts trapped behind rostra either side of him, aghast at his misjudged off-the-cuff remarks. The same thing happened in the US when Trump put forward his theory that injecting with disinfectant was a possible cure, to the visible horror of a woman scientist on the platform. One can't help thinking there must have been some relief when Boris caught the virus and was whipped off to hospital, then down to Chequers to recover and play with his newborn son for several weeks. Not to mention be with his probably fed-up fiancée. John's impersonation of Boris – as people still call him, albeit more derisively than chummily of late – would have been cherishable; upper-class twits were his speciality. He would have had even more fun with the wretched Matt Hancock – no relation, I hasten to add – chosen as secretary of state for health, one suspects more for his support of Brexit than any qualification for that or indeed any job in government, and unexpectedly confronted by a catastrophic problem way beyond his skill set to deal with. On days when the news is dire Boris does not appear at the daily briefing, lumbering Hancock with announcing all the bad stuff. To begin with he was quite perky as he read out manipulated statistics, but gradually his eyes have glazed over, and he is stiff with fear when confronted by questions from the press, as he tries desperately to stick to the party line, rehearsed with Cummings, and cunningly constructed to avoid answering any questions truthfully, or comprehensibly, or, when at a loss, at all, ignoring the question completely and rambling on with another random set piece.

I see that look in my mirror too. Rabbit in a headlight. A very shabby rabbit. I am not a pretty sight. My Social Services Outfits, which I favour in France, are positively Vogue front page compared to my London Lockdown Look. I wear tracksuit bottoms which are two sizes too big for me since I became a shrunken vegan, so I either roll them at the waist or, for a change, turn up the trouser legs, or, on particularly wizened days, both. With them I sport old, only occasionally washed T-shirts, one saying, ironically, 'Funny Women', coming from a goodie bag given to us at the show a few weeks ago when Lola and I were so happy.

People often say I look young for my age, an effect mainly achieved by having a good haircut. My hairdresser being closed, I now have to sport a cute headband to keep my growing thatch from obscuring my vision, and I look like a disturbing, ancient child. My body is brown thanks to extraordinary weather and having time to sunbathe, but my face is ashen, because I get cold sores if I expose it to sunlight, so when I go out I wear a big battered brown felt hat. It was actually a beautiful hat once, made for me by the very trendy George Malyard, whose revolutionary designs are now archived in the Victoria and Albert Museum. When I wore it in the sixties I was the height of chic. Now, worn over my wan face, a mask over my mouth and nose, and with straggly wisps of dead white hair escaping, I look as though I too should be in a museum. Maybe there is a History of Plagues Department somewhere in which I could feature as a 2020 Pandemic Victim.

18 May 2020

Conscious that my mind is ailing even if my body is not, today I broke all the rules, made a desperate break for it and drove into the West End. A journey that in rush hour can take forty-five minutes or more took me ten. Instead of sitting in the customary traffic jam, I only passed about three other cars. I parked easily behind John Lewis – it really is upsetting to see that stalwart national institution closed down – and I walked to Oxford Circus, half expecting to be arrested, but not only were there no police, there were hardly any people at all. I actually stood in the middle of the road on Oxford Circus and looked down Oxford Street. In the middle. Something that has probably never before been possible in daytime. No buses, taxis or cars, nobody on the pavements. For the first time I noticed that the street is lined with trees. Without all the usual tourists and out-of-towners – Londoners usually give Oxford Street a wide berth – the street is an impressive avenue; a sort of Champs-Élysées. Regent Street too was silent, some shops ominously boarded up in a way that suggested they are permanently closed. There was nowhere to have a coffee. I passed a fabulous Indian restaurant near Regent Street, and it had signs of life. I looked through the window and the waiters, who would usually be the acme of elegance, were lounging around in shirtsleeves. The manager came out and we chatted, at a distance, and I was upset at the awful calamity this is for people who have worked hard for years to build up a much-loved business. Ahmed told me that if they were not allowed to open soon, they would have to go bankrupt. The same thing is happening to my son-in-law, who recently celebrated ten years' work to create a successful theatre production company, and now has to close down, there being insufficient support for the arts from the government. It is not even mentioned, despite being a huge earner for the revenue, providing thousands of jobs, attracting tourism, enhancing British reputation abroad, and especially helping disadvantaged children with all the outreach groups throughout the country, a few of which the John Thaw Foundation is proud to support. The theatre, music, museums and art galleries are vital to the well-being of our nation. For the Boris/Cummings lot, getting the pubs open takes priority over preserving our cultural life, or even our kids' education. They think that is what the public wants. Their numerous focus groups have misjudged a lot of the public's reaction to the situation so far, so they may be wrong. But I suppose our arts and entertainment institutions will remain some way down the list of priorities for a while.

It did me a lot of good to look at the architectural marvel of Regent Street and my beloved Broadcasting House, still trying to function to keep the news being communicated truthfully, as opposed to some of the dangerous stuff on the web. Sometimes I just have to stop watching and listening to the events as they occur. I turn to BBC Radio 3, where the music I cherish continues to soothe me, and all the presenters are carrying on calmly chatting to us, now from their various homes, in their usual gentle tones.

I had arranged to meet a friend of mine in Soho Square to pick up some masks she had made for me – a worthy reason, I felt, for breaking my sheltered status. It was a glowing sunny day. I walked, a bit tentatively, to the square. There, people were basking in the sun, reading papers, chatting, or just sitting, like me, looking around. The two permanent table-tennis tables were occupied by Chinese men, local waiters, judging by their outfits, playing with skill and courtesy; none of the shouts and squeals that happen when I play table tennis, just soft laughter. A group of five scruffy, shiny-eyed disciples were sitting on the grass, ringing bells and tinkling little cymbals, whilst tentatively chanting 'Hare Krishna', a cry that in the sixties echoed round London, when Hare Krishnas used to dance ecstatically, garbed in orange cloth, harmonising their mantra, totally ignored by the shoppers and office workers as they weaved around among them. I then wandered around the virtually deserted streets, smiling and greeting the other few strollers. The roads were closed to traffic. The friendly atmosphere was like it was when I was a young girl lodging in the Theatre Girls Club hostel in Greek Street, apart from the absence of the women stationed along the pavement politely selling their wares (who, as they got to know me, gave me advice on make-up, as long as I didn't stand around too long on their pitch). I am probably romanticising the scene and their lives, but they weren't the cowering, drugged-up, trafficked youngsters you see in shady hallways, nail bars and massage parlours nowadays.

20 May 2020

Every Thursday at 8 p.m. many of the population go into the open air and clap for the NHS and care workers, who are courageously fighting this malignant virus. Those front-line workers are trying to do their usual job of healing and comforting, with a few ineffective weapons, and under threat of coming down with the disease themselves. In fact, many have died. The politicians make sure that they are filmed clapping along with what they interpret as public unity, but I detect in the applause a hint of anger that the NHS has been neglected by the government, along with all the care workers, dustmen, shopworkers and delivery people who are now keeping us going, and have been shockingly underappreciated. Captain Tom Moore, a one-hundred-year-old ex-soldier, is marching up and down his garden, and Margaret Payne, a woman of ninety, is going up and down her stairs to replicate a childhood memory of climbing my beloved Suilven, both of them raising huge sums of money for the NHS. They, like me, remember how awful it was before the availability of healthcare for all, and they are demonstrating that money can, and should, be found to fund that.

22 May 2020

My body is not happy. Idleness makes me aware of pain. Because I am not working – no new scripts to learn, no nightly performances plus two matinees, no singing lessons, or visits to the gym to keep fit – my engine is no longer throbbing and I am becalmed. I have persevered with practising mindfulness, living in the moment and accepting whatever is happening in an interested, unemotional way. Not easy for me, but using an app from the University of California, Los Angeles, which sounds suspiciously Hollywood, but seems medically sound and not New Agey, I have found it a help.

One of the main benefits of this enforced idleness is the discoveries I have made about my body. I was alarmed the other day when I climbed a flight of stairs and was breathless. Because I was not, as I normally would be, rushing off somewhere, I stopped and thought about it, and realised I had not been breathing. I had run up the whole staircase holding my breath. When I did it again, breathing normally, I was fine. From there, I went on to observe myself in other situations, and discovered I frequently held my breath, particularly when doing something tricky.

Another thing I have found time to work on is a long-term practice of tensing my body against life. The smallest undertaking will cause the muscles in my neck, across my back, in my arms and hands and my diaphragm, to clutch in apprehension. I have tried to relax by practising yoga, Pilates, tai chi – to no avail. In fact, the effort to get the practices right, in my perfectionist way, has made the condition worse. Now something very strange has happened.

My body is teaching me a lesson, sending me a message. It is using my illness to cure a lifetime's destructive habit. With nothing better to do, I have had time here on my own to notice that every time I go into Clutch Mode a streak of pain goes through my body, and lo and behold my reaction, to stop it hurting, is to release the tension. This lifelong habit of living in constant preparation for fight or flight, in my body, and even my mind, is being driven away by pain. What an irony. I do not grasp this pen I am writing with like a last straw, as I was wont to do, because it hurts, whereas using just enough effort to hold and guide it does not. My poor body. All my life I have gripped it in an iron vice of unnecessary effort, and now, in the last lap, as a last resort, it is forcing me to relax. When I discovered I had rheumatoid arthritis, I thought my body had turned against me, allowing my immune system to attack me rather than defend me, but now I like to think it is trying to teach me a new approach to managing movement. If somewhat brutally.

23 May 2020

Another bloody letter from the NHS. In fact an email and a letter to make sure I don't forget that I am Extremely Vulnerable. Although there is actually no clinical evidence yet to prove that people taking my medication are more at risk; it is just a supposition. When I suggested to my medical team that perhaps a drug that makes the immune system behave, like tocilizumab, might be useful in treating coronavirus, in which inflammation is a huge problem, I was surprised and a little gratified to be told that they were in fact doing clinical trials to see if it does. Epidemiology appears to be another talent I have acquired.

All in all, although resenting the 'vulnerable' label, I do now accept that I am old. I cannot avoid it, since we oldies are constantly in the news as being in need of protection. It still surprises me a bit when very old ladies tell me they were at school with me. I opened a wing of an old people's home where ancient folk were mumbling to themselves, shuffling around on Zimmers, and the matron told me they were excited about my visit because 'You're their generation, aren't you?'

One of the things that depresses me most about getting old is all the things I will not have time to learn. And this bloody virus is wasting what time I have left.

I curse it for forcing the cancellation of the canal series I was doing with Gyles, which was proving the most fulfilling job of my career. In the two episodes that we managed to complete I not only learned to handle a canal boat, but had a rowing lesson from the Olympic medal-winning crew, and did interviews with many intriguing people who live on or alongside these historic waterways. I was doing a job that satisfied my avid thirst for knowledge, and being paid for the privilege. Tempus is fugitting.

24 May 2020

Had a lovely email from Norbie, my Hungarian friend, telling me to take care of myself. I am thinking a lot, in my lonely, disconnected state, about how lucky I am, in normal life, to be the recipient of sometimes quite profound affection from strangers, who have been touched by something I have written or acted in. I am at the age when women are normally invisible, treated unkindly.

Coming back from a gig in Inverness in those days when we could travel around, there was a mistake in my booking and a uniformed official at the airport berated me loudly, in front of the crowd in the waiting area, rudely accusing me of daring to sit on some seats reserved for business class, which I had actually been booked in, but for which I had been given the wrong ticket. It was humiliating and upsetting, but then a woman from the ticket desk swooped on us, told the man off and apologised profusely, saying that she recognised me, and was really sorry that I had been treated so badly.

'I know who you are.'

Had she not 'known who I was', I fear I would have just been a stupid old woman, fair game for humiliation. It was a salutary lesson, reminding me how fortunate I am to be treated so well. Because I pop up in people's drawing rooms on their television screens they think they know me, and kindly share with me stories of their lives, pouring out their hearts, knowing I will not share them with their friends or family. That is why I got hundreds of letters from readers when The Two of Us was published, and still get many, some sixteen years later, discussing addiction and bereavement, saying things to a sympathetic stranger that they cannot to people close to them. The marine in the hotel, and Tom in the pub in Cornwall too, felt able to share with me the secret sorrow they had to withhold from colleagues and loved ones.

I remember feeling sad that Tom had lost out on a prosperous life that he was entitled to. Thinking of it now, with the pace of my life reduced to a standstill, and a new consciousness of the enjoyment to be found in small natural things, it was arrogant of me to think he would be missing out by rejecting what I deemed exciting new experiences.

Sitting here alone staring at four walls, I would give my eyeteeth to be in that pub with a plate of chips, a glass of cider and amusing company. That is Tom's everyday life. Why on earth would he want to endure an airport, and flying, to be at a party with a lot of rich people he has nothing in common with, except a father who deserted him?

I will go to that pub again after this is all over. I bet he will still be there, smiling at his mates.

What're you going to have, Tom? Oh, if only.

25 May 2020

Stay at home; protect the NHS; jobs, jobs, jobs; stay alert; control the virus; save the NHS; keep two metres apart; wear a mask; don't cough; flatten the curve; whatever it takes; and now 'Get it done' – referring to ridding ourselves of the virus as well as Europe, which is still worryingly going on behind our backs, whilst we focus on this new government endeavour.

Slogans are still the order of the day. An approach that fills me with trepidation. Hitler recommended in Mein Kampf that short slogans should be used to appeal to 'the primitive sentiments of the broad masses . . . These slogans should be repeated until the very last individual has come to grasp the idea that is being put forward.' One of his favourites was 'Germany first', which I hope Trump is too stupid to have known about when he made his inaugural speech as president, otherwise he is even more dangerous than I thought. We have even endeavoured to obey our prime minister's Delphic maxims to 'whack a mole' and 'squash the sombrero', though his classics tutors at Balliol may flinch.

The instructions have become ever more complicated and contradictory. The comedy actor Matt Lucas's impersonation of Johnson dithering summed it up perfectly:

'So, we are saying, don't go to work, go to work, don't take public transport, go to work, don't go to work, stay indoors, if you can work from home, go to work, don't go to work, go outside, don't go outside, and then we will or won't . . . er . . . something or other.'

I have always believed that the British sense of humour is one of our strongest weapons against extremism. The strutting absurdity of Hitler, Mussolini and the rest of his murderous gang, with its ludicrous goose-stepping soldiers, would surely have been laughed out of court in Britain. Indeed, they were, in the playgrounds in England during the war, which resonated with songs about the relative merits of the Nazi leadership's balls.

But we mustn't forget that these ludicrous cartoon figures ended up killing many millions.

Social media is, I'm glad to say, full of ridicule of our present leaders. Cabinet ministers are wont to say, of things they want us to believe, it is 'the will of the people' or 'the country has spoken'. All I can say is they can't be looking at social media, or chatting in the queue at Tesco.

25 May 2020

A distressed phone call from Joanna. My youngest daughter has a rental home in St Ives. After it was permitted to make a short journey, she drove the three children down from Devon to check on the house. She met no one, and went nowhere apart from her house. The work on the house went on till late in the evening, and the kids were tired, so she decided to stay the night, but at 9 p.m. a neighbour came to the door and threatened to report her to the police if she did, because overnight stays were not allowed. For God knows what reason. His belligerent visit felt a bit like the Stasi in East Berlin. She was no threat whatsoever to anyone. But her neighbour was drunk with the power of self-righteousness. My daughter was disobeying the rules. Never mind how pointless they were. And she must be punished.

I have always had a reluctance to obey rules. Maybe growing up in the shadow of the rise of the Nazis had some effect. My mother was reluctant to let me join the Brownies with their lovely brown uniform, and utterly refused to allow me to become a Girl Guide, because she had heard of, and been frightened by, the Hitler Youth movement in Germany.

It seems to me that, if you are going to obey rules, you have to double-check that they are necessary, and made by people with good motives, who know what they are doing. We do not seem to be controlling the virus as well as some other countries – 65,000 people have died so far. Despite numerous prior warnings of a potential pandemic by scientists and the likes of Bill Gates, we were not prepared at all. Johnson likes to think of himself as a Churchillian figure, but he has none of the honesty with which Churchill warned us of the inevitable tragedies of war, and it is hard to trust him after the lies of the Brexit campaign.

The new rules have come at us thick and fast, and to begin with we nearly all did as we were told. We locked ourselves away, trusting that the government was dealing with it. But the daily briefings, with multiple charts and facts and figures, have not inspired us. Schemes like the Test and Trace app, tried out on the Isle of Wight and hailed as 'the cherry on the cake' of getting the virus under control, have not filled us with confidence in our leaders. South Korea and Germany have effective systems up and running, but we were supposed to be getting our own 'world-beating' version. I personally never really understood it. It seemed to be a few operators waiting for people to phone them to tell them they had the virus, whereupon these observers would inform those people's friends, telling them to quarantine for two weeks. I could not grasp what function the app had in the process. Anyway, it has disappeared without trace. Or track. Together with the millions it cost to invent and trial it.

Nevertheless, people are still loyally trying to abide by the rules, whilst not being sure they are sensible. The economy is inevitably going to be wrecked by the shutdown. The NHS is forced to delay all other life-saving treatment whilst it deals with the virus casualties. My profession faces ruination under the disastrous rules whereby no theatre, cinema or museum can operate. It seems young people just get a mild version of the infection. So is there not an argument for locking away and protecting just us vulnerable ones, and letting the rest of the population carry on as normal, apart from a few bouts of fluey illness, so that the economy continues to operate, avoiding the potential disaster of a massive recession?

Although I admire the way my fellow countrymen are obeying the rules, it makes me nervous. I have already confessed that I have disobeyed them. That is partly because of my reluctance to kowtow. I need to respect a person before I do as they say.

26 May 2020

There are rule-breakers even in their own ranks. Svengali Cummings has himself transgressed. As a rule-breaker myself, I was prepared to give him the benefit of the doubt when he sat in the rose garden of 10 Downing Street – a setting usually reserved for major governmental announcements, not scruffy backroom advisers – and rambled on about why it was all right for him to go gallivanting up to his family estate in Durham, and then have a nice little drive, and a sit by the river with his wife and child, while the rest of us sweltered behind closed doors. The mockery of his excuses – driving over fifty miles to see if his eyes were good enough to drive, not having enough childcare – has been wonderfully funny, covering the profound anger at his hypocrisy for which 'the will of the people' was definitely that he should have been sacked. But, of course, he wasn't. How on earth would Michael Gove, and the man Gove stabbed in the back during the leadership battle, our prime minister, know what to do without him?

27 May 2020

Went to Hammersmith Hospital, where I was five minutes late getting back to my parking meter. The attendant was already tapping into his machine and, remembering previous similar occasions when I have been told that, once started, the process of issuing a ticket has to continue, I was reduced, at the thought of yet another fine, to whimpering, 'Oh, please.' To my utter amazement the man tapped a few more keys and said, 'All right, love, but don't do it again.' He abandoned the protocol, maybe risking getting into trouble with his boss, who presumably would be able to see evidence of his having given away the revenue. In the afterglow of his kindness, I decided we can and definitely should break rules.

In 2015 – God, that seems another world – I went to the magnificent Alexander McQueen exhibition at the V&A.

From an apprenticeship in tailoring, this genius of haute couture soared into his own unique stratosphere, saying, 'You've got to know the rules to break them. That's what I'm here for, to demolish the rules but to keep the tradition.' That is something that could be said by all creative people who have moved their particular Art forward – whether Stravinsky, Picasso, Pinter, Defoe or Sondheim. For humankind to survive there have to be laws and rules, but these must be constantly tested and challenged, and improved upon, and we are indebted to the individuals who do this on our behalf, sometimes at great cost to themselves – the suffragettes, the Peterloo martyrs, the conscientious objectors, the ordinary folk who sheltered Jewish families during the Nazi period.

Is the pandemic making us too compliant? Anxious to avoid risk? Should we just do as we are told? Maybe in this instance it is for the public good. But we must not lose the duty to question received opinions, and if, after examining them, we find them wanting in their contribution to the nurturing of humanity, we must reject them. We must refuse to toe the line. We must rebel. It is so difficult to avoid being seduced into prejudice by peer pressure, political jargon, religious dogma and press distortion or government edict.

Before the virus attacked us, we witnessed many acts of civil disobedience by the people involved in Extinction Rebellion. They are passionate in their battle against our headlong plunge into climate disaster. There are other groups and individuals engaged in obstructing the development of the HS2, a vastly expensive high-speed rail link from London to Birmingham, and eventually further north. Now that so many people are working at home and finding it possible, and maybe even preferable, spending £106 billion to take thirty minutes off a train trip to Birmingham, at the cost of destroying homes, woodland and wildlife, seems folly.

Like all peaceful protesters, the Extinction Rebellion campaigners are prepared to go to prison for us. If flouting the law is the only way to draw our attention to destructive developments that stand in the way of a greener lifestyle, they will do it. Now is the vital time to take action, when the country has had a taste of what life can be like without so many aeroplanes, cars and pollution of every kind. We have heard the blackbird sing. And we like it.

In my profession there are many rules. Punctuality is necessary. You can't keep an audience or a film unit waiting by turning up late for work. The superstitions, like not whistling in the theatre or saying the name of the Scottish play, are too myriad to mention. Most of them are dying out anyway. Even 'the show must go on' is less abided by. I love the story that John was told by the lugubrious comic Max Wall, with whom he was appearing in a play at the Royal Court Theatre in Chelsea, about one old trooper who did break the rules. 'Monsewer' Eddie Gray, as he was known, sported a huge moustache, glasses and an ill-fitting top hat, and spoke in Franglais. An expert juggler and slapstick comic, he was apparently an odd bloke who didn't stand fools gladly. One matinee, when Max and Eddie were playing the Ugly Sisters at the notorious Glasgow Empire, Eddie, dressed to the nines in wig, bosoms, elaborate woman's costume and absurd make-up, the full pantomime-dame drag, abruptly stopped struggling to make himself heard over rioting kids in the stalls, turned to Max and said calmly, 'I'm not 'avin this, mate – I'm off.' Whereupon he left the stage and drove back to London, leaving Max to adjust the plot for the rest of the show to involve only one Ugly Sister.

It is painfully obvious that my amateur theory is not scientifically or anthropologically sound, and must not be confused with Rees-Moggery, but I believe that, whereas other animals on the whole go with the herd, the propensity to break rules, disobey orders, question the norm and reject the accepted standards and beliefs is what makes us human. It could lead to anarchy, but without it you have slavery and stasis.

7 June 2020

One massive defiance of the rules has just taken place. People around the world are gathering despite the virus, marching in outcry at the death in Minnesota of a black man, George Floyd, who was slowly murdered by a policeman kneeling on his neck. He cried out for his mother, and said he could not breathe, but the murderer continued and his colleagues just stood and watched. A young girl, remonstrating all the while, filmed the nine minutes it took for George Floyd to die, as evidence. I confess that I have not been able to watch the whole nine minutes, it being so obscene, but suffice it to say that I was grateful that crowds of people, of all ethnicities, defied the lockdown rules and marched in protest. Worldwide. It could not wait, for memories are too short. The subsequent stories of racial harassment and injustice that have been told by people of colour have shocked me and I'm sure many others. I knew it existed but I've done nothing. If I look deep into my soul, I know that I too have questions to face.

I have not sufficiently considered the lack of people of colour in positions of power in all areas of society, including my own profession. On today's news I watched the statue of a slave owner being felled in Bristol, and realised I really do not know about my own colonial history. I never learned it at school, and, like women's history, it is grossly neglected to this day. My granddaughter has been involved in writing letters to schools, requesting them to change the curriculum into something more accurate. Great Britain has a proud history in many ways, and no harm will come to it by facing the bad bits. I was impressed, when I went to Berlin, to see so many schoolchildren being taken round the Holocaust Memorial and other museums illustrating their country's Nazi past.

I honestly did not know what an appalling racist Winston Churchill was. In 1937 he told the Palestine Royal Commission:

'I do not admit for instance, that a great wrong has been done to the Red Indians of America, or the black people of Australia. I do not admit that a wrong has been done to these people by the fact that a stronger race, a higher grade race, a more worldly wise race to put it that way, has come in and taken their place.'

I cannot connect this white-supremacist garbage with the man I have long respected. I do not know how his brilliant brain could have overlooked the multiple flaws in this argument. I do know that he led us out of a terrifying war. I remember the comfort and inspiration his wonderful speeches gave to us. As a child I loved the pictures of Winnie in his siren suit, with his homburg hat and stick, a cigar in his mouth, stomping through the debris after a raid. Now

I am sickened by some of the things he said in the past. I am forcing myself to examine the disturbing things my hero did and said, and yet I would hate to see his statue removed from Parliament Square. Let him stay, but let it be known that even heroes, like all of us, can be ignorant and cruel. He was a brilliant maverick with huge talent, and I like to think that, if he had been tackled about his earlier racism, he would think again. Just as, to a lesser degree, my mother would have regretted using the N-word to describe the colour of her coat if she knew how hurtful that description was, and I would have thrown my beloved golliwog into the rubbish if I had known what it symbolised.

Whilst we struggle towards equilibrium in this necessary balancing of our society, there will be excesses. The other night I watched a streaming of the National Theatre production of Les Blancs, a searingly honest play about colonisation and apartheid in South Africa. There was an after-show discussion of the production between three women of colour. They all concurred that this subject must only be directed by a person of colour. I wondered if they felt that all the many shows about white stories should only be directed by a person of that colour. In my opinion theatre and the arts as a whole should be free of all restrictions and rules. Just as we now have had a black Henry V, a female Hamlet, and are about to have an eighty-year-old interpretation of the same role, we should not categorise or limit our approach to art. However, because of the paucity of diversity in directors, perhaps it is time to positively discriminate for a while, as we have regarding women. When I was young it was unheard of for women of any colour to direct. I was always on my own at meetings of the belligerently male managerial team at the Royal Shakespeare Company in the 1980s.

I really believe that the Black Lives Matter movement, by breaking the pandemic rules and going on marches, awakened the awareness of many of us, and achieved a massive step forward towards a genuinely understanding, integrated, respectful and peaceful world. A world where everyone believes the Quaker faith that there is 'that of God in everyone'. Everyone. Including Churchill.

14 June 2020

Tonight we had a Zoom book club meeting, a dozen women from disparate backgrounds meeting to discuss Elizabeth Bowen's In the Heat of the Day, and I got unattractively angry about its obtuse description of life in wartime London. Everyone agreed that, despite it being acclaimed by the literati, we found the style impenetrable. I am always irritated by the gulf between a lowly but enjoyable read and literature, which often seems to demand obscurity and no satisfactory ending. This book is full of passages which a group of very intelligent women, all better educated than I, found impossible to understand. The others were calmly analytical, but I let fly with lots of highbrow critique along the line of: 'It's wanky and up itself.'

This was a study of a much more elegant wartime than I remember. Classy people continuing to smoke and chat on vaguely about their love affairs while an air raid is in full blast outside. Not an Anderson or crowded underground shelter in sight. A lover who is a fascist spy with no explanation as to why he should support a regime that he would have known by then was slaughtering millions, except that he has a slightly nasty mother and sister, and a vast home that he does not like much. Anyway, after my out-of-proportion Zoom tirade, causing, I noted in my gallery view, several raised eyebrows, I ended up feeling worried about my mental state. Being isolated for months with my own thoughts, and little face-to-face discussion, has addled my brain. Yet, like others, I am frightened of emerging from this exile. I cannot visualise what the future will be. How it will end. Mainly because it won't. There will be none of the much-desired closure.

I am puzzled by our current fashion for bringing about closure. There is no such thing. If someone's child is murdered, the punishment of the miscreant does not bring an end to the parents' suffering. The severance of our link with Europe will not be over and done with on 1 January, when the Brexiteers will be rejoicing about the 'closure' of their fifty-year struggle to get away from unity with our neighbours. It is the ongoing adventure of living that nothing is irrevocably ended. Germany did not find closure on the Nazi period with the squalid death of Hitler; there followed a long struggle to reinvent itself. Today its chancellor, Angela Merkel, is one of the world's most admirable leaders. (It is interesting that all the countries that have calmly acquitted themselves well through the pandemic, free from all the 'we will fight this war' rhetoric, have been led by women – Taiwan, New Zealand, Germany.)

18 June 2020

Strange that I was remembering Vera Lynn a few weeks ago. Her death has just been announced, at the age of 103.

'She had a good innings,' as my dad would say. Such a British, crickety tribute is right for her, because she truly was quintessentially English. She could not have been any other nationality, with her tall, slightly gawky body and toothy grin. Like my sister Billie, she worked all over the world with ENSA during the war, sleeping in mud huts or in the backs of cars, entertaining a handful of troops in a clearing, lit by jeep headlights, or on a makeshift platform somewhere, in front of hundreds of men, who sometimes hadn't seen a woman for months. She was unthreatening and likeable. Her voice was pitch-perfect, unaffected, with that pure, resonant London simplicity. Every word was as clear as a bell, so that I discover that, eighty years later, I can remember all the words of every song she sang, not just 'Goodnight, Children Everywhere'. They spoke of all the things we most longed for during the ugly conflict. Beautiful fantasies. There may never have been bluebirds over the White Cliffs of Dover, or a nightingale singing in Berkeley Square, and certainly not angels dining at the Ritz, but, sitting on a bunk down in the air-raid shelter, listening to a crackly radio, that was what she promised us. And, more realistically, that 'Jimmy will go to sleep in his own little room again.' Just what eight-year-old Sheila would have loved. Vera Lynn said it would happen – 'Just you wait and see' – and we believed her. She sounded so honest. And in the newsreels, we saw she meant it. She didn't dance about and pull silly faces; she just stood there, and told us in her strong, unaffected voice that everything would be all right.

How important words were during the war. We only had the wireless, so we interpreted events through our ears.

When Churchill made his poetic, vivid speeches, we were stirred; when the obviously ailing king struggled to master his heart-stopping stutter to address us, we wanted to be brave for him; and when the It's That Man Again gang fooled around, it cheered us up. It was our ears that they had to appeal to. Maybe nowadays, if a woman stood, without a backing group, stock-still at a microphone, and made no attempt to be sexy or provocative, just sang the words and meant them, we would not be impressed. But that's what Vera did. And we were impressed. More: she was our sweetheart – and we loved her.

I remember a poem that sums up the value of entertainers such as her. It is by Louis MacNeice, a neglected poet I used to see often with Dylan Thomas in the Soho dives I visited in the fifties and sixties with Alec. When I was appearing at the Garrick Theatre in 1963 in a play called Rattle of a Simple Man, he staggered into my dressing room one night, paralytically drunk, a sorry sight that made his death a few months later no surprise. This poem, 'Death of an Actress', which could've been written about Vera, expresses a love of performers that makes me proud to be in a profession that fulfils the need that he describes.

I see from the paper that Florrie Forde is dead –
Collapsed after singing to wounded soldiers,
At the age of sixty-five. The American notice
Says no doubt all that need be said

About this one-time chorus girl; whose rôle
For more than forty stifling years was giving
Sexual, sentimental, or comic entertainment,
A gaudy posy for the popular soul.

Vera was never knowingly sexual but, like Florrie,

> She threw a trellis of Dorothy Perkins roses
> Around an audience come from slum and suburb
> And weary of the tea-leaves in the sink;
>
> Who found her songs a rainbow leading west
> To the home they never had, to the chocolate Sunday
> Of boy and girl, to cowslip time, to the never-
> Ending weekend Islands of the Blest.

Vera, like Florrie, had a potent song, 'We'll Meet Again' – cherished by what Vera called her 'boys'. As for Florrie,

> . . . she made a ragtime favourite
> Of 'Tipperary', which became the swan-song
> Of troop-ships on a darkened shore . . .

But MacNeice's Florrie died in a military hospital, whilst Vera lived happily to 103. Florrie took her last bow, as MacNeice put it,

> Correctly. For she stood
> For an older England, for children toddling
> Hand in hand while the day was bright. Let the wren and robin
> Gently with leaves cover the Babes in the Wood.

Maybe Florrie Forde's particular style, like Vera's, is now dated, and tea leaves in the sink are a rare occurrence, but there is still a need for entertainers who make us laugh and sing, and look forward to better times involving bluebirds, cowslips and rainbows.

19 June 2020

Last night I watched an episode of the television detective series Vera. I remembered meeting Brenda Blethyn many years ago after doing a broadcast in the old BBC Bush House studio. She was on the verge of giving up the profession because she seemed stuck in a casting rut. Her performance last night, in a well-directed episode, surrounded by top-notch actors, was faultless. The character she has created is odd, detailed and hypnotic to watch. Her walk up a bleak moorland road after the death of a colleague was as profoundly moving as any highly praised Shakespearean performance. I salute these members of my profession. Their expertise can be overlooked by critics, and some people in our industry, but the public embraces them with gratitude.

John always referred to himself, and was referred to by others, as 'just a telly actor'. Television is more respected now than when John did The Sweeney, but I maintain, looking back at some of his work, he was a superlative actor, truthful, intelligent and charismatic. His portrayal of the old man in Goodnight Mister Tom would compare to many a much-lauded Lear.

I sometimes anguish about my eclectic career and my questionable contribution to the culture that I consider essential for our society. The Wildcats of St Trinian's is one of the worst films ever made – I suppose that is a sort of distinction. Mercifully it seems to have got lost in the ether, so it does not pop up to bite me on some obscure satellite channel, but attempting to follow in the footsteps of the sublime Alastair Sim, and play the headmistress of the school with, for some unknown reason, a Dutch accent, cannot claim high status in the British film canon. My performances as Senna Pod in Carry On Cleo or my impersonation of Margaret Thatcher in a weird episode of Doctor Who will not get me listed on anyone's roster of great performances. I did do some posh work at the National and the RSC – the British premiere of Stephen Sondheim's Sweeney Todd, classy bits and bobs – mixed with Just a Minute-type comedy shows. Altogether, a regular hotchpotch of a career. Difficult to categorise.

If asked about my future ambitions, I usually reply: 'To pay the bills.' I am a working actor. It is my job – just as yours may be plumbing, or nursing, or shopkeeping. In the middle of a twelve-month run of a strenuous musical, performing eight shows a week and doing morning class to keep my voice and body fresh so that I can keep the hundredth show still looking like the first, audience members often say, 'You must have fun', 'You look as though you are enjoying yourself', as though it is some kind of hobby. I have been known to snarl ungraciously, 'It's my job.' The same reply applies to 'How do you learn all those words?', albeit with the addition, in old age, of 'With a lot of difficulty.' The actor and comedy performer Peter Jones would always solemnly say to me, 'Better than working in a glue factory', haunted as he was by a visit to one that he made for some obscure reason. Of course, he was right.

I think what I would like to be known as is a popular entertainer like, but nowhere near in the same class as, Vera Lynn. The thousands of letters and warm greetings in the street I have received during my working life are honestly more satisfying to me than the odd rusting awards I have on my lavatory shelf.

I hope I have, as they say, done my bit. I have always, as John put it, had to 'earn a crust'. It was, and in my case still is, my job. I have done a hell of a lot of work, most of which I, and the public, have long forgotten – 'Weren't you Sheila Hancock?' – most of it undistinguished, but over the years I have raised a few laughs, I have heard audiences having a good time, so when I feel a bit inadequate I remind myself of some advice Martha Graham gave to Agnes de Mille. It is valid for anyone attempting anything creative.

'There is a vitality, a life force, an energy, a quickening that is translated through you into action . . . It is not your business to determine how good it is nor how valuable it is nor how it compares with other expressions. It is your business to keep it yours clearly and directly, to keep the channel open. You do not even have to believe in yourself or your work. You have to keep yourself open and aware to the urges that motivate you. Keep the channel open . . . No artist is pleased . . . No satisfaction whatever at any time . . . There is only a queer divine dissatisfaction, a blessed unrest that keeps us marching and makes us more alive than the others.'

Come to think of it, that is a pretty good credo for life.

5 July 2020

We have been told that poetry will now become an optional subject in GCSEs. The powers that be have declared that it is hard for students 'to get to grips with complex literary texts remotely'. It is tragic how we underestimate our children's ability. People think Shakespeare has to be simplified, bowdlerised or cut, but when we did the RSC small-scale tour, after one workshop to prepare them, I never met a single child who didn't comprehend the plays and the text. If they didn't understand every word, they still liked the sound of it. In fact, nowadays, with rap and performance poetry, the younger generation are discovering a new delight in the use of language.

Some kids will never know about poetry, or hear classical music, unless they are introduced to it at school. That is just not fair. My existence would have been pretty barren if teachers had not opened up these worlds to me. A poem can crystallise a complex mindset and help you understand what you, and others, are grappling with. Coincidentally, today I received from a friend a poem by Jacqueline Saphra, one that helped me deal with my present unease.

Obviously worried about the economy, the government (or Boris, desperate to be loved) has relaxed a lot of the restrictions. So, of course, everyone is celebrating en masse. Except me. While the people in the pub down the road seem to be having a wonderful time, and my family are going on holiday, and the square I live in is empty with people away enjoying staycations, I am still quarantined and nervous at this sudden change of direction. Everyone is moving on, but I still feel guiltily wretched. As we Quakers say, this timely poem 'spoke to my condition'.

> The Sad is feeling it today, it's had enough.
> The Sad is feeling bad for being sad, but no,
> don't talk at the Sad and tell it to buck up
> when the Sad is falling into its own shadow.
> Don't give the Sad the 3rd degree. It runs
> with pain, it bonds with fear and faith, it gets

to grips, applies the balm of sorrow to its own
beleaguered eyes. The Sad will not accept
comparisons, knows only the soft strands
of itself, the briny reaches of the soul.
The Sad understands; it lies down in the hot land
of the heart and weeps: it keeps you whole,
it does the human work. Hold tight. Believe
the Sad, give it some air and let it breathe.

Spot on. How dare we deprive our children of lifelong
comfort and revelation.

10 July 2020

The slogans have an air of desperation about them now.
'Keep our distance, wash our hands, think of others and
play our part. All together.' This one has not had a lot of
coverage – perhaps even the writer felt uneasy about its
clumsiness. Is it still Dominic, I wonder, or is he too busy
planning the destruction of the civil service and the BBC?
I suppose the introduction of the word 'our' is intended to
shift the effect from scary orders to a matey appeal to our
finer feelings.

So, the slogans keep coming at us. This government has
never been great at judging the mood of the country, despite
all its focus groups. Now it appears to have lost its hold
completely.

We are told that, at the start of the pandemic, ministers
hesitated to lock down because they thought the British
population would not comply, and certainly could not
be trusted to sustain the discipline for long. Hence they

were slow off the mark, compared with all the other more successful countries, in containing the virus, at the cost of thousands of lives. Far from not complying, we have taken to it like a bunch of ducks to water, staying in our nests for near on five months. Now they are panicking because we will not come out.

This latest one has really confused us. 'Eat out to help out,' they plead. Is that really a good idea after all the hiding away? We will pay half the bill. Get on public transport, get your hair done, have your eyebrows plucked, go to the pub, get tattoos, anything, anything, so long as you spend money. Richmond, Chiswick, and further afield, are all coming to rowdy life again. People are queuing at Primark to buy more landfill throwaway clothes. One pub open near me in Hammersmith is packed with customers certainly not observing any social distancing rules. Boris Johnson assures us now that he expects 'a significant return to normality by Christmas' and that he is 'hoping for the best and planning for the worst'. So that's all right, then.

1 August 2020

The deaths predictably are going up. Johnson is looking gloomily crumpled. The job, which he visualised as a child as being a beloved 'world king', signing a few papers that Dom put in front of him and playing cricket at Chequers, is actually no fun at all. He says he is now working on a complicated scheme that will pass the buck for keeping his subjects safe to local councils, bosses and us. Since when he is nowhere to be seen. The leader of the opposition, Keir Starmer, struggled to discuss a paper about the threat of a deadly third surge with a vague Johnson. Eventually, in exasperation, he wailed, 'Has the prime minister actually read this document'?

'Waffle waffle – well, of course I am aware of – mm, mm . . .'

Starmer's mouth actually dropped open, as the few people on the benches behind their flailing leader shifted uncomfortably on the green leather.

Prime Minister, we have had enough of your inexplicable changes of direction. You told us, in your early gung-ho days, that masks were a waste of time and we should not bother with them. At the time the medical profession was desperately ill-equipped and all the masks were needed for the NHS. Fair enough. We are grown-ups. If you had just told us that, we would have made our own. As we will now that you have admitted we need them.

Do we want the 'normality' back that you are promising? Some of us would prefer for the moment to be seized to make radical changes. Rather than try to shore up an outgrown retail sector, with shopping malls and superstores, we think we may prefer delivery, and smaller, more friendly shops. Perhaps we would like city centres to be rid of identical chain stores and cafés, and replaced by an eclectic mix of homes, clubs, libraries, specialist shops, family butchers and greengrocers, green spaces and no cars. Never has the public been more ready to rethink a stressful, greedy, crowded existence, and you are just trying to drag us back to the old ways. There are architects and visionaries who have ideas to bring about the way of life that we have tasted and still be commercially viable. Some of us don't want to go back to your concept of normality – an unpleasant everyday normality that most of you have never experienced. There is not much overcrowding in Eton. So no. No go. Not yet. No fear.

3 August 2020

Martin is selling his beautiful estate, which has been a refuge of peace for many of his friends. The time has come for him to move on, so the house is on the market. I feel quite brave venturing out of London to stay with him for one last time. Today a woman came for a viewing. She recognised me, and by a curious coincidence she had, the night before, been watching John in Kavanagh, as well as at the same time reading one of my books. An auspicious start. The estate agent told us that she was moving from Hong Kong, so I tentatively asked if it was because of the current situation with China clamping down on Hong Kong democracy.

'No,' she said, 'my daughter and son-in-law were killed in a car crash in January, and I'm going to bring up their three-year-old son. We need a fresh start.'

I was stunned. She had, in a few months, completely changed her life, and for the sake of her grandson was creating a new one with him. I asked if her husband was still in Hong Kong organising this upheaval, and she said, 'No, he told me he didn't want to look after a two-year-old child, and I haven't seen him, nor do I want to, since that day.' By this time I was distraught for her and in awe of her valour.

She did a tour of the elegant house, walked to the lake and through the woods, and came back ecstatic. She looked me in the eye and said, 'I want it.' I actually cried with delight. I knew that this house which has had so much love poured into it would be a healing place for her and a joyful adventure playground for a child to grow up in. We cracked open a bottle – several, actually – sitting by the swimming pool, to celebrate. As she mellowed, we discovered that she had worked in the law, but was mainly now an ideas woman, backed by Amazon. She had invented edible diamonds, but somebody stole the patent and she was now working on something with Liberty fabrics. In every way – for her work, her grandchild, her visiting daughters, her love of solitude – the house was perfect for her. We were very happy. I hadn't quite grasped all the things she told us, but decided her talent for original inventions came from the sort of slightly eccentric brain that my boring rationality finds difficult to comprehend.

We sat around the pool for a couple of hours discussing how she would adapt one of the barns as a workplace, make the pool secure for Oliver, her three-year-old. Martin explained the quite onerous task of managing the estate – the woods needed managing well, as they supplied the woodchip for the heating system. The wildfowl in the lake have food left on an island that has to be rowed out to in all weathers, and the swimming pool is apt to go green without constant attention. All this she shrugged off, so deeply had she fallen in love with the place that would be her salvation from appalling tragedy. I felt such compassion for this gutsy woman. Notwithstanding coronavirus, I gave her a hug as we said our goodbyes.

After all the excitement we began to mull over the whirlwind three hours. Niggling inconsistencies were explained away. Was the grandchild two or three? Maybe he had had a birthday since January. Her interest in the CCTV cameras, which Martin dismissed as 'not connected, just a deterrent', and her seemingly strange enquiry about a gun room, were explained by a woman on her own in this isolated location needing good security. Again, close examination of the walk-in safe was natural for a rich woman with a Gucci handbag and nice jewellery.

When I went down for breakfast the next morning, my two friends were huddled over a mobile phone.

'We have a problem.'

Philip, Martin's partner, should start a new career as a private detective were he not infinitely more valuable as a paramedic. Through the internet he had discovered the full name of, and one or two pseudonyms for, our new friend, plus the fact that she had served a prison sentence for multiple crimes, ending in an open prison, from which she absconded and committed fifty-one more offences. She had indeed got a job in the law, by pretending to have been to university to get a non-existent law degree. We traced a history of what seemed like petty crime and deception.

So who was she? What was her motivation for spinning a web of lies? Was she staking out the joint for a future burglary? Did she really watch Kavanagh and read my book? Or did she just think that I would be flattered? I discovered that there had been an article in the Daily Mail property magazine, saying that I was a regular visitor to Martin's home. Did she read that and gen up on me? But why? She didn't know I was going to be there. Like all good fraudsters, had she prepared herself for a topic of conversation with the owner, who had declared in the article, 'It is too big for one person'? Did she think she might woo a lonely, very rich man? If so, she was barking up the wrong tree; as Martin pointed out, 'make-up man to the stars' should have given her a clue.

I am haunted by a documentary in which a very intelligent young man seduced a much-respected teacher into thinking that he loved him. The teacher wrote a diary about this 'great love' that he had never dreamed he would have until this beautiful young man entered his world. For two years the teacher was radiantly happy, and then he started being ill. Having got him to change his will and go through a gay wedding ceremony, and convinced the teacher's many ex-students and friends that it was a surprising but wonderful thing to see him so happy, the young man had then started to slowly poison him. He got away with the cruel murder of this deluded teacher until, a while later, he started the same performance with a lonely old woman living a few doors away.

I don't think for a moment our visitor was that sort of evil. I think she was a fantasist. As someone who is brutally, sometimes harshly, honest, this is a mindset that I can't begin to understand. She was with us for three hours, weaving a tragic story around herself. She was completely relaxed and seemed to be enjoying herself. We also traced a young woman, who could have been her daughter, who was involved in a road accident in January, the same time she said Oliver's parents had been killed. In this accident a girl was killed and the young woman, possibly our visitor's daughter, was sent to prison for negligence, leading to a manslaughter charge. From the newspaper report, the prison sentence seemed totally unjustified and counter-productive, but was this the true fact that had catapulted the woman into her invention of a tragic accident?

She said she was going to sort out the finance and would phone the estate agent the next day, but of course she didn't. Nor did she respond to the agent's calls. So we will never have the much-vaunted 'closure' on this.

My theory is that something dreadful happened to her, possibly as a child, that made her own life unbearable, so she invented a new one, and this became a habit. When I was evacuated I created a twin called Wendy, after Sheila had punched a girl and all the girl's brothers were out to get her. 'Don't hit me, it wasn't me – it was Sheila. I'm Wendy, her identical twin.' Sheila became nasty but Wendy was gentle and sweet. I kept up this subterfuge for several months.

The encounter with this woman has affected me profoundly. As an actor I always need to know the character's back story, and I fear I will never discover hers. Does she just like seeing how other people live? She has apparently viewed other houses. Does she hope to slip a watch or some cash into her pocket during the viewing? Nothing was missing after she left. Is she incredibly lonely and this is a way to meet people? I doubt if she often gets the welcome she got from us. Did that affect her? Does the fact that she hasn't made an offer – which she has on other houses and then withdrawn – mean she felt a tiny bit touched by how deep-felt was the sympathy engendered by her lies? Or was she chuckling about how she got one over on the rich bastards?

She has probably forgotten all about the adventure, and moved on to another. But I will never forget her. Or cease, strangely, to care about her. Today I have the worst flare-up of my rheumatoid arthritis since it started three years ago.

I actually can't walk, as my knee is agony if I bend it even slightly. Mine is a systemic illness. It affects my whole being. I will one day get a lot of laughs when I tell the story of this woman, but for now, it hurts.

7 August 2020

I am in danger of losing touch with my grandchildren, so I assured Lola that, if we keep our distance and stay outdoors, we are quite safe to explore London. The centre of London is still deserted, so I have decided to luxuriate in this curious calm before the office workers storm back from their homes, and tourists flock to crowd the pavements and parks again. Lola decided we should start with an area she has passed through but never explored. The centre of government. The hub from which we trust our Members of Parliament, elected, as they keep reminding us, by a vast majority of us, and the prime minister whom they choose for themselves, are sorting out our salvation.

For the first time since lockdown I travelled in my car with a passenger. I wiped down the car with sanitiser, Lola sat in the back, both of us masked, and the windows open, hopefully blowing away any virus. If the virus actually does form globules that may, or may not, float in the air, or possibly land on a surface, which we might touch, and then touch our faces, unless you keep two metres, or maybe one metre, apart, and only meet in the fresh air, and then only facing forwards, and not going indoors, but forming a bubble of only family, or two households, or perhaps four households, or just two people, or maybe six, we should be all right. The blizzard of information about this nasty little killer is always changing, but that is where we are at the moment. I think.

There were even more parking spaces in Westminster than Soho. We started our tour at Victoria Tower Gardens. We had all the literature, and an audio guide, and the weather was perfect, but it did not start well.

There was no one around. Usually there would be workers from the various government offices enjoying a lunch break in the sun, but we were completely alone. We found the statue of the Burghers of Calais and were a little mystified as to why these French guys who defied the cruel English have pride of place next to our seat of government, but decided it was because we are good sports, and Rodin has done a lovely piece of sculpture.

We searched the entire gardens but could not find the memorial to Emmeline and Christabel Pankhurst anywhere. There is a delightful children's adventure playground up one end, but no sign of the militant feminists. Eventually we gave up and crossed over the road to see if we could get into either St Margaret's Chapel or Westminster Abbey. Both were firmly closed. One would have thought they could have recruited a few odd Christians to supervise safe entry given that we are now officially allowed to worship. Primark has managed it. Mammon is obviously more efficient than God.

The Houses of Parliament are entirely enclosed in scaffolding, whilst they work on removing the asbestos, rot and rats from the decaying Palace of Westminster. Perhaps we should just turn it into a museum, and build a new circular House of Commons, where there is no nonsensical uncrossable symbolic line the length of a sword, though shouting and abuse now replace duelling in our adversarial chamber. Since lockdown, Prime Minister's Question Time is being held with a few socially distanced members present, and the rest participating on Zoom. The speaker has said he misses the cut and thrust and fun of a crowded session, but I wonder if, like me, the rest of the electorate are enjoying the recent subdued debating, without all the schoolboy catcalls and infantile point-scoring. It certainly suits the new leader of the opposition, Keir Starmer, whose quiet, methodical, facts-based arguments put poor Boris Johnson in a terrible tither of lies and incomprehensibility.

Lola and I were the only people on the grass of Parliament Square, apart from a few coppers chatting near Churchill's statue, stationed to protect it from the Black Lives Matters supporters, who are attacking statues of slave owners and racists. The coppers were backed up by three very bedraggled men draped in Union Jacks, ready to stand up for Winnie, although, judging by the bottles around their feet, it was wiser to remain seated. I have never been close to the Churchill statue and Lola and I were staggered by its massive bulk. I think he would have liked it. Even his valiant, supportive wife, who destroyed a brutally truthful portrait of him by Graham Sutherland, might have approved. I wonder if she would have been so protective of him when, after he died, it was revealed he almost certainly had an affair with a woman he met in the South of France.

We wandered around the statues of impressive men, like Gandhi, Lloyd George and Mandela when – lo and behold – there was a woman.

Standing resolutely among the men, since 2018, is Millicent Fawcett, holding a banner quoting from the speech she gave after the death of Emily Davison at the 1913 Epsom Derby: 'Courage calls to courage everywhere.' Engraved on the plinth are a job lot of names of fifty-five women and four men who fought for the rights of women, showing every bit as much courage as any of the men standing grandly on the other plinths in the square. The courage to suffer imprisonment, verbal abuse and assault by the police and passers-by when arrested, being held down whilst a thick tube was thrust down their throats into their stomachs and choking liquid food poured down it. Courage to withstand prejudice and ridicule and the apathetic condescension of the political class of the time, including Asquith, the prime minister. Lloyd George's statue raises its arm in protest at the presence of these women who actually bombed his house. Still no Pankhursts. Maybe the powers that be melted them down to make Millie? We should not be greedy. After all, 2.7 per cent of statues in this country are of women, not counting royalty. We must not get above ourselves.

Millicent Fawcett was known as a suffragist rather than a suffragette, as she rejected a violent approach. She did not go to Regent Street with an ice pick to break all the windows, or chain herself to railings, or throw herself under a horse, but quietly campaigned persistently, at the same time supporting her blind husband in his liberal political endeavours. I have sympathy, pacifist though I am, with the suffragettes, who were tired of this measured approach. They wanted 'deeds not words'. Dogged Millicent Fawcett spent her whole life fighting in campaigns for many causes – against child abuse and the appalling concentration camps for families of the Boers, and in favour of higher education for women and fair treatment of prostitutes.

I have profound admiration for women like her, and her sisters. Well-educated, dedicated reformers, part of the now somewhat maligned middle class, which is behind much progress in the world. At the beginning of the pandemic, the television news featured a story on two hearty country women who were taking food to a row of cottages near their homes. The people who answered the door were astounded and grateful, and one of the women said, with touching honesty, that she was ashamed that only now did she realise how neglected these people were, and she would make sure in future that everyone knew each other better. She was the sort of woman who will do that with dedication. She will be called bossy, interfering, a busybody, a do-gooder and nowadays a virtue-signaller, but she will just get on with it, because she, and those of her ilk, are just kind and good.

Millicent Fawcett's whole family of ten siblings were activists, relentlessly arguing and writing about their demands. One of their suffragist friends, Emily Davies, co-founder of Girton, the first women's college in Cambridge, was once talking to Millicent Fawcett and her sister Elizabeth Garrett Anderson, who became the country's first woman doctor. Emily is reported as saying to them both: 'It is quite clear what has to be done. I must devote myself to securing higher education, while you, Lizzie, open up the medical profession to women. After these things are done, we must see about getting the vote' – whereupon she turned to Millicent Fawcett: 'You are younger than we are, Millie, so you must attend to that.' All of which the three of them did.

Wonderful. Lola and I looked at Millicent's statue, and read their names on the base, with pride and gratitude. Good on you, girls. A hundred years late, so about bloody time.

We then sauntered down Whitehall. The audio guide Lola found on her phone warned us it would be difficult to cross to the Cenotaph because of the mass of traffic. There was hardly a car or bus in sight.

We pressed our noses against the iron railings at the end of Downing Street and stared in at the grim men in full protective gear, carrying evil-looking guns. I reminisced about the days when the public could wander up to the famous front door and watch the comings and goings of famous folk and more lowly secretaries and other staff – even having a chat with them. Especially the one sole copper standing benignly by the front door.

I have several times been to grand functions inside. At one I chatted to Rudolf Nureyev, who proved to be wickedly mortal in real life but obviously took some magic elixir before going onto the stage and turning into a god. On another occasion I was invited to the fairly ordinary flat in which the prime minister actually lives, the rest of the house being for receptions and office work. Tony Blair was chatting up a few lefties before the next election campaign, and I was disturbed by what I thought was a policy to appease Rupert Murdoch. I voiced my unease, supported by Maureen Lipman and several others, and Tony was not best pleased. The sad truth was that he was right that the press could make or break a political party, certainly before social media, and in order to get anything done you have to be in office. It's no good being highly principled and constantly in opposition, something I have argued about the disastrous Jeremy Corbyn. Despite this slight dispute, his much-criticised, admirable wife, Cherie, was gracious enough to attend John's memorial. Lola and I hung around by the railings for some time, hoping Boris or someone recognisable would drive, or maybe cycle, through the gate, but like everyone else they had disappeared, and no one went through the hallowed door at all.

We wandered up the street, passing the Trafalgar Studios, as the Whitehall Theatre is now called, still with its stage photos outside but, like all of the London theatres, closed, or, as we say, 'dark'. The situation regarding the theatre is dire, as it is impossible to make a show financially viable if social distancing in the auditorium means fewer bums on seats.

I imagined the desperate sadness the cast must have felt on the night the company manager told them to pack away their make-up and go home indefinitely. Actors are now trying to create things on phones and iPads and in pub gardens, but there is no paid work at all in the theatre, and many are packing shelves in supermarkets – if they are lucky.

I found the dusty deadness of this theatre particularly upsetting, as, when it was called the Whitehall, it was famous for its farces. Brian Rix led a superbly skilled company of actors in plays, often by Ray Cooney, that made this building shake with laughter. I myself did a TV play here with Dickie Henderson and Brian, from whom I learned the technique of not just a double but a triple take.

At the end of Whitehall we stopped to look at a deserted Trafalgar Square, and found it hard to believe that it was eighteen years ago that a four-year-old Lola, with her little brother Jack and cousin Molly-Mae, let off a host of balloons saying goodbye to their grandad, after a glorious remembrance ceremony in St Martin-in-the-Fields. We brought a crowded square to a standstill. I am pretty sure Lola does not really remember much about it. We talk of him often, though. And I feel his presence every day. Usually, as today in the square, with a smile on my face.

Lola and I felt our mood lift as we turned into St James's Park. For many years I had only driven past it on the Mall and Birdcage Walk. In the past, when appearing in the West End in the summer, some of us would take a sandwich and go, between the matinee and the evening shows, to listen to the music playing on the bandstand in the park, but I have not walked round it in decades. Today it is ablaze with borders of summer flowers, and the fountains are cascading brilliance on the lakes, whilst the hundreds of birds make up for the lack of humans by crowding the shores, showing off their feathers. The park is renowned for its collection of rare waterfowl and don't they know it, strutting and flapping right up to your feet, noisily demanding to know where everyone has gone with their titbits and admiration. Lola and I were a poor substitute for hundreds of tourists and government staff.

On a little island, Duck Island, is a rustic cottage with a perfect small country garden of flowers and vegetables. We were told the Birdman, one of the staff, lives there, in which case, I want that job. I will happily feed the pelicans and chase off the foxes. I would have a perfect view of any events on the Horse Guards Parade, and up the Mall at the Palace. Once it opens again, I could even do a play in the evening at the Trafalgar Studios, just round the corner. It would be the best digs ever. Except, of course, in normal times, there would be hundreds of people around, not just me and the birds. So perhaps not so ideal.

On our next stop, on the other hand, we found what really would be our perfect home. If you walk along Birdcage Walk towards the Palace, there is a little passageway on the left leading to heaven. Queen Anne's Gate, particularly at the moment with no parked cars, all the owners being locked down in their country or overseas estates, looks just as it did when it was built in around 1700. Standing looking at the exquisite detail on the elegant houses, with no sound but birds, and a very distant low hum of traffic, it is breathtaking. Literally. We found ourselves talking in whispers. As we crept awestruck around this secret area, we decided that, of all places in our capital, this is where we want to live. We were in luck. Lola's phone informed us that one of the houses overlooking Birdcage Walk and St James's Park at the back is on the market. For £41,500,000. So, I hope some work turns up soon. The royalties of £57.38 on the DVD sales of Bleak House, which is all I've earned in the last months, falls somewhat short.

Lola said, 'It's all so close together.'

With no crowds to push through, or traffic to impede us, it is true that a short walk encompasses the majesty of the Gothic grandeur of State and Church, the wealth of treasures in art galleries and the site of public protest and celebration in Trafalgar Square, the horticultural beauty of a park with lakes and fountains and multitudinous rare birds, and an unspoiled architectural gem from the eighteenth century.

'Isn't London lovely?' said Lola.

It is, it is, and it has taken an ugly virus to remind me how much I love it.

1 September 2020

Things are on the move. Fast. I drove into Chiswick this morning for the first time in a couple of weeks. Two of the roads that I drive down seemed strangely devoid of traffic. I had seen plenty of temporary barriers marking out cycle lanes before, but only when I parked in a back street and read the new signs at the end of these two roads did I discover that they are now closed to cars and motorcycles. No warning, no public meetings – not even on Zoom. Seemingly overnight, planters with green leaves have appeared, blocking all the parking places, and the road is open for cyclists and pedestrians only. The High Road, as a result, is at a standstill.

My first reaction was rage – I am used to feeling fury about idiots in Lycra who jump lights, and sneak up on the inside of your car, and then swear if you don't see them – then delight. Must be the pandemic effect. There will be, is already, on social media, outrage from motorists, but I will put my money where my mouth is and force myself to use public transport or walk, whenever my unreliable joints will allow me. It is a great first step. Now the council has to choose carefully how they replace the empty shops and cafés in the streets that they have closed, so that people will go there to enjoy the ambience that a lack of cars can provide.

There has to be a major rethink of transport in our area. Hammersmith Bridge has now been closed to traffic for months, and a couple of weeks ago another dangerous crack in its ancient structure was caused by the heatwave, so it is now closed to bikes and pedestrians, and boats are even barred from going under it. The nearest crossable bridges either side are miles away, so just to get to the other side of the river, with the doubling-up of traffic, is a journey of about an hour. Just to cross the Thames. The water buses have stopped and people planning holiday boat trips to the City or the coast will have to make do with the upper reaches of the Thames. I have quite enjoyed watching posh yachts sailing by, the people on deck quaffing Champers, only to be stopped abruptly by the rude honk of the rusty old ship straddling the river by the bridge, barring their passage, then coming back past me again, the guests and crew shouting and gesticulating in disbelief. The closure is a terrible inconvenience for the locals. We will have to resort to swimming across, or reinstate the old tradition of the ferry man. Some lads were already running rickshaw rides across the bridge before the latest closure. Maybe this is taking slowing down our lifestyle too far.

The other big step forward for me is the decision to film two more episodes of our canal programme. It will be quite tricky to keep two metres apart on a narrowboat, but with strict testing, wearing masks when possible, and constant hand-washing, disinfecting and finger-crossing, Channel 4 have decided to take the risk. I am delighted. I need work. I need the creativity, the comradeship, the fun, the excitement of making a show. I am a bit nervous about it. It is a big jump from months of isolation to being crammed in a boat, and meeting and interviewing a wide variety of people, but the challenge of inventing a whole new approach to filming is exciting. I am proud that my industry is finding new and innovative ways of surviving.

11 October 2020

The most uplifting event for me is the opening of our new Quaker meeting house. Fourteen years ago we were told our place of worship was to be knocked down, first to be replaced by a Tesco store, and several revisions later to accommodate a car park for the new development of Hammersmith Town Hall (which I forgive, for they are still flying a European flag). We can sit in a silent gathering anywhere – a specific building is not necessary. Nevertheless, Quakers have a tradition of creating lovely homes for themselves, and we decided to erect one nearby that fitted our era. After endless discussion, and much dedication by a few, we now have a state-of-the-art, environmentally visionary place of great beauty, and we move in next week. It is sad that because of the coronavirus we cannot, as we planned, throw open our doors to everyone, and celebrate with our new neighbours, but we are determined to use this lovely home to serve and, maybe, help repair and progress our world. Quakers are good at supporting those in need, and I am sure our new meeting house will be a refuge, and an engine for change. We had a socially distanced last meeting for worship in our old premises, to say goodbye and thank you. I remembered nineteen years ago calling upon Friends to 'hold in the light' my four-year-old grandson Jack as he underwent a radical operation for a brain tumour at Great Ormond Street Hospital. He starts his first teaching job next week.

2021

January 2021

The reaction to the announcement of my damehood has been astonishing. All the letters and emails from people from my past and present swept away my embarrassment with their obvious delight. It was like reading one's own obituary but doubtless a lot more loving than the real one will be.

February 2021

In lockdown three, my life continues to be a tragicomedy.

Just before Christmas two of my daughters arrived with my present. They both looked a bit nervous and at first I didn't see what it was. Nestled in Jo's hand was a tiny jet-black kitten. 'We thought you needed company.'

They piled into my house baskets, litter trays, furry beds, scientific kitten food and pussycat toys. I have always had cats and love them, so was bewitched by my tiny frightened new friend. He had been taken from his mother too soon and was very needy. There followed hours of rescuing him, comforting him, playing endless games, teaching him to use the litter tray, stopping him biting, tending the scratches on my legs and hands, bending, twisting, lifting, until last week my eighty-eight-year-old body revolted and I felt an excruciating pain in my back. Used to pain with rheumatoid arthritis, I thought that I could cope, but I couldn't. An MRI has revealed I have a compression fracture in my spine. Serious stuff. So darling Bobby has been found a new home and is now very happy to be with two adoring little girls rather than a grumpy old woman. And I have to cope with a new battle with my body.

March 2021

Forcing myself to keep active. On my morning walk along the river, I stood outside William Morris's home and thought of Auntie Ruby. When I was a child, Ruby lived in Red House Lane in Bexleyheath, opposite a mysterious big house set behind a six-foot wall, which we all had to give a wide berth during the war. It was only years later that I realised it was William Morris's house, a wonderful example of his work, and possibly a centre for covert operations during the war.

Ruby was not my real aunt. That was Auntie Cis, short, I believe, for Cecilia, whom I met on rare occasions and did not like very much. Cis was my father's sister, but there was no love lost between them. Her beautiful face had been ravaged by childhood smallpox, which may also have accounted for her withdrawn manner. Or was it her relationship with the besuited woman she lived with, Auntie Teddy, that made her uncommunicative in those unenlightened times? I only know that having tea with them in their gloomy house in Bromley was a scary ordeal. The real role of auntie in my life was taken by dear Ruby, my mother's loving best friend.

Auntie Ruby was a spinster who lived a blameless life. A member of the Women's Voluntary Service, she was a firefighter during the war, and continued to serve her community in peacetime. She ran a small business and it was suspected that the owner, who died and left it to her, had been in love with her. Or maybe I made that up. I inherited a blue sapphire engagement-type ring from her, which probably prompted the romantic idea. (Such a situation would never have been discussed within the family.) Auntie Ruby seemed to me the height of elegance. She was a cut above my family. Her father had been a high-ranking naval man and her mother was a sweet rosy apple of a woman. I often stayed with them, or visited for meals, when my parents' work made it necessary.

Just when I needed it, Auntie Ruby opened my young mind to simple pleasures and social responsibility. She had a car, a dear little grey box of an Austin 7 in which she would take me on trips to see the Kent orchards in bloom. She also took me up to London to the ballet and plays, the highlight of these trips being an ice-cream sundae at Lyons Corner House. She gave me books I could own, not just borrow from the library. She was politically aware, and introduced me to things my overworked parents had neither the time nor the energy to dwell on.

After her parents' deaths, having tenderly cared for them in old age, she moved to a pleasant flat overlooking a cricket ground. Teas with her were a blissful contrast to those with Auntie Cis – bone china cups of fragrant tea, and pretty plates of home-made Victoria sponge, eaten to the sound of a cricket match, which we watched but neither of us entirely understood. I always left with a beautiful perfumed rose from the flats' communal garden, which of course Auntie Ruby supervised and tended.

She enriched my understanding, and that of several other children she took under her wing. When she died she left a note to say that we were not to be sad, because she had had a wonderful life, and I think that was true. She was a fulfilled woman whose apparent lack of a conventional partner was amply recompensed by her many other relationships, mainly with children. Later she sat with me by my mother's, and then my first husband's, deathbeds. She was quite simply one of those middle-class good women I have spoken of before.

February 2021

John always said that, if it had not been for two teachers who encouraged him to become an actor, he would've been a criminal. I've been enjoying rereading a letter from a radio listener that shows me how far he came.

'Dear Sheila,

'I would like to say how much I enjoyed your interview on BBC Radio 2. It prompted me to share with you a little anecdote from my childhood which I thought you might like.

'I was raised in Burnage, Manchester in the 1950s & 60s, as just another council house kid. But I have to say I am quite proud of our heritage of successful people from the area. The Gallaghers, the actor and musician Max Beesley, and of course, the most famous of all, your wonderful actor husband John Thaw.

'A story you may be interested in concerns a young boy, sent on an errand to fetch a gallon can of paraffin for the kitchen heater by his Mum, to the Handy Shop on Kingsway, in said Burnage (John would have known it well, it was the local "we sell everything" shop). Having arrived at my destination (you may have guessed by now I was the young lad in question) I reached into my pocket only to find the crispy new folded green pound note I had been given, with strict instructions to "keep a tight hold", was not there! I searched fervently through all of my pockets to no avail. Now, if you knew my Mother, a scouse lady with matching "temperament", and indeed my Police Officer Father, you would have known that to return home without the fuel, and more importantly the correct coinage in change, was definitely NOT an option!

'My only recourse was to re-trace my path to the shop, searching, vainly, for the missing note. Crossing the road in what I estimated to be the approximate place I had crossed before, I glanced up to see a young man stooping to pick something up from the pavement. At this point I should say that whilst I cannot claim to have known John personally, I knew him vaguely by reputation. You must understand that Burnage, being a relatively small, suburban community, most of the local population knew something, perhaps too much, of one another's business. He was the elder of those boys from the bottom flat who looked out for his kid brother because they had no Mum at home, and their Dad was a lorry driver. Hmm, not to be messed with!

'Quickly, I assessed my options. Return home with floods of tears and a severe grovelling act, (unthinkable), run away to sea, (better by far than facing the wrath of my Mum), or suicide. Well, given the look of "it's my lucky day" on the face of the big guy (John of course), it seemed a sure bet he had recovered my lost treasure. So, somewhat bravely I have to say, I addressed my fears and plucked up the courage to stutter, "Excuse me, but was that a pound note, my pound note, you just picked up?" . . . and closed my eyes waiting with bated breath for the reply.

'To my great surprise, I was relieved to see the lost pound being thrust into my outstretched hand, accompanied by a wry smile and a rather severe, "You ought to be more careful!"

'Needless to say, there was a distinct skip in my step as I returned home with the fuel, thinking "life is good, and those Thaws are not such bad people after all". And, as my Mother carefully scrutinised the change for the correct amount, I was secure in the knowledge that there were just two people in the whole world aware of my day's adventures.

'As I watch the reruns of the excellent Morse series, I often recall that day, and also, were John around to read this tale, even though he may not remember it, I like to think it would bring back that same wry smile.

'I hope this gives you a little giggle, Sheila, and may I take this opportunity to wish you much success with your new play,

'Donald Brown (a fan)'

It did give me a giggle, but also respect for Donald and all the other people that make good from unpromising backgrounds. I met one of the Gallagher boys on a chat show, and his cocky walk and wary, slightly dangerous, air reminded me so much of John.

April 2021

I am finding this new venturing out into the big wide world very difficult. The effort of making myself look presentable, finding things to talk about other than coronavirus, looking beyond the four walls of my house, is proving a challenge. Today my friend Julie organised a trip to help me out of my shell.

Julie has always enhanced our friendship by dreaming up lovely outings for myself and her husband, Simon. She finds all the best restaurants and shows, organising our visits impeccably. She is a perfect travel companion. Like me, she is an avid guidebook addict; she is even more voracious for new experiences than I, and I sometimes trail behind her, as John did me. Even on the earwigging stakes she exceeds my effrontery. Years ago, sitting in Florian, the café in St Mark's Square, we watched and listened to a classic Death in Venice scenario: beautiful young Italian boy leading ageing American man a hell of a dance. Said American offering all sorts of goodies, beautiful boy shrugging indifferently, exquisite lips pouting. Eventually beautiful boy flounces out of the café, American pays the bill and flies after him. And so does Julie. Even my nosiness wouldn't stretch to sleuthing so diligently. She came back, breathless, to recount heart-rending scenes, before she lost track of them.

Today she arranged a glorious outing to a hotel called Gravetye Manor, which is ingeniously providing gourmet picnics in its spacious grounds, obeying all the social distancing rules. The food came in a box full of exquisite vegan goodies, the wine was poured by masked and gloved waiters, and everyone kept two metres away from one another.

The garden is one of the most beautiful I know. Everything is underplanted so that a bed of tulips stands proud above buttercups and bluebells. The impression is of a wild garden but it's actually planned with consummate skill. The trees are a medley of leaf and bark colour and shapes and one wonders at the generosity of the people who designed a garden that they themselves would never see in its full glory. I was overwhelmed with gratitude towards these ancestors that had laboured to provide balm for a later generation's pain.

9 April 2021

Prince Philip died today aged ninety-nine. He has been ill for a while so it is no surprise. What is a surprise is the man that emerges from all the tributes. I fear he has been unfairly treated. He was not just the gaffe-making joker he was portrayed as. He actually worked hard to promote British industry and manufacturing, and in the process avidly studied the subjects he involved himself in and made excellent speeches at events that he organised. He was not just a man who walked two steps behind his wife.

Prince Philip did his best to modernise the monarchy, having been a victim of its old-fashioned attitudes when his wife became queen. It seems he welcomed Diana into the fold and tried to support her. I suspect the royal family, and above all its advisers, are finding it hard to adapt to new ways. The people who look after them come mainly from their own class – sometimes jobs are handed down from parents to children – nor are there many black or brown faces to be seen at Buckingham Palace, but I am sure that will change.

I put some of Prince Philip's more dodgy remarks down to being a member of the upper classes. They are so ill-informed as to what is unacceptable language. Prince Andrew's teeth-gritting interview about his friendship with Jeffrey Epstein was a classic example of upper-class-twit talk. The prince's self-awareness, and his awareness of ordinary people, was so awry that he could not see how disastrous his pizza-in-Woking stuff was, on every level. I am pretty sure he thought all those appalling folk he mixed with were rather jolly, and that the young girl he cavorted with was there because she liked him. His 'honour' was to stand by his friend even if he was a convicted sex offender.

The upper classes are big on loyalty to their own and sticking up for their friends. I am touched by the story of Nicholas Elliott, who considered Kim Philby a friend, both being alumni of Trinity College, Cambridge, and members of the old-boy network. Elliott requested that he should be entrusted with a last private meeting with Philby, the day before his arrest as a spy, to get a full confession from him. Philby duly spilled out his guilt to his friend, but postponed signing the written confession till they next met. Trusting upper-class loyalty and honour, Elliott left. Philby defected to Russia the next day. There is a naivety in these old-fashioned values of honour and loyalty that can be dangerous, but as embodied in our Queen they work.

I am of a generation that has a respect and affection for the royal family that is difficult to lose. I know the organisation has to change and it will probably become redundant.

I cannot give a logical reason why, but that saddens me. I am glad it won't happen till after I am dead and gone, for I have little confidence in some of the ideas about what will take its place.

18 April 2021

My darling friend Brenda died today. Her son tells me she had all my books on her bedside table. I hope they made her realise how deeply I loved her.

May 2021

On my way to one of my endless visits to Charing Cross Hospital, I go through a really scrubby little park with mounds reminiscent of those left from piled-up air-raid destruction rubble. This spring, as every spring, it is transfigured by a beautiful perfume.

It reminds me of France, where we discovered that a similar perfume came from a tree by our house that was alive with frantically working bees. Denis identified it as un tilleul – a linden tree. Ellie Jane and I have become slightly obsessed with these – apart from their fragrance – rather unimpressive trees.

I have always liked trees. There is a gigantic oak that grows in our hameau. Estimates of its age vary wildly between 300 and 800 years. Even, as I tell the children of our community, older than me. I visit it regularly to lie against its slightly sloping trunk, trying to absorb its strength. Nowadays my back does not lie so flat, slightly humped over as it is by the weight of life's burdens. My fracture will make it even more difficult when I am eventually allowed back to my French home. When I try to embrace the tree, my arms stretch barely a third of the way round its trunk and my fingers delve two inches into its gnarled bark. It is alongside an ancient track and I wonder how many generations have lingered in its shade. Occasionally what seem like votive offerings appear in its roots, grotesque clay heads and animals and a precarious pile of stones. No one, not even Denis, knows who puts them there and this is a place where everyone knows one another. Maybe folk come from afar, maybe even the shades of the Gavots who, centuries ago, came to our precious plot looking for work in the fields, worship our tree, and we all accept that it is its due, and the offerings are left until they eventually crumble away into the sacred earth beneath, awaiting the next tribute.

I treasure a print of a Van Gogh painting that hangs on the wall of my house in France. It is a picture of an old couple in a wood. Van Gogh shows rows of stark tree trunks, with a strange-looking tiny couple standing deep in colourful, burgeoning undergrowth with no route through it. On his last visit to France, John and I were sitting on the sofa whilst I carried out a medical procedure which we usually did with laughter covering our concern, but on this occasion John stared long and hard at the Van Gogh. He used to jokingly say the couple was us. Now he said very solemnly, 'That definitely is us. Lost in the woods but it is still beautiful, kid.' I responded with some joke. I discovered later that Van Gogh committed suicide a month after painting it. Maybe John recognised the artist's state of mind whilst he was working on it and identified with the figure of the man standing amongst the tangled undergrowth wearing a top hat and funereal black. Which begs the question whether, despite his apparent denial that he was dying, the superhuman effort I made to shield him from the truth was a terrible mistake. Was he doing the same for me? Did he hope I might understand his interpretation of the picture? He also stopped listening to his beloved classical music some months before he died because 'I don't want to get weepy.' Maybe I should have talked more about death, the most important challenge of all our lives. On the other hand, perhaps it was best that he turned his back on death as he had always done with anything that troubled him. And that I did the same.

Together we found a way through the forest.

May 2021

Really glad to be back on a canal boat with Gyles. When I fractured my spine I lost two inches in stature and gained a bit of a hump in my back which they told me couldn't be made better. They were wrong. With the memory of my sister's determination and lots of physio I can now stand up more or less straight but have to be careful when I bend forward, which has been a perfect excuse on our latest canal trip to force Gyles to do all the crouchy things on the boat, grovelling around on the floor, while I stand looking noble at the tiller.

One of the hardest things as you get older is admitting defeat. I hate having to say I can't do things or I feel tired. This is the woman that climbed a mountain, for God's sake. The other day the boat was about two feet above the footpath and I had to admit I could not safely jump down.

There was some unkind comfort in the fact that Gyles, who is over ten years younger than I, did jump, fell flat on his face and got a black eye.

'Pride cometh before a fall,' said his wife.

June 2021

I had a long chat with Jack. It is deeply satisfying for me that my grandson has chosen to enter the profession that is the most important for our country's future. The pandemic has revealed to the public the huge divisions and injustice in our education system. In the mixed school where he teaches he has the challenge of helping some kids who, during the extended absence from lessons, have been coached by loving parents with the help of virtual learning, whilst others have had no access to a screen, with parents either unequipped to help them or in some cases unwilling. There will be those kids for whom lockdown was nothing but trapped abuse, away from the protection of their teachers, who in these days have to double as social workers.

News of positive change comes from, would you believe, Eton. There is a new headmaster, Simon Henderson, since I visited with the children from Tower Hamlets, and he seems to be genuinely aware of the schism in children's education that the coronavirus has exposed. What's more, he is taking steps to put his ideas into practice. Back in the first lockdown he allotted £100 million to support less advantaged children, laying on free digital study courses, so that now 115,000 children and increasing all the time, around the country, did the same lessons as Etonians. Key workers' children, and some who are vulnerable, attended

Eton College during the lockdown. No doubt this has unsettled some of the parents who pay £42,000 a year to give their boys an elite education, but he says, 'I feel the right thing now is to share our wealth, resources and expertise. It is the right example to set our boys.'

It would be easy to sneer, as I once did, that Eton is just trying to justify its existence. That it is paternalistic. But I don't want it to be abolished. I want some of that for all children. There is a portrait of a teacher there with, above it, a Latin quote that translates as: 'The excellence of a teacher is to identify differences in talent.' That is my ideal. It is what the comprehensives were intended to do. Accept that every child is talented, and should be taught to be the very best of their personal ability. And no talent is any better than another. We have discovered in the last year that we cannot manage without care workers. They should receive an Eton-standard education in their very skilled jobs, as well as all the lifestyle delights like art, music and sport to give quality to their lives. If Simon Henderson is making things happen to give more children a share in Eton's wonderful education, which it is, whatever the opponents say, I am with him all the way. Maybe change will come from the top down. At least all the other Etonians in top places will listen to him. I don't give an idealistic damn how it happens, as long as it does.

So, is change beginning to happen? Certainly we are more aware that it is needed. In my profession the changes are fundamental. Everything is digital. During lockdown I have done television interviews, made little films at home on my laptop. I linked up with a producer and director in Los Angeles, two actors in Madrid and two in London, to do a reading of a potential film script online. It was as if we were in the room together. Extraordinary. Rather a nice script that will probably never be made, but it was an enjoyable adventure. The film is about a relationship struck up between an old lady with the virus, and a young exhausted doctor. We all chipped in with ideas, and I managed most of the mechanics of recording something in three different places. It went quite well, but nothing replaces being together in the flesh.

One thing that came out of that film job was a poem by Kitty O'Meara that the producer, Darwin, sent me.

And the people stayed home.
And read books, and listened, and rested, and
exercised, and made art, and played games, and
learned new ways of being, and were still.
And listened more deeply.
Some meditated, some prayed, some danced.
Some met their shadows.
And the people began to think differently.

And the people healed.
And, in the absence of people living in ignorant,
dangerous, mindless, and heartless ways, the earth
began to heal.

And when the danger passed, and the people joined
together again, they grieved their losses, and made
new choices, and dreamed new images, and created
new ways to live and heal the earth fully, as they had
been healed.

I feel it starting. We are exploring the new.

June 2021

Had a lovely message from Jonny, an invaluable friend, who had seen an interview I did in Chichester Theatre last November which has now been streamed – whatever that is. When the director of This Is My Family, Daniel Evans, asked me to do it, I was embarrassed. It was to be about my career in musicals. 'What career in musicals? I didn't know I had one.' But the interviewer, Edward Seckerson, had done a massive amount of homework and dug up clips from many shows I have appeared in over the past sixty years. Including a wonderful clip from a secret recording of the last night of Sweeney Todd, in which I heard the audience going wild as I came on stage and started my opening number. The reaction was deafening and, in true Theatre Workshop style, I told them to shut up because I couldn't hear the band. Then, after a chat with the conductor, and resetting the pies I had to make during the number, we started again. Stephen Sondheim would have been gnashing his teeth. The audience reaction was ecstatic, and listening to it affected me deeply to realise that I had received such love from an audience.

In some of the other clips, which I was forced to listen to despite my phobia about seeing or hearing any work I have done, it was like listening to someone else. And unexpectedly I thought that someone else was rather good. It was like seeing young photos of yourself from a time when you agonised that you were ugly, only to discover that actually you were quite pretty. Or at least had nice teeth. I felt enormous regret that all those years I had not appreciated the generosity of audiences, and allowed myself to feel some pride. My regular advice to my embryo-actor grandchild Lola is: 'Enjoy it.'

On the day we recorded the interview, I took a break before we started and wandered over to the cathedral. I was allowed in although it was officially closed to visitors because of Covid. I had it to myself. It was a disturbing experience. I was aware of generations of people entombed here, their often important lives over, and in most cases forgotten. Maybe, like my sister in the notebook I found by her body in 2017 BC – Before Coronavirus – they wondered, in old age, what it was all about.

Me too. I wonder. Who am I? What have I done with my numerous years' worth of living? Materially, between us, John and I achieved more than our parents could have imagined. I sit here writing this on the balcony of a stylish house overlooking the Thames in London. John's mother, Dolly, a woman with star quality, who deserted her sons to try to achieve her potential, ended up alone and in poverty, unfairly hated by the lad for whom her genes, and inadvertently her behaviour, had provided the spur for his comparatively stratospheric success. The lad's father, coal miner, lorry driver, wheeler dealer, was able to share in his achievement with profound but wryly dismissive awe. My parents were happy to end up in a comfortable mobile home, in a caravan park, where Dad worked part-time in the bar and Mum became president of the local Women's Union. They too were proud of, but afraid for, their high-flying daughter, with her extraordinarily luxurious way of life.

None of them would have deduced that their children's achievements were due to the seeds they sowed. The desire to please them, to make them proud, or in John's case with poor Dolly, to show her what she had rejected. John did very well indeed, and, at least in those musicals, I did not let my parents down completely. We have not done badly.

But who cares?

Success, as defined by the world, now means little to me. Money, name in lights, even – forgive my ungraciousness – damehood. Ironically, nearing the end as I am, I find that it is completely irrelevant what I personally have, or have not, achieved for myself. The test is whether I have, like our parents, intentionally or inadvertently, passed on something that will contribute to the future.

I do not remember any other time when we have had the stark option of ominous disaster or, potentially, glorious change. We thought the atom bomb might end civilisation, but so far it has not. Although it is still there and so are the madmen. What we are now doing to our planet, and to one another, could, I honestly believe, destroy us. There is a possibility that life once existed on Mars. We too could end up as a dead star shooting round the sky, all its magnificent achievements wiped out. Or, maybe, providentially, the seismic shock of this worldwide pandemic could be the blessing that will save us and propel us into a period of regeneration.

It will be a hard fight to convince some that change is necessary. Donald Trump has gone from office, but he is holding rallies with an eye on a return to the presidency. He has already done irreparable harm and must be kept from doing more. Depressingly, I understand some old Etonians are doing their best to discredit and get rid of their visionary head. In Chiswick, most people have been enjoying the closed roads, new street cafés and cycle lanes, only to find that some Tory councillor has rallied the scheme's ill-informed opponents and the streets are going to be given back to the polluting cars. A tragedy. If we are to survive we have to make sacrifices. Alter the whole ethos of the profit motive and embrace simpler lives. Challenge the party system that has resulted in such nincompoops at the helm. I can't believe I am saying this, but the disgraced Dominic Cummings might be the most radical thinker we have. It's a shame that he is so unpleasant because we need an inspirational leader with new ideas. It will be a massive challenge.

I, of course, will not be here to see that change if it happens, and I am too old to be much help, but I sense something is happening of which I might live to see the beginning. My contribution has been made. For some unknown reason, which cannot be my parenting, my three daughters, together with their partners and my eight grandchildren, are ready for a new start. They are thinking, observing, marching, planning, learning, teaching, determined. It is no longer a right/left political struggle as it was in my youth; it is much broader than that. Change will take a long time, but they and their contemporaries are ready to go.

It is impossible to gauge exactly what each of us have contributed to posterity. I know nothing of the lives of the 10th Earl of Arundel and his wife, Eleanor of Lancaster, but I know about their deaths. In Chichester I several times visited the Arundel tomb mentioned in Philip Larkin's poem, and I was as moved by it as he was. The fact that Larkin has been revealed as a racist and anti-Semite for me adds even more potency to the lines he wrote; it is as though he is challenging himself to think the best of mankind. What touched me most was that the earl has one of his gloves in the other hand.

One sees, with a sharp tender shock,
His hand withdrawn, holding her hand.

He has taken it off before putting out his bare hand to his wife, which she has reached across her body to hold. Was he in need of comfort, or offering support to the woman lying by his side? Either way I find the gesture has more resonance, thinking back about it now, than when I first saw it.

Never has there been more need for each and every one of us to take off our gloves, and reach out to support each other, to make sure that 'what will survive of us is love'.

Love of all the creatures, the brilliance, the beauty, the overwhelming magnificence of this well-worth-saving planet on which I have been privileged to exist for eighty-eight years.

Old Rage paperback

I have somehow agreed to add a few diary entries for 2021 and 2022 for the paperback of this book. I am already regretting my decision. In the avalanche of awful, ludicrous, tragic, inspiring, downright weird events of the last two years, how do I select just a few occasions? Well, I suppose I could start, as I did last time, with my damehood.

9 November 2021

Any qualms I had about my worthiness for a damehood were banished by the sheer delight of this day. I prepared for it with my usual lack of grace towards compliments, then ended up basking in them. I was persuaded by my daughters that I needed a new outfit for the occasion, but refused to go shopping, so a super-calm stylist, Rachel Fanconi, brought things to my house and draped my reluctant, grumpy person in a selection of fabulous gowns. Eventually we settled for a trouser suit that was comfortable as well as, I had to admit, extremely elegant. She also persuaded a jeweller, Hancocks – sadly no relation – in one of my favourite London places, Burlington Arcade, to loan me some exquisite vintage diamond earrings, worth a small fortune and frightening me to death lest I lost them.

So, this morning I donned my designer suit, my borrowed earrings and my neck chain on which hang the wedding rings of my two husbands and my mum and dad – I wanted them to come with me – and felt, as John would say, 'the business'. My chaperone was Charlie, the grandchild chosen for the adventure as it coincided with his seventeenth birthday. He too looked 'the business'. His usual attire being shorts, jeans or a wetsuit, he was wearing a proper suit and tie for, I think, the first time, which he carried off with dashing aplomb.

The day started overcast and grey. The car taking us nearly missed the turning, the road leading to the palace looked so unassuming. Until we were on it. Miraculously, the sun came out, and there, at the end of the long straight approach, glowed Windsor Castle. We both said 'Wow' and from then onwards we wallowed in the sheer beauty of the next two hours.

Inside, we were led through several galleries of superb furniture, gold wallpaper, lavish carpets, tapestries and pictures. There were lots of dignitaries in splendid outfits smiling and greeting us. One man covered in feathers, braid and medals clanked up to us and whispered that 'We' – presumably he and other staff members – 'are all delighted about your award.' Another, seeing me gawping at a Rubens, asked if I would like him to tell me about the art. The whole occasion was an extraordinary mixture of ornate grandeur and cosy friendliness. Several of the officials pointed out that they were happy that the investiture was being held at Windsor, rather than the usual Buckingham Palace, so that they could welcome visitors again after the long period of isolation.

By the time we got to the ceremonial room for the actual
dameing – is that the feminine of knighting? – I was having
a ball. There was a chamber orchestra playing in the
resplendent big salon and Prince William greeted me with
a lovely smile. He is, surprisingly, very tall and had to bend
down to hang my medal on the hook that had been put on
my posh jacket in readiness. Unfortunately, I had opted to
wear a white as well as a red poppy, it being Remembrance
Week, and they got in the way of the hook, so the poor
prince struggled. 'Can I help you?' I said, thereby nearly
taking over my own investiture, which he hastily prevented
whilst explaining that, because of Covid, he hadn't done a
ceremony for two years and was out of practice. I assured
him he was doing very well. We had a nice chat and I thanked
him and the band and rejoined Charlie, who was watching
in the corner. He said that, despite my not curtsying on
account of my Quaker tradition, I walked backwards
very well. The press interviews were friendly and no one
suggested my award was unsuitable or hypocritical for an
erstwhile rabid lefty.

To confirm even further my joining the Establishment, my
son-in-law Matt Byam Shaw had organised a party at the
Garrick Club, that grand institution that still bans women
from being members. In my fiery youth I once went to
lunch there with Donald Sinden and deeply embarrassed
him by invading a curtained area where women guests were
absolutely barred. I was expecting to see some important
chaps engaging in serious Man Talk, when actually most
of them were fast asleep, several snoring loudly. This time
I was warmly welcomed by the doorman and conveyed to

the glorious library where my family awaited, all done up to the nines in bow ties, dinner jackets and party dresses. The staff were welcoming, the food and wine, chosen carefully by Matt, were fantastic, and I was embraced by their love. They told me they were proud of me. I held on to the rings round my neck and hoped that they were too. I loved every minute of it. This class warrior was utterly seduced.

3 February 2022

This morning I 'had a fall'. That's how falling over is described when you are old, and it takes on ominous implications. Relatives tut-tut and hmm. It is presumed you have become unstable, and unable to be on your own. A fall presages your imminent demise. A tragedy.

My old-lady fall, however, was more of a joke. Caused by childish behaviour. I was sitting on the side of my toilet shaving my legs in the bidet alongside. So far, so good. Then for some unknown reason I decided to stand up in the bidet in order to get out. I can't recall the details but a combination of soapy feet and slippery floor tiles found me semi-naked, flat on my back, on the floor. The very expensive watch thing which is supposed to summon help if I fall – and indeed incessantly asks me if I need help if I so much as lift my arm quickly – on this occasion chose to ignore me. Only when I decided to give it a poke did I discover that my left hand was dangling at an odd angle from my wrist. There followed an undignified wriggling on my bottom to reach my phone in the next room to summon my long-suffering daughter.

Whilst on the subject of embarrassing mishaps, I recently had another ludicrous emergency, caused by a vein in my leg bursting and spurting blood everywhere. That time too, the necessity to acrobatically hold my leg in the air, whilst pressing the hole in my leg with my thumb, made fiddling with my help-summoning watch impossible.

The truth is, although I have turned both episodes into good funny stories, they've left me a bit shaken. Living alone, I thought I had any potential accident covered with my emergency watch gadget. But for both events I needed my daughter to carry me to A&E. Although everyone is in awe of my usual health, there is no stopping the inevitable Decay which brings with it the other dreaded D – Dependency. On the other hand, both of these occasions could have happened when I was thirty, and I would have needed help then. I am falling into the 'she's had a fall' trap. Anyway, my friend Simon has come up with a solution, by attaching a tape to my phone so that I can wear it on my person at all times. Hopefully Siri will be listening, even if she can't drive me to A&E.

5 February 2022

My accident has thrown up another problem which is less easy to brush aside. The main disaster is that with my broken wrist I can't drive for a while. This is my worst dread come true, losing my car. I love driving.

From my Lambretta scooter in the sixties and my first car, a racy Morris 1000 convertible, I have always had beautiful vehicles – a Jaguar sports, an MG, a Morgan. All my life I have relished being in control of a machine and acquiring the skills of a good driver. I passed the advanced driving test with flying colours, and I enjoy the challenge of politely handling the complexities of modern aggressive driving – especially now cycle lanes are making it hard to negotiate the roads. Driving gives me freedom. On a bad day, my rheumatoid arthritis can immobilise me but, having reluctantly gone from gears in my cars to automatic, I can still drive.

Speeding through the French or English countryside with Beethoven, Elgar, Shostakovich feeding my soul is my idea of bliss – a feast of joy with no interruption. I even like driving in London. I have an encyclopaedic knowledge of back streets and detours to avoid traffic jams, picked up from seventy years of driving in the capital. After the no-travel rules of lockdown, I was a bit nervous of using the car again, especially in France, but I overcame my fear and it is a vital part of my life.

I am a very good driver, with a clean record. I will be furious if, because of my age, the insurance companies decide to further limit my freedom. I already pay a fortune for the sin of being over eighty, even though there is no evidence to prove I am more accident-prone. I will be desolate if ever I am forced to forgo one of my greatest pleasures in life. Although the planet may be grateful, I suppose.

April 2022

Spent the morning at the Quaker meeting house comforting women and children who have just fled from Ukraine.

Despite Home Office incompetence, the scheme of people opening their houses to refugees is working. Families have volunteered their homes, but both the refugees themselves and the hosts need support in dealing with the trauma of these perilous journeys to Britain, fleeing the violence of the Russian onslaught. Women and children have left behind their male relatives facing great danger, and they are naturally in a state of shock when they arrive.

In conjunction with Hammersmith and Fulham Council we have set our beautiful new meeting house to work, providing, through translators, advice on schools, medical help, English classes, but above all comfort and love.

I am especially preoccupied by the children, some of whom have spent days in underground shelters, listening to the sounds of a furious bombardment on the world above. I can remember what that feels like. I can understand when an ashen-faced little girl clings tightly to a knitted rabbit she has found, and screams and fights with her mother who tries to get her to share it with another weeping child. She has left all her toys, her clothes, her bedroom and her father behind, in a place where they will probably be destroyed. Nobody cares about her, so why should she care about the other girl? She desperately needs to hang on to this new woolly friend. I remember that too. During evacuation, my friend was a felt owl.

Not speaking their language makes it difficult to provide comfort, but acting the fool, clowning, invoking, eventually, cautious laughter, usually works with these anguished children. Followed by tentatively offered cuddles.

Russia's invasion of Ukraine is beyond cruel – for both sides. People are suffering dreadfully. I confess I barely knew where Ukraine was until now, but from what I have researched since the war broke out, as usual, an earlier intervention could probably have prevented this tragic devastation. Once again we have failed to avert 'the occasion of war'. And now it has happened, the newspapers and leaders in the West seem to be doing their utmost to push an already obviously unbalanced, despotic Russian leader into feeling persecuted and vengeful. Whilst leaders utter threats to one another of bigger and better weapons, the ordinary people are, as usual in war, cannon fodder. How is this massacre ever to end?

I hope and pray that Quakers are, as is their custom, intervening in some secret way. There is a Quaker meeting house in Moscow. Hopefully they are supporting any resistance in the population. Never has our Peace Testimony of not bearing arms been so difficult to defend. But the duty, and indeed deep desire, to help the victims of war is clear.

I am, however, a bit worried that this countrywide wave of sympathy for the Ukrainians is overlooking the equal duty of comfort we owe to the Afghans, whom we have betrayed so terribly.

June 2022

Old Rage is out there and I await the brickbats. I don't seem to be capable of writing with restraint; I forget people are going to read it. Then, when it is in the public domain, I am embarrassed by my emotional revelations.

I confess that nowadays I am sometimes nervous of expressing an opinion. (*Not often!* I hear you shout.) Because of the threat of being 'cancelled'. That word sounds so terrifying. Erased from life.

My grandchildren are constantly telling me 'You can't say that, Nana' or 'You can't use that word.' It seems to matter more that I say the right words than that I say what I feel. I know words can hurt so I will do my best to use the right terms so that I don't upset people, but I must be free to speak, challenge and disagree.

I have been touring all over the UK, talking about the book to wonderful, warm audiences. I confess I have done my best to incite them to revolution. They are usually well mannered (a kindly quality I like) and reticent. They don't like scenes. Yet I have had only one letter of complaint – from a woman who said she hadn't paid to hear 'a political rant' (I refunded her ticket money) – but I'm sure I have made many people squirm with embarrassment when I ridicule our politicians.

On the other hand, in the Q&A sessions, many have felt able to reveal a deep anxiety and even rage at the state of our country. In one place a soft-spoken woman, who I suspect had never spoken in public before, tremblingly said that she had lost faith in everything she had been brought up to believe in. The government, the Church, the police, the NHS, and even the Post Office, which had corruptly betrayed some of its employees.

I can't help but agree. We can't just sit passively saying, 'I can't watch the news, it upsets me so.' We must engage and take responsibility for what's going on, and try to stop it. But how?

I tell them we can offer our support to a local charity, or even stand for the local council. We can write to our MPs so that when they say 'My constituents tell me' they don't just mean a couple of people in their office. We can use our votes, not necessarily just voting for the party we have always supported, but trying to get some dedicated, honest people into Parliament. We can read the newspaper we don't ordinarily read, to get a different perspective and broaden our views. But above all, we need to listen – to the young. Find out what they want the world to be, after we misguided old folk have died off and stopped making such a mess of it.

And then I hope they take no notice of what I say.

I don't want to be a guru, or an inspiration, or a national treasure. I get nervous when people take me too seriously. Wisdom, in my case, has not come with age. I change my mind all the time. Sometimes someone will say, 'I was very interested in your last book, when you said . . . something or other.' My reply can often be, 'Really! Did I say that? Well, I don't think that now.' What kind of guru is that? I am not to be trusted.

Especially now. I've seldom been so confused. Copying the government, I blame everything on Covid. My thoughts are muddled. Like my audiences, I am emerging from our enforced hibernation bewildered, unnerved, cringing in the light at the end of a long, scary tunnel.

11 July 2022

The dreaded lurgy has struck at last. I have so far managed to avoid getting the virus by masking, and keeping away from public places, in fact by putting my life on hold for two bloody years. Now I am doing a TV series which is strictly monitored to prevent Covid – tests every day, keeping a safe distance from others, not mixing with people outside the unit. I was driven to Bristol this morning and my first test made them frown, then the second more serious test had everyone running around in circles. Positive.

I was shut up in my Winnebago with no one allowed to come near me, then hastily ferried back to London. Filming had to be suspended. I felt perfectly okay but very guilty causing such trouble. We were filming in a crowded room a couple of days ago. Everyone had been tested for the virus but the little bugger somehow sneaked in. I am furious that for over two years I've managed to avoid this bastard thing and then I get it when it is supposedly on the wane.

Now I am sitting at home waiting to be ill, feeling every bit as vulnerable as I have repeatedly been told I am. Can't pretend I'm not scared. Some people say it's just like a mild cold, but thousands, no, millions worldwide, have died from it. For years I have taken drugs to suppress my badly behaved immune system. Will it now take revenge, and refuse to fight the virus?

13 July 2022

Oh boy, do I feel ill. 'Mild cold'? Are you kidding? Appalling sore throat, raging temperature, violent cough causing bleeding in my throat. Rushed to A&E by my son-in-law. It was packed. I was quickly shoved in the corridor with a couple of other plague victims.

For the entire day they tested every crevice of my anatomy, and kept taking my soaring blood pressure and temperature. I was not permitted to move from my corridor bed, and my son-in-law refused to leave my side. I ended up feeling more embarrassed than ill.

I noticed that every single medical person, nurses, doctors, trolley pushers, cleaners, ran everywhere. The feeling of a lack of staff and inadequate facilities was shocking. None of them rested for a second, and they were on duty non-stop for the length of my stay.

Eventually I persuaded them to let me go and die at home. Though saying that, I am determined that, having fought off a myriad of other illnesses, this bugger is not going to see me off.

8 September 2022

I was enjoying myself taking part in the light-hearted chat on a live broadcast of *Steph's Packed Lunch* when the floor manager whispered in my ear, in a moment when the camera was not on me, that something was happening with the Queen. My heart missed a beat, but before he could explain more he cued me to continue. In the next commercial break I cornered a young runner and asked her, with dread in my heart, what was going on.

She looked at me anxiously – 'Are you alright?' – and used a tissue to wipe away what I realised were tears on my cheeks.

'The Queen,' I hissed. 'Is she dead?'

'I think she may be, but don't upset yourself, Sheila. She's an old lady, after all.'

Never has the generation gap seemed so wide.

In the next commercial break the first assistant hastily explained to the studio that it had been announced that the Queen had taken a turn for the worse, but we weren't to mention it, although I could, if I liked, as I was elderly, say something nice about her. I didn't, I couldn't. I was too upset.

So on I went with my jolly prattle. It wasn't my best performance.

As the day progressed the news gradually unfolded that the dear woman had indeed died. Two days ago she was photographed as she said goodbye to the current prime minister, who had resigned, and welcomed the new one, Liz Truss. She probably knew she was dying, but I suspect that she wasn't going to miss the opportunity of seeing the back of Boris Johnson, or giving the new woman, who seemed to have popped up from nowhere, the once-over.

And now she's not there anymore.

The whole country has gone very quiet. Of course it's not surprising that she died at the age of ninety-six, but somehow we are still shocked. She has always been there. Through wars, recessions, terrorism, appalling governments, royal family ups and downs, she has remained steady. She has performed her duties impeccably, meeting and greeting with a smile some pretty awful people – Trump and Putin amongst them. She has never shown the rage or boredom that she sometimes must have felt when carrying out her official jobs. Did she think, at the opening of Parliament, as she looked at the latest batch of MPs crowded at the entrance of the House of Lords, 'All these peers and earls sitting here may not have been elected, but they are a damn sight more civilised than that lot from the Commons. What a shower! In my seventy years in charge, these prats are the worst. And this bloody crown is killing me.' If she did think that, not a glimmer of a smile or frown did she ever show. She was a consummate actress.

I hope I am right in thinking that lockdown was a pleasure for her. Prince Philip had retired and I like to think they had a nice cosy year living a normal life in a cottage in the grounds of Windsor Castle. Just the occasional gallop on one of her favourite horses and a few staff looking after them. No banquets or receptions. No need to stand about for hours shaking hands and asking people if they had come far. Just the two of them.

I fully realise the indifference of the young runner is shared by many nowadays, and things will have to change, but I am grateful for her service. Ever since those messages that the princess sent to us kids during the war, I have liked her being there. All those parties we had of which she was the centre. Standing with happy, usually rain-drenched, crowds on the Mall, cheering big events like her wedding and her coronation. The military bands, the incomprehensible rituals, the Jubilee and VE Day street parties.

All the recent photos in the press remind me how beautiful she was, with that rationed, radiant smile. In the grey years after the war, she was often resplendent in silk and satin and diamonds, or handsome, saluting in uniform, sitting sideways on a horse. As the years have progressed she has not fallen into the trap of trying to look young, but has aged with frumpy dignity. Possibly the image that best illustrates her spirit is that of the frail, bent old woman in Balmoral, greeting the ludicrous Boris Johnson and Liz Truss, probably racked with pain, but still managing that familiar, glorious smile.

She is revered worldwide, as the reaction to her death is proving. For the last eighty years she has met every major figure in the world, and they, however elevated, have deemed it an honour. And yet she always seemed and probably was quite ordinary. A unique achievement.

What will give us dignity as a nation now she has gone?

19 September 2022

The period of mourning for the Queen seems a little overstretched. The royal hearse leaving Balmoral and travelling through the sunlit hills and dales of Scotland was stunning. Then clattering up the cobbled streets of Edinburgh, crammed with quiet, respectful subjects, was timelessly impressive, as was the service in the starkly plain kirk. The sober respect was embellished by swishing radiant kilts and mourning bagpipes. The Scots swallowed their resentment towards England and demonstrated a deep regard for the monarch who seemed to relish living in their country.

After the Scottish trip, the arrival of the hearse in England at the dreary RAF Northolt airbase, followed by a drive along the ugly A40, was a bit of a let-down. Nonetheless hurried drivers stopped respectfully as the cortège passed.

The lying-in-state went on for days to accommodate the thousands who wanted to pay their respects. I began to feel a bit uneasy that, whereas when she first died the grief was genuine, with a palpable sense of loss, now it seemed there was a somewhat desperate demand from the media that tears should be shed. It was almost obligatory.

After the funeral, the hearse was to pass the end of our road on its way to Windsor. We were very excited about this as the street had been thoroughly washed and scrubbed in readiness; they even repainted the lamp posts. By the time the cortège was due, champagne was flowing (maybe a bit inappropriate, but it had been a long day) and spirits were high as we waited on the pavement.

Then two cars went by at top speed and we weren't sure if they held the coffin. We realised they were behind schedule and the roast venison for the banquet must be getting cold, but hey, look at our lamp posts.

Then, on its own, came a big, slower car. It was her. She looked lonely. She probably was sometimes, especially after Philip died. Alone on her pedestal. We all fell silent.

'Goodbye, darling,' I whispered.

September 2022

My first time in France in two years. Everything seems altered – including me. The journey there now seems arduous and environmentally unjustified, the track down to the house feels perilous, as does climbing into the bath to shower, and descending the steep stairs with no handrail. I am two years older. Either I spend money on making it more old-lady-friendly, or I pass it on to someone else to experience its joys. So – I can hardly bear to write this – my beloved French home is on the market. It feels like a betrayal – of the thirty years of refuge and solace it has given John and me.

So I have been showing possible buyers round and it is upsetting. For a third of my life, I have loved my home and thought it beautiful. I know it is simple, without a pool or central heating, but I thought people would see its glory and fight to own it. But that hasn't happened. What they see is cracks in the walls, the lack of privacy, the neglected grounds, the potholed track. One potential buyer even complained when he heard Denis's cock crow. Admittedly the old bird is tone-deaf but if he gets too rowdy a bit of Mozart usually shuts him up. The buyer (or not, as it turned out) couldn't get away quick enough when I told him that.

I now realise I have neglected the poor little house since John died. I hadn't noticed there really are huge cracks. This year has been scalding hot with hardly any rain, and these medieval houses have no foundations, so the walls do move. The locals ignore them. When I told Denis next door, there was a lot of French shrugging. Ah, Denis! If a buyer wants to be private, I suppose this is not the house for them. I enjoy having chats with the neighbours, and in the summer seeing Lydie's little ones jumping around naked outside my kitchen window. The close relationships between the inhabitants are a big bonus for me. They are my European family. How will I bear eventually to say goodbye?

13 November 2022

I am fascinated by Liz Truss. She has seemed to thoroughly enjoy destroying the economy and nearly democracy itself. She was thrown out, but she is still having a ball. She has a new outfit for every event, and obviously a hairdresser and maybe make-up artist in tow. I was open-mouthed to see her at the solemn Cenotaph ceremony today. She has been prime minister for only a disastrous forty-four days, yet she saw fit to attend.

Has the woman no shame? No awareness of what is right and proper? She pranced on in the new black hat, lipstick to match her poppy, with all the living prime ministers. As is the tradition. But even Boris Johnson served a few years. Is it perhaps something she has to do to prove her right to an ex-prime minister's lifetime pension? That would certainly be Boris's reason. Or is she just terminally stupid?

It terrifies me that our political system has allowed these cretins to rise to the top. Albeit briefly. And what must the new king think? It's taken him seventy-four years to get there.

November 2022

On the opposite bank of the river from where I live there is a venerable private school. A few years ago, we residents on the other side received a letter informing us that they were seeking permission to do a major development. I was suspicious that the trees in front of the school, which for most of the year make it invisible to us and the thousands of people that walk on our side, would be sacrificed to give the splendid new building a good view of the river. So, of course, I trekked along to take a look at the designs, duly made an objection, even demanded a meeting with the then headmaster, was given lots of promises and have kept an eagle eye on the now neglected and sickly trees ever since.

Today I received another letter about more permission for further major developments. The school now has its first female head, so, in a sexist way, I hoped she might agree that ignoring all those who take pleasure from the seasonal changes in the ancient trees as they use the river path, in favour of the view for a few privileged young men, might be unfair.

So what am I going to do?

Nothing.

I considered going into battle again. But then I thought: 'Sod it. I can't be bothered.'

This is new behaviour for me.

I have begun to believe my sense of duty is a destructive element in my life. It has made me a censorious, boring and above all exhausted human being.

It stems, I suspect, from my childhood.

For instance, I think how appalled my father was by my school report that said I was 'inconsiderate' and 'a born leader but [she] must be careful to lead in the right direction'. He actually wept when he read it. The war had given him an understandable horror of leadership in the wrong direction.

But was I really such a self-centred dangerous child? There was that time one of the teachers found me doing a striptease on a wet indoor break time. I had got down to my green serge knickers, which I was slowly rolling down in a twelve-year-old's version of sexiness, when Miss Carter intervened. In those pious days I suppose it was the equivalent of children looking at porn. I was made to feel dirty and dangerous and repentant. Was it my teachers' dismay and my father's concern that condemned me to a life of – that amorphous word – duty? Filled me with a desperation not to let people down?

I know it deprived me of a hell of a lot of fun.

But who am I letting down now anyway? My teachers and parents have gone their way. My children have left home. There's only me, and the world won't miss my input.

So bugger the trees.

November 2022

Our former health secretary has just eaten a cow's anus.

Matt Hancock has also swum with eels and crawled through a tunnel full of rats and maggots. Maybe standing stoically at that lectern during the pandemic, lying about how well he was doing, was good preparation for dealing, seemingly unemotionally, with the horrors of *I'm a Celebrity . . . Get Me Out of Here.*

Dear God, what have we come to?

I've tried not watching the news or reading the papers, but the sense of a country in decline permeates my indifference. I'm not sure how we got our current prime minister, Rishi Sunak. The electorate had nothing to do with it. He seems a nice enough little bloke. We haven't heard much from him. Even though inflation is sky-high, the whole country seems to be on strike, or threatening to be, and my lovely GP is too overworked to answer her phone, Covid is still rampant, climate change is causing floods and fire and bringing bewildering scorching then freezing weather, and people are queuing at food banks.

Inconvenient though they are, I feel the strikes are a sign of the electorate determined to make their voices heard. It was their pressure that got rid of Boris Johnson. A loss of trust in politicians is making people seek other solutions than government. I have been thrilled to hear of several areas taking a community responsibility for their energy supply – getting together to install solar panels, or insulate, and one place even having its own windmill.

December 2022

Something strange has happened. As part of the BBC centenary celebrations (bless them!) I was invited to appear on the *Today* programme where they would show me some correspondence discovered in the archives. Letters from me, seventy years ago. I have absolutely no recollection of writing them, so the girl that emerges has taken me by surprise – as was clear in my reaction on the programme. They were lucky I didn't use really bad language, as is my wont, on their live broadcast.

Garry Richardson, who presented the programme, agreed to take me to the BBC Archives in Reading so that I could take a proper look at the material.

The first letter was beautifully written on lined paper sent from a YWCA hostel. It is addressed to *Dear Sir* – it not occurring to me in those days that an important person could be a woman – and signed *Yours Faithfully*, and it explains that I have enclosed a stamped addressed envelope for them to tell me if there is any possibility of having an audition.

It was written in 1949 when I was sixteen and just starting my training at RADA. In those days the Academy was like a finishing school. There were a few older ex-servicemen there on state scholarships, like my dear friend Tony Beckley who was in the Navy, or Paul Eddington, who as a Quaker was a conscientious objector, and who spent his war in ENSA, the theatre organisation that entertained the troops. But apart from me, I only remember one other working-class person there at that time – Shani Wallis.

I was miserable at RADA. In those days received pronunciation was essential for an actor. Getting rid of my accent in voice classes, where everyone else effortlessly spoke with elegant vowels and said 'going' not 'goin'', was humiliating, although I pretended that I too found it funny. Thank God regional accents are cherished now.

And yet RADA didn't crush me, because here I am in 1952 writing to the BBC declaring 'I am a 19-year-old struggling actress who knows no one with influence.' There follow several more letters begging for an audition, culminating in one saying 'I may say this audition has become a positive obsession with me and you will get no peace until I do it – I only want an opportunity to show what I can do – even if you hate me.'

In the early fifties I was playing in tatty repertory companies and touring to second-rate theatres, staying in grotty theatrical digs, so the desperation is understandable, but the bold determination in a girl from the lower class is extraordinary. We were just not supposed to be so pushy and unladylike. For heaven's sake, I still wore a hat and gloves when I did the round of agents in Charing Cross Road and Shaftesbury Avenue. But behind the scenes I was obviously full of suppressed rage.

In the archives is a report of the audition that I eventually had, although I have no memory of this event that must have meant so much to the young Sheila. It made me spit with rage reading it.

For Diction it said 'perhaps a little over-careful' – thank you, RADA, for two wasted years of torture. For Tone – whatever that is – it said 'Would pass for educated.' What? What the bloody hell does that mean? She is obviously ignorant but might hoodwink people into thinking she went to Cheltenham Ladies' College?

The adjudicator gave me an A for Acting, so he must have thought I was talented, but his closing comment was 'I have a feeling this actress might be useful for character juveniles.' The Juvenile Character category was for people playing maids and similar subsidiary roles. Not leads. Good God, no. Not from her background.

Fortunately, I obviously did not see or hear about the report at the time – or hear back from the BBC. There is a pathetic letter from me saying 'You haven't even acknowledged my being there.'

There was a happy ending, though. Also nestling in the archives is my 1961 contract for *The Rag Trade*. I played a lead – a gawky, vacuous girl with a cockney accent. And it was a huge success. And it was a lead. The era of the emergence of the working-class actors and subjects had arrived.

I asked the archivist why these letters had been kept, and she suspected that somebody in the department had been intrigued by this frustrated girl and wanted to follow her story. In one of my letters in 1959, still pleading for a chance, I say 'I beg of you to allow this as I should hate to be inscribed as hopeless to the end of time in the secret BBC files.'

So, thank you to that imaginative archivist for pursuing my youthful journcy. It sheds a different light on the wilful, slightly dangerous child mentioned in that school report. That stroppy girl survived.

Looking back, this lack of recognition of her existence was obviously what hurt – the shut doors, that injustice, that rejection. I am proud of that unsupported girl's ability to keep fighting indifference. I guess that might also be the root of my sense of duty – to see that it doesn't happen to others.

Try as I may to shirk it, that is actually who I still am.

December 2022

Nearly ninety. I have never been one to make much of a fuss about birthdays. Especially since 2002, when John died the day before my birthday, so I tend to remember that event more – for the first few years with grief at his absence, now with gratitude for the years of his fabulous presence. But now everyone keeps demanding to know how I am going to celebrate 'the big one'. I actually hate parties. My deafness is such that in a crowded place I can't hear even people close to me. I hate standing around juggling plates and glasses and ending up having nothing to eat and drink. But my family and friends will not permit me to avoid a 'do' of some sort. To refuse would be ungracious. For I am deeply, deeply grateful.

I will have a party to say thank you to my dear, funny, honest, sympathetic, endlessly supportive friends. And I will take my family to Bailiffscourt Hotel for a few days (I'm spending the kids' inheritance). It is a wondrous, crazy place, compiled in the twenties and thirties by the, I suspect, slightly mad Lord and Lady Moyne, of buildings and bits and pieces and furniture from ruins all over the country, to create a fantastic mock medieval dwelling. I have been going there since the hippie fifties. I went on several occasions with my dear husband Alec, and later

John. Now I will go with the family that they fathered, but were not, like me, privileged to see turn into a fascinating, loving, powerful entity.

We will be in the wonderful Sussex countryside near to the vast elemental sea, a fitting setting for me to give thanks for my enormously blessed existence.

And to contemplate what's next. It's like Mary Oliver says in her poem, 'The Summer Day':

I don't know exactly what a prayer is.
I do know how to pay attention, how to fall down
into the grass, how to kneel in the grass,
how to be idle and blessed, how to stroll through
the fields
which is what I have been doing all day.
Tell me, what else should I have done?
Doesn't everything die at last, and too soon?
Tell me, what is it you plan to do
With your one wild and precious life?

Yes, what is it? We'll see.

ACKNOWLEDGEMENTS

From the bottom of my heart I thank the following people, without whom this book would never have happened.

Victoria Millar was at my side again, guiding, calming, and prodding me at all the right times.

Silvia Crompton's attention to detail and morale boosting were invaluable.

Paul Stevens, the Rottweiler, got me organised.

Clare Eden, Melanie Paskin and Dorothy Kazimierczyk kept my chaotic life in order, so that I could find time to write.

Everybody at Bloomsbury has been a joy to work with.

Above all, Alexandra Pringle has inspired and guided me for nearly twenty years, as she has many authors. She is my mentor, comforter, inspiration, friend. As an iconic feminist she won't like me saying this, but I also relish her glamorous beauty.

A NOTE ON THE TYPE

The text of this book is set in Linotype Sabon, a typeface named after the type founder, Jacques Sabon. It was designed by Jan Tschichold and jointly developed by Linotype, Monotype and Stempel in response to a need for a typeface to be available in identical form for mechanical hot metal composition and hand composition using foundry type.

Tschichold based his design for Sabon roman on a font engraved by Garamond, and Sabon italic on a font by Granjon. It was first used in 1966 and has proved an enduring modern classic.